KANT ON GOD

Peter Byrne presents a detailed study of the role of the concept of God in Kant's *Critical Philosophy*. After a preliminary survey of the major interpretative disputes over the understanding of Kant on God, Byrne explores his critique of philosophical proofs of God's existence.

Examining Kant's account of religious language, Byrne highlights both the realist and anti-realist elements contained within it. The notion of the highest good is then explored, with its constituent elements – happiness and virtue, in pursuit of an assessment of how far Kant establishes that we must posit God. The precise role God plays in ethics according to Kant is then examined, along with the definition of religion as the recognition of duties as divine commands. Byrne also plots Kant's critical re-working of the concept of grace. The book closes with a survey of the relation between the *Critical Philosophy* and Christianity on the one hand and deism on the other.

ASHGATE STUDIES IN THE HISTORY OF PHILOSOPHICAL THEOLOGY

Ashgate Studies in the History of Philosophical Theology provides students and researchers in the field with the means of consolidating and re-appraising philosophy of religion's recent appropriation of its past. This series offers a focused cluster of titles presenting critical, authoritative surveys of key thinkers' ideas as they bear upon topics central to the philosophy of religion. Summarizing contemporary and historical perspectives on the writings and philosophies of each thinker, the books concentrate on moving beyond mere surveys and engage with recent international scholarship and the author's own critical research on their chosen thinker. Each book provides an accessible, stimulating new contribution to thinkers from ancient, through medieval, to modern periods.

Series Editors

Professor Peter Byrne, King's College London
Professor Martin Stone, Katholieke Universiteit Leuven
Professor Carlos Steel, Katholieke Universiteit Leuven
Doctor Maria Rosa Antognazza, King's College London

Other titles in the Series

Hegel's God
A Counterfeit Double?
William Desmond

Aquinas on God
The 'Divine Science' of the *Summa Theologiae*
Rudi te Velde

Duns Scotus on God
Richard Cross

Mill on God
The Pervasiveness and Elusiveness of
Mill's Religious Thought
Alan P. F. Sell

Kant on God

PETER BYRNE
King's College London, UK

ASHGATE

© Peter Byrne 2007

All rights reserved. No part of this publication may be reproduced, stored in a retrieval system or transmitted in any form or by any means, electronic, mechanical, photocopying, recording or otherwise without the prior permission of the publisher.

Peter Byrne has asserted his moral right under the Copyright, Designs and Patents Act, 1988, to be identified as the author of this work.

Published by
Ashgate Publishing Limited
Gower House
Croft Road
Aldershot
Hampshire GU11 3HR
England

Ashgate Publishing Company
Suite 420
101 Cherry Street
Burlington, VT 05401-4405
USA

Ashgate website: http://www.ashgate.com

British Library Cataloguing in Publication Data
Byrne, Peter, 1950–
 Kant on God. – (Ashgate Studies in the History of Philosophical Theology)
 1. Kant, Immanuel, 1724–1804 – Religion. 2. Religion – Philosophy.
 I. Title.
 210.9'2

Library of Congress Cataloging-in-Publication Data
Byrne, Peter, 1950–
 Kant on God: / Peter Byrne.
   p.   cm. -- (Ashgate Studies in the History of Philosophical Theology)
 Includes bibliographical references and index.
 1. Kant, Immanuel, 1724-1804. 2. God. I. Title.
 B2799.G6B67 2007
 211.092–dc22

2006018445

ISBN 978-0-7546-4022-6 (hbk)
ISBN 978-0-7546-4023-3 (pbk)

Printed and bound in Great Britain by MPG Books Ltd, Bodmin, Cornwall.

Contents

Preface		vii
	Acknowledgements	viii
	References	viii
1	God and Kant's Critical Project	1
	The aim and the problem	1
	Sources and strategies	3
	Does Kant's life settle the interpretative questions?	5
	The *Weltanschauung*	7
	The context of religious philosophy	9
	The Critical project in outline	11
	Coda on transcendental idealism	15
2	Kant on Natural Theology I	19
	The ontological argument	22
	The cosmological proof	31
3	Kant on Natural Theology II	37
	The physico-theological proof	37
	The argument from possibility	40
	Arguments from probability	44
	God as an object of intuition	52
4	Religious Language and the Boundaries of Sense	57
	Kant the positivist?	57
	Kant on God-talk: the fundamentals	61
	Analogy	69
	Wobbles?	72
5	The Positive Case for God	77
	Teleology	77
	Moral teleology	
	The moral proof in the second *Critique*	84
	The force of the postulate	86
	Doing without the highest good	94
6	Kant on the Elements of the Highest Good	101
	Happiness	101
	Virtue and holiness	110
	The highest good as an immanent or transcendent end	117
	The cogency of the moral argument	120

7	Kant's Moral Theology Explored	125
	God and the foundations of morality	125
	Morality, commands and legislation	128
	Kant on radical evil and divine grace	139
8	Kant, Christianity and Deism	153
	Kant and Christian truth	153
	Kant as pure rationalist	159
	Kant as naturalist	163
	Kant and deism	167
	Conclusion	172
Bibliography		175
	Kant sources	175
	Non-Kant sources	176
Index		181

Preface

The aim of this study is to expound and discuss the concept of God in the philosophy of Immanuel Kant (1724–1804).

Since there have been many other books in English with this same aim, some sort of excuse is needed for yet another attempt. One excuse I have is that this study will concentrate on an issue that has still, I believe, to receive due attention in treatments of Kant on God, namely the status of claims about God in the Critical Philosophy.

Another excuse is that each generation of philosophers, including philosophers of religion, has to get stuck into Kant. Taking his philosophy of religion in isolation, he remains and will remain one of the most important contributors to debates in the subject. His treatment of the proofs for God's existence is still much discussed and is seen, even by those who disagree with it, as a major challenge to natural theology. His so-called 'moral proof' of God's existence serves as the paradigm of an entire approach to reasoning from the moral life to God's existence. His moral philosophy remains a front runner in ethical theory and it has important implications for perennial topics such as the divine command theory of ethics. Kant is part of the contemporary philosophical scene and books that expound, defend, or attack his ideas on topics in the philosophy of religion and ethics are often contributions to current debates.

The picture of Kant as a thinker in the philosophy of religion changes from generation to generation. As philosophical movements come and go, so do ways of interpreting Kant. As Chapter 1 indicates, there have been some attempts in recent English-speaking philosophy of religion to interpret Kant in the light of the current fashion for 'Christian philosophy'. This means assimilating his views to those of orthodox Christianity and downplaying the apparent religious scepticism present in his writings on religion. With this current movement in mind, I endeavour, by reference to Kant's account of religious language and religious truth, to give a clear overview of his relationship to Christianity and deism.

In plotting Kant's account of God, I have endeavoured to give an interpretation which arises from a direct reading of his own words, with as few references to secondary sources as possible – though readers will see that I am indebted to a number of recent studies of Kant's treatment of natural theology for the content of parts of Chapters 2 and 3.

In what follows it will be assumed that readers have a basic understanding of the Critical Philosophy, that is Kant's system as it developed in and after publication of the *Critique of Pure Reason* in 1781. In the later sections of Chapter 1, I shall give an outline of the main features of the Critical Philosophy, but this will be a thumbnail sketch only.

Acknowledgements

I am greatly indebted to my colleague Dr Maria Rosa Antognazza for her comments on a draft of this book. I was able to discuss a number of interpretative matters with my colleague Dr Christopher Hamilton. He also provided assistance in the translation of passages from Kant, and in particular one from *Moral Mongrovius II*. I am grateful to Charlotte Byrne for her many helpful corrections of matters typographical. In the course of writing about Kant on religion as the recognition of duties as divine commands, I was assisted by correspondence with Dr Patrick Kain (Purdue University). Dr Patrick Frierson (Whitman College) also shared his thoughts with me on Kant on grace during the composition of Chapter 7. Neither correspondent should in any way be associated with the accounts of these matters I subsequently produced.

References

References in this book are via the author, date, page number system, save for those to Kant's own works. In citing Kant I generally provide an abbreviated English title followed by page reference. The page references are to volume and page numbers of the Academy Edition of the *Gesammelte Schriften*, with the exception of the *Critique of Pure Reason* – here the usual first edition (A) and second edition (B) numbers are used. Abbreviations of English titles for Kant's works are provided in the text in accordance with the following key:

Anthropology – Anthropology from a Pragmatic Point of View
Conflict – The Conflict of the Faculties
Critique$_1$ – Critique of Pure Reason
Critique$_2$ – Critique of Practical Reason
Critique$_3$ – Critique of Judgement
End – The End of All Things
Groundwork – Groundwork of the Metaphysics of Morals
Logic – Immanuel Kant's Logic
Lectures Ethics – Lectures on Ethics
Lectures Logic – Lectures on Logic
Lectures Metaphysics – Lectures on Metaphysics
Lectures Theology – Lectures on Rational Theology
Morals – The Metaphysics of Morals
Natural Science – Metaphysical Foundations of Natural Science
New Elucidation – New Elucidation of the Metaphysical Principles of Cognition
Only Possible Ground – The Only Possible Ground for a Demonstration of the Existence of God
Orientation – What Does it Mean: to Orient Oneself in Thinking?
Peace – Toward Perpetual Peace
Proclamation – Proclamation of the Imminent Conclusion of a Treaty of Perpetual Peace in Philosophy

Progress – What Real Progress Has Metaphysics Made in Germany since the Time of Leibniz and Wolff?
Prolegomena – Prolegomena to Any Future Metaphysics that Will Be Able to Come Forward as a Science
Religion – Religion within the Boundaries of Bare Reason
Theodicy – On the Miscarriage of all Philosophical Trials in Theodicy
Theory and Practice – On the Common Saying: That May Be Correct in Theory, But It Is of No Use in Practice

Where other Kant texts are mentioned readers should find the title I used self-evident, for example: *Correspondence* (for *Briefwechsel*) *Opus Postumum, Reflexionen, Über Wunder, Moral Mongrovius II*. A full citation for all of Kant's works referred to in the text is provided in the bibliography, where the German titles are spelled out.

The translations of quotations from Kant are my own (with help – see above). I have tried so far as is humanly possible to be faithful to the punctuation of the original. I have rendered Kant's emphases on words and phrases by the uniform use of italics. On occasions when I have added my own emphasis, I have said so. 'A priori' is italicised in the Academy text. In keeping with usage throughout this book, I have put the phrase in Roman.

Chapter 1

God and Kant's Critical Project

The aim and the problem

The theme of this book – the status of claims about God in the Critical Philosophy – gains its importance from a number of facts. One is that the Critical Philosophy displays an obvious bi-valence or paradox in its use of the concept of God. One the one hand, God and related concepts are used, appealed to and depended upon by Kant in many key passages of thought and argument. On the other hand, the Critical Philosophy tells us that we can have no knowledge of the divine nature and existence. Early on in the first *Critique* (in the Preface to the second edition) we encounter the famous statement concerning the notions of God, freedom and immortality: 'I therefore had to deny *knowledge* in order to make room for *faith*' (Bxxx). We will come across many such statements to this effect as we proceed. Further, readers of the first *Critique* will be familiar with other passages that entail that statements about a transcendent divine being are without sense. So Kant not only denies that we can have knowledge of God; he also *appears* to deny that there is any meaning to talk about God. This latter point is controversial. Many commentators on Kant's philosophical theology ignore or deliberately discount Kant's apparent commitment to the meaninglessness of claims about transcendent entities such as God. And one can see why they do. If the interpreter of Kant on God takes this commitment seriously, then the problem of making sense of Kant's dependence upon, and positive use of, the concept of God becomes that much more difficult.

It is my contention that Kant's Critical account of God cannot be properly interpreted unless Kant's account of the meaning and reference of religious language is taken seriously. The effort must be made to disentangle the threads in it and present it as both coherent and intimately connected with other facets of the Critical Philosophy. I do not claim that I am the first on this particular scene – indeed what I have to say on this score is indebted to others (notably to Keith Ward – see Ward 1972:81ff.). But I will focus on this issue to a greater extent than is usual in English-speaking commentaries on Kant's philosophy of religion.

I will contend that there is a real sense in which, for Kant, talk about God is meaningless – albeit he thinks we can give it a sense! There is in the Critical treatment of God a passage of thought of the following form: 'try to construe talk about God in the "normal" way and its meaning evaporates in our hands; to restore that meaning re-interpret it an a radically new (and subjectivist) way'. This is to say that he is a radical revisionist in the philosophy of God: his own account of the limits of knowledge, thought and meaning block off traditional uses of the God-concept, so he must construct a new understanding of what it means to talk of God. The reconstruction Kant offers is undertaken in the spirit of trying to retain key features and uses of the traditional concept of God, but there is radical change nonetheless. Thus my interpretation of Kant on God will yield the conclusion that he was not a theist or a Christian in anything like the standard ways those stances are understood. If we must use modern jargon, we can say he was a post-Christian and post-theistic thinker. Something like this verdict must be entered at the same time as we give due acknowledgement to the fact that the concept of God (and allied concepts such as immortality) played a key role in his Critical system. Here is the tensive, paradoxical character of his philosophy of religion again.

From the above it will be seen that this study will set itself in opposition to a certain trend in recent English-speaking philosophy of religion. This is a trend that turns to Kant and discounts the religious scepticism that I and others see in the Critical Philosophy. Kant is reclaimed for theistic and Christian philosophy. An article in a leading philosophy of religion journal proclaims in its title 'Immanuel Kant: a Christian Philosopher' (Palmquist 1989; see also Palmquist 2000). In a clutch of articles, John E. Hare contends that Kant had (contrary to virtually all standard interpretations of his moral philosophy) a divine command theory of ethics (Hare 2000a, 2000b, 2001). Here it is implied that Kant's ethics actually demands a personal deity who commands, rewards and punishes. Note what is at issue here between Hare and earlier interpreters of Kant with whom he is in dispute. There is an abundance of textual material in post-1780 Kantian texts that show Kant thinks we must use *the idea of God*, and which indicate that this idea includes in its content the notions of a holy lawgiver, a beneficent world-governor and a just judge of all human conduct (see, e.g., *Critique*$_2$ 5:131$_n$). The interpretative question concerns what Kant thinks the use of the idea amounts to. Is the use literal or metaphorical? Is it assertoric or does it merely have the force of an 'as-if' posit?

Palmquist and Hare on Kant on religion may be styled 'revisionists'. They are going against a consensus that has seen Kant as a powerful religious sceptic. The sceptical side to his Critical metaphysics and philosophy of religion serves as a standing challenge to the many philosophers who think that, now Positivism is dead, rationalist philosophical theology can be launched again. Some contemporary philosophers want to do 'old-style' philosophical theology. They also respect Kant. So they want to show that he is on their side. There is in addition a very powerful movement in contemporary English-speaking philosophy of religion that is Christian philosophy. Some Christian philosophers want to reclaim Kant. They want to show that Kant was much more religiously orthodox than older interpretations allowed.

Let us return to the topic of Kant as a religious sceptic. Interpretations of Kant on God that see him as an arch-sceptic are very old. Heinrich Heine's 1835 book *Zur Geschichte der Religion und Philosophie in Deutschland* signals a common view of Kant as the ultimate religious sceptic. Heine contrasts the quiet external life of the scholar Kant with his destructive, world-crushing ideas (Heine 1979:81). Kant is the great destroyer in the world of thought (82). In contrast to the destructive power of Robespierre, who merely killed a royal family, Kant produces the greater terrorism. Kant killed God (82). This act of assassination was completed in the *Critique of Pure Reason* through the means of confining human thought to that which may be encountered in experience. The Critical boundary on valid thought leaves us like the prisoners in Plato's myth of the cave. Plato's prisoners only know shadows and images of the real things that make up reality outside the cave. Kant's prisoners can only know of things as they appear to, as they are reflected in, the human mind. Things in themselves, independent of us, are unknowable. God, as a putative thing in itself, thus becomes *nicht anders als eine Dichtung* ('nothing other than a work of fiction', 86). Thus Kant's message to humanity on the front of his great work should have echoed those of Dante: 'Abandon hope'. (Heine's suggestion is unwittingly ironic: it is one of the aims of the Critical Philosophy to assure its students that there is an answer to the deep human question 'What may I hope?') Kant, the Robespierre of thought, is, according to Heine, not content with his deicide. He cannot forget about his old servant Lampe and the ordinary good-hearted people he represents. Lampe stands before his master, tears in his eyes at the prospect that the consoling thoughts of traditional religion are delusions. Kant has pity on him. He says to himself: old Lampe must have his God and so I will give him his God back by letting practical reason vouch for God. Thus Kant, having killed God with theoretical reason, tries to enliven God's corpse through the magic wand of practical reason (89). This is Heine's reference to Kant's claim that, though God be unknowable (and perhaps unthinkable) through theoretical reason, practical reason needs to postulate God in order to meet our deep-seated ethical needs. This does not impress Heine. It reminds him of his Westphalian friend who destroys all the street lamps on the road and then, standing in the dark, waxes at length on the practical necessity of street lamps on a dark night. He has only destroyed them in order to show how necessary they are (90–91).

Kant has destroyed God, for Heine. The reintroduction of God through appeal to ethics does not really complete a resurrection of the corpse. It is merely a sop to those with the human weaknesses of his old servant.

We have got two tensions in front of us up to this point. There is the primary tension: on the one hand, we have bucketfuls of religious scepticism in the Critical Philosophy, and, on the other hand, we have a plethora of seemingly positive uses of the notion of God. There is the further tension among his interpreters: between those who accept the scepticism at face value, explaining away the positive uses of 'God', and those who accept the positive uses of 'God', while ignoring or mitigating the scepticism: Heine versus Hare. I will come down closer to Heine as this study proceeds, but with one major qualification. Any credible study of Kant on God must acknowledge and demonstrate that the positive uses of the notion of God post-1780 are grounded in concerns integral to the Critical Philosophy. They are certainly not there because Kant was worried by the tears of the lower classes, or even because he was anxious about the Prussian censor (though he was worried about him). This desideratum evidently increases the first tension.

Sources and strategies

Consider some strategies for dealing with the primary tension. One such is the invocation of inconsistency. Kant just is an inconsistent writer – some may contend. The negative and positive statements about God in the Critical Philosophy indicate a thinker who cannot make his mind up on the truth and coherence of theism. But this clearly will not do. *Critique₁* Bxxx has already been quoted: Kant places limits around what may be known and cognised in order to make room for faith. The Critical limits on cognition do rule out forms of dogmatic religious and metaphysical claims. Yet from the beginning those same limits are there to rule out dogmatic materialism, fatalism and atheism (*Critique₁*:Bxxxiv). This philosopher's aim was actually to set up a tensive account of God. The atheists and their allies are defeated not by proving religious dogmas, but by showing that no one has any right to dogmatic assertions, negative or positive, in this area. Religion is saved through a meta-scepticism that undercuts the religious sceptic's claims, while at the same time it deprives the believer of objective certainty that his or her beliefs are true (or even, perhaps, meaningful). It is intended to be a defence through a kind of undermining of all previous positions on the nature and reality of God.

Having made this point, it must be said that Kant tests the patience of any interpreter committed to a principle of hermeneutical charity. There are things in his philosophy of religion that reveal a mind unresolved or unable to enunciate a single perspective. My discussion of Kant on the so-called 'moral proof' in Chapters 5 and 6 will illustrate this point. On this topic he says things which are difficult to make consistent and in some places he does not seem to realise the plain entailments of what he has written elsewhere. While violations of interpretative charity must be kept to a minimum, for otherwise they undermine the very notion of a correct interpretation, we shall not be able to avoid some such violations in what follows.

The issue of the consistency of the post-1780 Kantian corpus on religion raises the important question of what counts as belonging to that corpus. The three great critiques obviously do: the *Critique of Pure Reason* (1781, second edition 1787), the *Critique of Practical Reason* (1788) and the *Critique of Judgement* (1790). The major and minor works from 1780 to 1800 whose production was actually overseen by Kant must also be included. There are legitimate debates, however, over the relevance of other sources. One such set of sources is the texts created by Kant's colleagues and students from his lectures. The Academy text of Kant's *Schriften* contains lectures on, amongst other topics, ethics, logic, metaphysics and rational theology. The notable lectures on ethics and metaphysics are compilations of notes taken by Kant's pupils at one or other of his annual lecture series on the relevant subject. Some of these pupils were very eminent thinkers in their own right (the *Lectures on Ethics* includes a set of notes by J. G. Herder). Most of them were not. It is obvious that we cannot rely on them 100 per cent for completeness and accuracy. The status of the notes on Kant's lectures on rational theology is relevant to interpreting Kant on God, particularly the *Philosophische Religionslehre nach Politz*. These lectures date from the early 1780s and were edited by Karl Heinrich Ludwig Pölitz and first published in 1817. They contain some affirmations that are more religiously conservative, less sceptical, than those found in the critiques. They are thus ammunition for those interpreters of Kant's philosophy of religion I have crudely called 'revisionists'. This portion of the lectures on rational theology show a Kant apparently more content with traditional, rationalist metaphysics about God than one would expect from the author of the *Critique of Pure Reason*. A. R. Wood accordingly uses these lectures to suggest that the Critical Philosophy is to a large extent compatible with traditional, rationalist philosophical theology (see

Wood 1978, especially 149). The problem we will find in Chapter 4 is that there is one place where the account of religious language in these lectures contradicts that contained in the three critiques, and in numerous other places in the Critical corpus. It seems evident to me that a broad interpretation of Kant on God must be established from the post-1780 writings that he saw to press, and within those particularly from the three critiques, and that this interpretation must take priority in any conflicts with such sources as the lectures on religion. There are comments on God as the legislator of the moral law in notes taken by C. C. Mongrovius of lectures on ethics from the session 1784–85 that provoke similar issues of consistency – this time in relation to Kant's rejection of theological morality. In the case of *Moral Mongrovius II*, ways can be found of harmonising Kant's reported comments with those on the same issues in the critiques.

My interpretation will emphasise the subjectivist strands in Kant's treatment of religion, even while it acknowledges contrary tendencies toward objectivism. These are strands that make the truth and meaning of religious affirmations relative to human needs. In the jargon of contemporary philosophy of religion, there is a strongly anti-realist thrust in Kant on God. That anti-realist thrust is strikingly supported by the *Opus Postumum*. This is a set of loose, unbound, remarks written by Kant largely between 1796 and 1803 which were to be the basis for a statement of his final metaphysics. He did not complete the remarks or bring them to an accomplished order. They abound with 'subjectivist' comments on God, comments that identify God with the moral law and deny that he is a reality independent of the human mind. To interpreters of Kant who wish to see him as within mainstream theism, the *Opus Postumum* must be dealt with. It can be seen as embodying a radical change in Kant's view of God (as did the first editor of the notes, Erich Adickes – see Ward 1972:160). Or it can be dismissed as the unfinished ramblings of a man who was clearly very weak in mind and body in his last years. A contrary tale will be told by those who want to interpret Kant's account of God in the completed Critical works as being radically subjectivist. Thus Paul Guyer claims that the *Opus Postumum* makes explicit what is implicit in Kant's prior writings and that it is wrong to suppose that he would undertake a radical break from earlier views in the last years of his life (Guyer 2000:405). My use of the *Opus Postumum* will in general terms follow Guyer's lead.

Does Kant's life settle the interpretative questions?

If there is some tension within and controversy over Kant's religious views, may one sort matters out by reference to his life? Do biographical materials enable a clarifying light to be shone on his philosophy of religion? The answer to these questions is: there is some light to be shed from study of Kant's life, but it is not as decisive as we might hope for.

We must first acknowledge the usefulness of the extensive private correspondence of Kant's that has been preserved. One thing that the correspondence does for us is show that this man set great store by sincerity in speech. In a letter to Moses Mendelssohn of 6 April 1766, Kant stated that the greatest evil that could befall him was losing the self-respect that comes from a sense of honesty. He would never become a person who indulged in fraud. He distinguished between, on the one hand, lacking the courage to affirm in public all the things he was completely convinced of and, on the other, making statements in which he did not believe (*Correspondence* 10:69).Kant must therefore be read as capable of holding things back in his writings on religion, but we should be wary of accusing him of deliberately saying what he did not believe.

Does a study of his further correspondence tell us what he believed in matters of faith? Kant's *Correspondence* is remarkable for the lack of letters in which he writes directly about his religious faith. There is, however, a notable exception in the case of a letter to J. C. Lavater of 28 April 1775 (10:175–9). In response to Lavater's request for Kant to comment on his (Lavater's) account of faith and prayer, Kant distinguishes between the teachings of Christ and the report that we have of them. To see these teachings properly we must separate out the moral instruction of the New Testament from its dogmas: 'These teachings are certainly the fundamental doctrines of the Gospels, what remains can only serve as auxiliary teachings to them' (10:176). Thus Kant seems to commit himself to a fundamentally deistic view of Christ: he was but a moral teacher. The similarity is strengthened by Kant's equation of the non-fundamental doctrines with those that we could only know through knowing a historical revelation (10:177–8). Thus: the essential truths of Christianity are its moral teachings and no reliance on historical revelation is necessary to know these. The unspoken but obvious implication is that these moral doctrines are truths of reason, and as such accessible to anyone, anywhere and any time. The letter then adds the thought that we will be conscious of the gap between our evil doings and the holiness of the law and must rely upon some inscrutable means or other by which God will justify us in despite of that evil. In a follow-up letter to Lavater, Kant summarises the essence of his account of true faith as: 'the sum of all religion consists in righteousness and that we ought to seek it with all our power in the faith i.e. unconditional trust that God will then supply the good that is not in our power [to bring about]' (10:180). In both letters Kant says we need not strive to know any more about how God might supplement our efforts. We should equally not venerate the teacher of this simple message (Jesus) rather than the message itself or think that anything other than moral conduct will do in orienting ourselves toward God. We should not think that religious ceremonies or confessions of faith are any help in this task.

In these letters Kant seems to lay his own religious commitments clear: faith in a God (the precise kind of God is left undefined); commitment to a moral law; faith that there is some divine mechanism for overcoming the gap between our moral obligations and our evil ways; and an assertion of the irrelevance of dogma, revelation in history and ceremonies to true faith. At first glance, this comes close to the standard package of eighteenth-century deism. On the surface, it seems to scotch the notion that Kant was a Christian in any substantive sense of 'Christian', since it marks the rejection (as necessary to salvation) of belief in the *religion about Jesus* which the Christian church has constructed and which it has claimed to anchor in the New Testament. It is notable that the text of these two letters to Lavater does not assert that humanity needs a Redeemer. The question of how exactly to place Kant in relation to Christianity and deism will be taken up more thoroughly in the last chapter of this study.

Moving from Kant's correspondence to biographical sources, we find that these contain some striking facts. One is that Kant was believed by many of his close acquaintances to be some kind of unbeliever (see Kuehn 2001:120). This reputation was based on Kant's behaviour. For most of his adult life he seems to have played no part in organised religion, keeping well clear of the Lutheran churches and practices of his native Königsberg. Many biographical accounts have the following famous story: Kant was to be seen in his academic finery processing across the university square toward Königsberg Cathedral to inaugurate a new Rector only to walk past the building at the last moment while others went in (Kuehn 2001:318; Kant would enter only when it was his turn to be the Rector). Contemporaries who published accounts of his private conversations and table-talk record that Kant had no time for prayer or for hymns, and, more importantly, that he expressed his unbelief. Kuehn records that one such companion, J. G. Sheffner, often heard Kant 'scoff' at prayer and other religious practices. Kuehn's verdict is that 'It was clear to anyone who knew Kant personally that he had no faith in a personal God. Having postulated God and immortality, he himself did not believe in either' (2001:3). Kant's long-time acquaintance K. L. Pörscke recorded that Kant had often assured him that, though Kant had not doubted any of the dogmas of Christianity even after being a *Magister* for a long time, 'by and by one element after another fell away' (*nach und nach sei ein Stück ums andere abgefallen*, Vörlander 1977:155).

We thus have some limited autobiographical and biographical data that tell us that the man Immanuel Kant had lost faith in the Christianity of his youth some time after becoming a *Magister* (Kant became a full professor in 1770, at the age of 56). However, for all his scepticism about revealed and organised religion, he avowed belief in God in private correspondence. We have a hint that he was a deist (yet we shall see below that he repeatedly denies being a deist – another conundrum).

The *Weltanschauung*

Kant's writing career stretched from 1749 to the early 1800s. Lewis White Beck claims that, through the many changes in his detailed philosophical positions, Kant remained committed to a general *Weltanschauung* that can be summarised in 11 theses (Beck 1969:427–9):

1. Philosophy/metaphysics can be scientific.
2. Philosophy/metaphysics is not merely a technical subject but is important for humanity.
3. The interests of humanity are identified in the ideals of the Enlightenment and centre on freedom of the individual under strong government.
4. The progress of the human race is not measured by the amount of happiness it enjoys but by the development of moral character and freedom on the part

of human beings.
5. There is a God and an immortal soul.
6. Moral duties are not founded upon or derived from belief in God. Though morality supports religion, religion is a problematic support for morality.
7. Historical revelation may instruct people morally, but moral truths do not depend on historical revelation.
8. Human beings have free will.
9. The Newtonian, mechanistic view of nature is correct.
10. The physical world, by virtue of being a machine, is not the product of chance but is a teleological whole.
11. From (6) and (10): the science of nature, as well as morality, leads to a theistic metaphysics, in which the doctrine of humanity remains all-important.

Beck seems to me to have got it about right. We will see as we proceed that there are problems about, qualifications in, the belief in God and immortality in (6). We will find that the assertion of the theistic-teleological world-view in (10) and (11) is also subject to some qualification in Kant's mature writings. Despite this, the above list points to an enduring world-view in Kant's thought. What his philosophical progress amounts to is a journey through different ways of defending and articulating that world-view.

The elements of the world-view show that Kant was keen to defend and reconcile what appear to be conflicting demands of the Enlightenment: commitment to human progress and commitment to the completion of the scientific project. The first commitment shows in a belief in the perfectibility of the human race. Kant sees that perfectibility in moral terms. We have a duty to become morally perfect. The goal of the individual is the cultivation of the worthiness to be happy conjoined with happiness itself. The second commitment is based on the assumption that Nature is in harmony with the human intellect. Human reason seeks as an end the thoroughgoing explanation of all natural facts through subsumption of facts under laws and the unification of those laws in theoretical systems. These two commitments are made by one and the same human reason, which in Kant's special sense (when not identified with our cognitive powers in general) is the faculty of ends and principles. Reason sets the human being its key goals and provides it with overarching principles of thought and action. Reason appears to be in conflict with itself because its first goal, human-perfection-through-morality, seems to demand that human beings stand in some significant sense outside the world of natural causes. If they are wholly part of it, then they have no free will and their perfection and happiness is entirely at the mercy of blind, natural causes. On the other hand, if they do stand outside the world of natural causes, then the project of science cannot be completed, for scientific explanations could not then extend to human nature and human actions.

One of the chief aims of the Critical Philosophy is to resolve this tension. The idea of God, in the traditional lineaments provided by Western philosophical theology, is central to the resolution and thus central to the Critical Philosophy. The notion of God is necessary to sustain the belief in the completion of science, since we cannot (affirms Kant) support the notion that the world is intelligible, and thus open to human understanding and reason, save through the thought that it is the work of a designing intelligence. The idea of God is necessary to sustain belief in human perfectibility, since through the idea of God we maintain the thought that something other than blind natural causality controls the world and thus our destiny. Rather, the world can be thought of as a teleological whole – a whole working toward an end in which the human good will be realised – and as controlled by an agency that is morally aware. What the Critical Philosophy does is both enable this dual use of 'God' (to refer to a world designer and to a providential planner of history) and resolve the tension between the commitments behind the dual use. It does these two things by relativising and restricting the scope of the commitments reason makes in both the realms of theory and practice.

Heine must be wrong: the concept of God is not an afterthought designed to comfort the vulgar. This point about the centrality of God to Kant's entire project tells in favour of seeing Kant on God as within mainstream Christianity and philosophical theism. It will have to be balanced by stress on the radical character of the relativising and restriction of the import of the concept of God arising out of Kant's account of the boundaries of reason.

The context of religious philosophy

In his biography of Kant, Manfred Kuehn states that there were two main influences on German philosophy at the time Kant was developing his ideas: Wolffianism and British philosophy (2001:183–4). In philosophical theology the importance of Wolffianism was in its promotion of a God whose existence could be proved by pure reason alone. Appeal to the mere idea of a God as an all-perfect being, or to the principle of sufficient reason, was enough to prove the existence of a being in which essence entailed existence. The religiously conservative character of the German Enlightenment showed in the fact that such religious rationalism was not perceived as a threat to Christianity's status as a true but revealed religion. The influence of the British tradition was present through knowledge of Locke, Hume and Hutcheson (among others). In general philosophy, the impact of British thought was shown in the concern of Kant and his contemporaries to give due weight to the claims of sensation, feeling and perception alongside the claims of reason. The task set by the British thinkers for German philosophers was to balance the role of pure intellect in knowledge and morality alongside against the importance of sensation and feeling in those areas.

In the person of Hume and the English deists, Kant would also have encountered striking forms of religious scepticism. Hume's *Dialogues concerning Natural Religion* (published posthumously in 1779) were read by Kant in translation in time to be mentioned in the text (dating from 1782 or later) of his lectures on rational theology. (10:1063). The *Dialogues* contain sceptical reflections on the cosmological and design arguments. In the closing paragraph of the third dialogue and the opening paragraph of the fourth, they present the charge that the traditional concept of God in philosophical theology is an incoherent mixture of anthropomorphism and mystery. The anthropomorphism stems from the desire to present God as a person with a mind and will. The mystery stems from the desire to present God as an absolutely necessary, simple and timeless first cause (see Hume 1976:179–81). The thought behind Hume's charge was not lost on Kant, as we shall see later. There are, in addition, strong resemblances between Hume's strictures on the bad effects of popular religion (Hume 1976:251ff.) and Kant's attacks on the corruptions of 'statutory faith' that abound throughout his writings. The thought that religion as an institutionalised system is riddled with superstition and false ways of serving the perfect being are the stock-in-trade of Enlightenment reflections on religion and Kant signed up to them wholeheartedly. We have seen that in his personal life he had a marked aversion to organised religion and public religious devotions.

Kant must also have been aware of English deism and its critique of revealed religion. One of Kant's most important teachers when he went up to the University of Königsberg was Martin Knutzen. Knutzen published a defence of Christianity against the attacks of the deists in the year Kant went up to the *Albertina*. It beggars belief to suppose that Kant was not fully aware of the main outlines of the critique of Christianity contained in the writings of the likes of Tindal and Toland (see Kuehn 2001:80). He was certainly aware of German proponents of deism. There are six references in his works to the writings of Herman Samuel Reimarus, author of the posthumously published *Apology for the Rational Worshippers of God* (see, for example, *Religion* $6:81_n$). The positive and critical views of Reimarus are very similar to those of the English deists. Such thinkers undertook a root-and-branch critique of the truth and authority of the Christian scriptures and the doctrinal system of Christianity. Anything in these that went beyond the preaching of a plain, natural religion was false, corrupting, religiously unnecessary and lacking in any authority over the rational mind whatsoever. A natural religion – consisting in a belief in a perfect being, providence in this life and the next and the accessibility and bindingness of the moral law – is the universal, timeless essence of true religion.

Our discussion of Kant on revelation in Chapter 8 will show striking parallels between Kant's thought and the deistic critique of Christianity (likewise between Kantian and deistic accounts of true religion). Deism was part of the common currency of German thought of the latter half of the eighteenth century, as is shown, for example, in the writings of the likes of Reimarus. If Kant was influenced by English deism, as I assert must have been the case, he certainly hides his tracks. The only explicit reference to an English deist in his writings that I have been able to come across is a brief mention of Toland in a list of sceptics (*Reflexionen* 16:450). He uses the word *deismus* in a number of places, but his definition of deism (belief in a non-personal, lifeless God akin to blind fate; see, for example, *Lectures Religion* 28:1047) is not close to deism as it is set out by English deists.

Kant deals with this diverse legacy in religious thought in the manner in which he deals with the whole of the history of philosophy. He seeks to hold together its incompatible elements. There are parts of his philosophy of religion that parallel Hume (his critique of the arguments of natural theology). There are parts that use the rationalist inheritance (his articulation of God as the original being, the sum of all reality). There are parts that cohere nicely with deism (his critique of historical revelation and defence of a pure, rational faith). And there are parts which speak highly of Christ and which use Christian symbolism. Once again, Kant's thought is tensive.

The Critical project in outline

Both of the conflicting commitments in the Enlightenment *Weltanschauung* that Kant takes over are, in his view, metaphysical. These commitments cannot be proved on the basis of experience. The belief about human perfectibility through morality relies on further beliefs about free will and about the co-operating influence of a deity that go beyond anything that can be vouched for in experience. Experience cannot assure us that the universe is such as to allow human beings to be free and to achieve the highest good. The belief that all things in nature are scientifically explicable through a unified system of theories goes beyond the mere empirical fact that, so far as we have discovered, most events appear to be connected with other events through laws. Kant accordingly took as one of his major preoccupations the settling of the due limits and scope of metaphysical knowledge. In outline, he sets about the reconciliation of the items in his Enlightenment world-view by limiting the pretensions of its competing scientific and religious metaphysics and thereby producing an outcome in which their conflicting commitments can be jointly maintained. This central preoccupation with metaphysics allows Kant to pursue another task of reconciliation, a reconciliation between the views of those, such as Wolff, who thought substantive a priori knowledge of the world was possible and those, such as Hume who denied it. This Kant styled the problem of how synthetic a priori knowledge was possible, if at all.

Descartes had set a standard for certainty in knowledge according to which true knowledge was demonstrable from intuitively known starting points. Thinkers in opposing camps, such as Leibniz and Hume, agreed that such knowledge was not available from the world as known through our senses. This fact could then be taken in one of two ways. Some took it as showing that the true object of knowledge was an intelligible, rational world behind the world revealed by the senses. Others, such as Hume, denied that pure reason alone could yield knowledge of matters of fact. They thereby confined our knowledge to the observable world but lowered its certainty and reliability in the light of the Cartesian ideal.

Kant's solution to the dilemmas outlined is found in the first *Critique*. It depends on the point that there have to be elements of universality and necessity in the guiding principles of human enquiry, or as he puts it: there have to be a priori contributions to our knowledge of reality. But he makes these a priori principles not descriptions of an intelligible, rational realm beyond the senses, but statements of the *form* to which the matter of our experience of the ordinary world has to conform. General metaphysics contains principles describing the fundamental nature of what exists. Its propositions now become statements a priori of the form any intelligible experience of the world has to take. Because we can be assured a priori that, for example, any experience we can make sense of must be of a world in which all events are causally interconnectable, so it is that our knowledge of the world of experience can be guaranteed to have the certainty that comes from its obeying rational principles of order.

The general metaphysical principles of reality turn out to be true when relativised into statements about the form and structure of empirical knowledge. This structure is dictated by two sources of empirical knowledge: sensibility and understanding.

Knowledge is of empirical things, their properties, relations, actions, etc. It requires that something be given to sensibility and that the experience so occasioned be ordered through concepts provided by the understanding. Sensibility has an a priori structure – the mode in which things are given to human beings is as objects in space and time. Something similar is true of understanding, which turns out to have just twelve 'categories' (or higher-order concepts/forms of judgement) under which all concepts applicable to experience can be subsumed.

More convincing than Kant's list of categories is his argument, sustained through the Transcendental Analytic of the *Critique of Pure Reason*, that any conceivable form of human experience must be such as to allow concepts of an objective world to apply to it (in particular concepts within such categories as cause and substance). The argument turns around the necessity of experience having the richness capable of giving rise to self-consciousness. This richness involves experience having a rule-governed structure. Such a structure allows the subject to take its experience to be of a causally and temporally ordered world – in other words: to be of an objective world of enduring, interconnected things.

From the a priori forms of intuition and the a priori categories of the understanding, Kant is able to demonstrate a range of necessary truths about reality that can serve as the basis of a scientific metaphysics (see item (i) in the *Weltanschauung*). But the cost of establishing these truths of metaphysics is a certain relativising of their validity. The demonstration, for example, that every event in the world must have some cause or other depends on the condition that the world is an object of possible experience: any world about which we can make empirical judgements must be causally ordered. On this ground, the principles of general metaphysics cannot be applied to items beyond human experience. Concerning aspects of reality that lie beyond all possible experience we can know nothing, either a priori or a posteriori. Kant's thought here involves three things: the 'Copernican revolution in philosophy', the distinction between appearances and things in themselves and the idea of a boundary to thought and sense.

Prior to Copernicus, astronomers took the apparent daily motions of the stars and planets to be real. After Copernicus, they realised that these motions were nothing but the motions of the Earth projected onto heavenly bodies. Prior to the Critical Philosophy, metaphysicians took it that they had to discover the objective, necessary features of an independent reality revealed in the first principles of thought. After the Critical Philosophy, we realise that such features are nothing other than the a priori necessities of human cognition that we falsely assume to be reading off an intelligible reality. Contrary to Hume, we can anticipate reality a priori and thus be assured of the grounds of empirical knowledge. But we can only anticipate it if it conforms to the a priori forms of sensibility and a priori categories of the understanding lodged in the knowing subject. In the *Prolegomena* of 1783 Kant links the question 'How is metaphysics possible?' to the question 'How are synthetic a priori judgements possible?' (see 4:255–6) Synthetic a priori judgements would testify to the 'real' use of human reason. They would be judgements that contained substantive knowledge about things, about reality, while being necessarily true and knowable in advance of experience. Yet how can a reality which is fully independent of the subject be knowable a priori by that subject? The only way such judgements are possible is if reality has to conform to the conditions laid down by the subject.

Out of the Copernican revolution in philosophy come two key ideas in Kant's thought: the distinction between appearances and things in themselves and the idea of a boundary to human thought. The ideas are interrelated. The boundary to thought comes with the line that divides things in themselves from appearances. We have cognition of reality only insofar as it appears to us. Cognition does not extend to things in themselves.

There is a great deal that can be said about the thing in itself/appearance distinction. Kant's language in expressing it allows the distinction to be interpreted in two ways. On a substantive, dualistic reading of it, there are two classes of object. We can have knowledge of objects in the class 'appearances' because these objects are in some measure or in some way part constituted by our cognitive activities. We cannot have knowledge of objects in the class 'things in themselves', not least because human knowledge depends on the a priori forms of intuition – space and time – and objects in the second class are non-spatio-temporal. Such a substantive reading of the distinction is plain contrary to the 'official' places in the first *Critique* where it is introduced. In such places the distinction is an adverbial one: objects as appearances are objects considered as knowable by a sensible intuition such as ours. Objects as things in themselves are those objects considered as knowable without reliance on a sensible intuition such as ours (see *Critique$_1$* A249). A letter to Garve of 1783 reinforces the adverbial view. It tells us that there are two ways in which objects can be taken: as appearances and as things in themselves (10:342). Kant links the appearance/thing in itself distinction to that between phenomena and noumena. In the second edition of the first *Critique* the distinction is initially introduced as a negative one, and as such it corresponds to that the appearance/thing in itself distinction, but the notion of a noumenon is made richer via a positive use of it:

> If under 'noumenon' we understand a thing *insofar as it is not an object of our sensible intuition*, because we abstract from our mode of intuition of it, then it is a noumenon in the *negative* sense. But if we understand by the term *an object of a non-sensible intuition*, then we assume a special mode of intuition, namely the intellectual, which, however, is not ours, and of which we cannot even grasp the possibility, and this would be a noumenon in a *positive* sense. (B307)

The things we know are known via the forms of a sensible intuition like ours: one that has to be affected by objects given to our senses. They can thus only be known insofar as they are phenomena. If we abstract from that way of knowing about objects, we cannot of course know anything about them, for that way of knowing is *our* way of knowing. It is not just a human way of knowing but characteristic of any finite, embodied creature's way of knowing. The act of abstraction may nonetheless be important because it reminds us that our modes of knowledge are limiting as well as enabling. This will allow room for the thought that things, reality, might have all manner of aspects which we, constituted as we are, could never be aware of. That thought is vital for the boundary drawing the Critical Philosophy wishes to undertake. We cannot make the world of phenomena co-terminus with all that there is. The positive sense of noumenon extends this thought to the conception of a knower with a 'non-sensible intuition'. Such a knower would know things without first intuiting them via receptive sense organs. This intuition would be creative. Things would be known and exist as objects of knowledge just in being thought of. This intuition would not be bound by space and time. It would not be bound by the categories, where they are thought of as general forms of judgement we use in ordering sensory input (see A256/B312). God's intuition would be creative in this fashion.

The concept of a noumenon is a boundary concept. It is there to curb the pretensions of sensibility (A255/B311). With this boundary concept Kant can cement the relativising moves he makes as part of his attempt to ground metaphysics as a science. The substantive claims of general metaphysics (such as those contained in the principle that everything that happens has a sufficient cause) become true a priori but only true of things *qua* appearances, *qua* phenomena. The boundary stops the principle 'Every happening in the world of sense must have a sufficient cause' being generalised to cover everything. We can at least postulate, or think of, realities that could lie beyond the boundary and we cannot apply the synthetic a priori truths of general metaphysics to those. These synthetic a priori truths are necessary conditions of the possibility of natural science's success in describing the world, but the boundary stops natural science being taken to be the complete description of all possible reality. This relativising of the claims of general metaphysics allows the claims of special metaphysics concerning the existence of God, the freedom of the human will (and thus the veridicality of the experience of being under moral obligation) and the immortality of the human soul to be thinkable, albeit not provable. Knowledge for beings with an intuition like ours is confined to appearances/phenomena. The problem with old-style special metaphysics is precisely that it has sought knowledge, and a priori knowledge to boot, of the things which, if real, would be beyond appearance. It is essential therefore for Kant's project that he expose the proofs of old-style special metaphysics as irredeemably flawed. We simply cannot have knowledge of objects that cannot be given in a possible experience. With the appropriate minor premise, it follows that we cannot have knowledge that there is a God, that we have free will, that there is an eternal life. Thus there arises the part of the first *Critique* which so struck Heine: the Dialectic wherein all the false metaphysical proofs of these Ideas of Pure Reason are exposed as resting on illusion.

But we can and we need to postulate the freedom of the will, the existence of God and some kind of eternal life for human beings. The needs that make us go beyond the boundary set by appearances/phenomena are not trivial or optional. They are the needs of human reason as such. The faith that the first *Critique* speaks of as transcending knowledge (Bxxx) is a not a passional affair. It is rather pure, rational faith (see *Critique*$_2$ 5:126). This is not reason directed toward the extension of our knowledge, but rather toward the founding of beliefs or working assumptions (there are ambiguities in Kant's thought on this which will be discussed in later chapters) necessary for steady pursuit of the goals in elements (3) and (4) of the *Weltanschauung*.

It is important to note that Kant distinguishes between *limits* (*Shranken*) and *boundaries* (*Grenzen*) in human thought and enquiry. Kant draws the distinction thus in the *Prolegomena*: 'Boundaries (in extended things) always presuppose a space, that is found outside a certain definite place and that encloses it; limits require nothing like that, but are mere negations indicating a quantity insofar as it lacks absolute completeness' (4:352). In mathematics and natural science we recognise limits. We know that our enquiries in such disciplines are limited in their scope. At any one time insight is finite in extent, but we could always take those enquiries further and discover more and more facts in mathematics and natural science. Says Kant: 'the enlargement of insight in mathematics ... goes to infinity; similarly there is no end to the discovery of new natural properties, new forces and laws' (4:352). Metaphysics, by contrast, leads us to boundaries. Notions such as God, freedom and immortality ('the transcendental ideas') show us those boundaries (4:353). We cannot coherently imagine our insight into these objects of thought expanding into infinity. These notions reveal boundaries because they are the alleged answers to important questions that human reason cannot give up. Yet at the same time, reason cannot answer these questions by providing us with *knowledge* of God, freedom and immortality. This because it is reliant, for knowledge, on the concepts and laws of the understanding, and they are only adequate for gaining empirical knowledge of things within the sensible world (4:353). Reason hits a boundary, realises that knowledge of appearance cannot answer the questions posed by special metaphysics, but is forced to postulate concerning what lies in the territory beyond the boundary. The boundary marks the edge of what can be cognised (4:357); beyond the boundary lies what can merely be thought, albeit on the basis of analogies drawn upon our knowledge of what lies inside the boundary. In this fashion metaphysical thought is bounded by the distinction between appearances and things in themselves.

Coda on transcendental idealism

In expounding the key themes in the Critical Philosophy we have hit upon the fact that Kant's system embodies the point of view he styles 'transcendental idealism'. He distinguishes this form of idealism from the 'empirical idealism' he finds in George Berkeley. That latter form states that those things we thought of as existing and enduring in space and time are nothing other than collections of perceptions in our minds. There are numerous passages in the first edition of the *Critique of Pure Reason* that are suggestive of a Berkeley-type view, passages such as 'appearances are not things in themselves, but rather the mere play of our representations' (A102). In the second edition he added a brief 'Refutation of Idealism' (B274–9) to rebut Berkeleyan views and to indicate that they formed no part of his *Critique*.

Transcendental idealism just is the claim that the objects of empirical knowledge are appearances rather than things in themselves. Considered from the standpoint of transcendental reflection these objects are appearances not things in themselves. Transcendental reflection takes in those facts that are necessary conditions for creatures like us (with sensible intuitions, etc.) to have self-conscious experience of a world that contains objects of ordered knowledge. To say, in the light of transcendental reflection, that we can only have knowledge of objects as they appear to us is, in one way, to utter a miserable tautology: we can only know objects in the manner in which creatures like us can know them. But the tautology is not so miserable given that transcendental reflection exposes the specific conditions under which creatures like us can know them. These are the conditions set by space and time as forms of intuition and by the categories as the fundamental ways of ordering the input received by a spatio-temporally conditioned, sensible intuition. Delineation of the conditions set by sensibility and understanding in the Transcendental Aesthetic and Analytic of the first *Critique* throws up the peculiar limitations of a way of knowing about objects based on sensible intuition and a discursive understanding. It thus gives some substance to the thought that we know objects only as our cognitive constitution allows us to know them.

Transcendental idealism concludes that we do not know things as they are in themselves. Once more, that looks like a miserable tautology, telling us merely that we can't know things if they are not accessible to the ways we have of knowing things. But the statement reminds us of the peculiar conditions under which we know things and thus allows us room to speculate about those aspects of reality that our limitations might leave forever unknowable to creatures like us.

We are reading transcendental idealism adverbially – along with an adverbial reading of the appearance/thing in itself distinction. A non-adverbial reading would have Kant telling us that the objects of our knowledge, being mere appearances, are constructed by us (using the forms of intuition and the categories) in response to the causal input of a class of non-temporal, non-spatial objects styled 'things in themselves'. The non-adverbial reading has allowed generations of Kant's critics to throw knock-down objections at the Critical Philosophy. How can things in themselves causally interact with a sensible intuition when causality, to the extent that we understand it, is a relation between things and events in time? The self that has empirical knowledge is also an appearance (see, for example, B158) and thus the causal transaction would have to be between the self as it is in itself and things as they are in themselves. This, apart from piling mystery upon mystery, raises further problems: how could, for example, the distinction between things and persons be made in a realm of things in themselves? The possession of reason, memory, consciousness, and the like is an empirical fact about selves. Selves could not be distinguished from non-selves in the realm beyond appearances by reference to these factors.

The adverbial and modest reading of transcendental idealism might suggest that Kant has in mind a 'filter' view as opposed to a 'creation' view of the knower–known relation. On the filter view, the subjective turn in epistemology and metaphysics at the heart of the Copernican revolution in philosophy serves to bring home the fact that human cognition limits those aspects of reality that we can be aware of. Our modes of sensible intuition are spatio-temporal. Thus the only aspects of reality we can be aware of will be spatio-temporal. The realisation of this limitation allows us to think that there may be aspects of reality of a non-spatio-temporal kind. This in turn allows us to suppose, though not to know, that human beings have a contra-causal freedom, something that they could not have if they were wholly spatio-temporal. In this manner, the picture of an epistemological subject with a sensible intuition and a discursive understanding kills off dogmatism. The fact (according to Kant it is a fact – see below) that human beings have no proof from experience that there is a God does not entail that there is no God. It remains thinkable that such a being exists in the realms of reality that our cognitive filtering apparatus will not let us reach. The

God and Kant's Critical Project 17

filter view preserves one of Kant's essential thoughts: the world disclosed in ordinary experience is empirically real but transcendentally ideal. That is to say, reflecting on the a priori necessary conditions of experience (that is, transcendentally), we see that our knowledge of this world is conditioned by our cognitive apparatus and thus contains a vital contribution from that apparatus. It is in that sense, but only in that sense, ideal or mind-dependent. It is like the sense in which the fisherman's net makes a contribution to the catch in the boat. The net does not create the fish, but it does mean that only a fish of a certain size will be caught.

The two-worlds reading of transcendental idealism makes the human subject the constructor of what it knows. The immediate objects of cognition are 'in the mind' in something like the fashion objects of perception are in the mind for Berkeley. A realm of things external to human cognition provides some causal (albeit it is an incomprehensible kind of causality) input to this process, but the specific character of the phenomenal objects thus created is down to our constitution. We have to accept this last claim, since the dualist reading of things in themselves excludes the thought that things in themselves could have the properties empirical objects have.

We have seen that the dualist reading of transcendental idealism encounters great difficulties, both intra- and extra-textual (see Allison 1983 for a full case against it). Does that mean that we must suppose that Kant views the finite knower's intuition and understanding as mere cognitive filters? Alas not. There are numerous passages in the Transcendental Aesthetic that state that the spatio-temporal properties of the world only reside in it *qua* appearance, not as it in itself. Just one example will illustrate the point. At A37–8/B53–4 Kant writes of time:

> Time is certainly something real, namely the real form of inner intuition. It therefore has subjective reality in respect to inner experience, i.e. I really have the representation of time and of my determinations in it. It is therefore real, not as object, but as a mode of representing myself as an object. If, however, I could intuit myself, or another being could intuit me, without this condition of sensibility, then these very determinations, which we now represent to ourselves as changes, would yield us a cognition, in which the representation of time and therefore of change as well would in no way occur. Its empirical reality therefore remains as a condition of all our experiences. It is merely that absolute reality cannot be granted it, according to the above. It is nothing except the form of our inner intuition. If one takes away the special condition of our sensibility from it, then the concept of time also vanishes, *and it does not attach to the objects themselves*, but merely to the subject, which intuits them. (my emphasis)

This is manifestly not the filtration view and the essential idea in this passage is repeated elsewhere in the *Critique of Pure Reason* – as at B148, where we are told, that beyond the boundaries set by the senses, space and time 'do not represent anything at all and outside of them have no reality'.

The core of the filtration view is simple. A given object can be viewed in more than one way. Viewed in a certain way, say by creatures with a certain cognitive constitution, only some of its properties are manifest. Viewed in another way other properties are discernible. But the one object has both sets of properties. However, Kant seems to set his mind against these plain consequences of the filtration model of the subject's contribution to knowledge. Kant's view is precisely *not* that objects have one set of properties considered *qua* appearances alongside, conjoined with, another set considered from another point of view. Rather: the properties they have *qua* appearances they *only* have *qua* appearances. (For further support of this reading see Allison 1996:12ff.) The thing in itself and the thing *qua* appearance may be the one thing considered in two ways, but the properties it has as an appearance it does not have as it is in itself.

The above problem more properly concerns a study of Kant's epistemology and metaphysics, but it does throw up an issue that pertains to Kant's concept of freedom, which conception is of importance for this study. Granted Kant has an adverbial conception of the appearance versus thing in itself distinction, and yet rejects the filtration model, he has a problem about identity. How can the one thing serve both as appearance and thing in itself? How can the one thing be a particular human being and also a thing in itself? In viewing it in the latter light, we will have to deprive it of its spatio-temporal properties since they only exist when it is viewed as appearance. But a human agent's very identity is given by him or her being born at a particular time and place, of certain parents, and as having certain memories and psychological traits. Kant wants to say of the given human being that s/he is part of a causal nexus considered as appearance, but has freedom of the will of a radical, contra-causal kind when considered as thing in itself or as member of an intelligible realm. He must therefore make an identity claim that his rejection of the filtration model makes very hard to comprehend. And if he were to accept the filtration model the reconciliation of universal determinism in the realm of appearances with free will in the intelligible realm would appear not to work. For the filtration model licenses us to give the thing in itself the properties of the thing *qua* appearance; these properties are merely a selection of the full set of properties it has. But then the human being as it is in itself would be determined by spatio-temporal causes and there would be no freedom in reality.

What we have learnt from this coda is that the modest, adverbial construction of transcendental idealism looks tempting. It enables us to see how Kant's Critical Philosophy allows him to place limits around certain kinds of dogmatism. It will, as noted, stop certain kinds of proofs of God's non-existence in their tracks. However, the adverbial reading requires an identity claim to be registered for it to be fully comprehensible. That claim is most easily made on a filtration model, but the filtration model hardly does justice to the full range of Kant's assertions about the subjective character of space and time. Here then is a conundrum in the interpretation of the fundamental thrust of the Critical Philosophy that we will just have to set aside. (Allison 1983, 1990 and 1996 open the door to the debates this conundrum has raised.)

Chapter 2

Kant on Natural Theology I

Kant's critique of the arguments of natural theology is justly famous. It is one of the crucial steps in establishing the point that knowledge of God lies beyond the boundary set for reason by the Critical Philosophy and is therefore impossible. It helped Kant earn the reputation of the philosopher who attempted to assassinate God. The critique has been much discussed and reactions to it have varied from warm endorsement to rejection. Endorsement is shown in those many thinkers who take it that, along with Hume, Kant dealt the deathblow to natural theology. A good deal of recent commentary on Kant has moved toward the opposite response, seeing Kant's objections to ontological, cosmological and design arguments as less than impressive (see the extended discussion in Wood 1978 for an example of this).

An initial problem with Kant's attempted refutation of the proofs of natural theology arises out of the extent to which they depend on the main tenets of the Critical Philosophy, particularly on embracing the Copernican revolution in philosophy and its attendant transcendental idealism. It is evident that elements of the refutation do so depend. Dependence is shown, for example, in the critical comment on the cosmological proof that castigates it for employing the principle that everything must have a cause beyond the world of sense. Kant's claim that 'the principle of causality has no meaning at all and no criterion for its use, except in the sensible world' (A609/B637) seems to depend on the previous pages of the *Critique of Pure Reason* and is likely to be seen as simply question-begging by a proponent of traditional natural theology. However, it must be noted on the other side of the scales that many of the chief points made against the traditional proofs in the *Critique* are to be found in a much earlier work (dating from 1763): *The Only Possible Ground for a Demonstration of the Existence of God*. There they do not depend on transcendental idealism, for Kant had not yet developed the doctrines of transcendental idealism. And the points in the *Only Possible Ground* themselves are foreshadowed by material in *A New Elucidation of the First Principles of Metaphysical Cognition* of 1755.

What these pre-Critical texts show is that from an early stage in his writing career Kant was sceptical of key elements in the ruling Leibniz-Wolff philosophy in Germany. A particular object of his scepticism is the use of the principle of sufficient reason and the principle of non-contradiction as the basis of metaphysics. Rationalist proofs of the existence of God were bound up with this use. They relied on the idea that there has to be a complete and sufficient reason accounting for all facts to get to the conclusion that there is a being whose existence was grounded in its very nature and concept. Such a being contains within itself the reason for its own existence. To deny the existence of this self-explanatory being is to violate the principle of non-contradiction. Postulating such a God then satisfies the demands of the principle of sufficient reason. The existence of such a being itself has a sufficient explanation (via its own nature) and in turn it provides the sufficient reason for the existence and character of everything else. The principle of sufficient reason and the God of rationalism are in a mutually supporting relationship. The principle enables a priori proofs of God's existence to be provided and thus assures reason of God's existence. God's existence in turn assures reason that the principle of sufficient reason holds throughout finite, mundane reality. This mutually supporting relationship forges a close connection between the goals of general and of special metaphysics. From one side of the relationship, reason armed with the principle of sufficient reason establishes God's existence. From the other side, reason armed with deductive, a priori proofs of God's existence is assured that the world exhibits the thoroughgoing rational order demanded by the principle of sufficient reason and is thus a fit object for scientific enquiry.

Kant objects from early on to those rationalist proofs of God's existence using the principle of sufficient reason. He summarises their form in *Lectures Theology* (12:1006) in the following terms:

1. All contingent things require a cause; why anything contingent exists at all requires an explanation.
2. The universe is a contingent thing.
3. The universe requires a cause/explanation.
4. The explanation of contingent things can only be a necessary thing (something that is explained *a se* – that contains the ground of its own existence).

He also objects in these earlier writings to what he styles in the first *Critique* 'the ontological argument' and its key thought that God's nature as the supremely real or perfect being includes or entails God's existence. Indeed in the *New Elucidation* there is an indication of his later thought that to reject the ontological argument (and the notion that the concept or nature of God is sufficient to establish God's existence) is to reject the argument from contingency. He moves seamlessly from rejection of the thought that God is the ground of his own existence to the impossibility of proving there is a God in reality from the mere fact that one has included existence in the concept of God (see 1:394–5).

We shall return to the *Only Possible Ground* in greater detail below, for it will be necessary to use it to help in the exposition of the critique of natural theology in the first *Critique*. Let us note at this point that, like the *Critique*, it yokes the Cartesian ontological argument and the argument from contingency to the teleological proof in a troika of traditional proofs for the existence of God. A hypothesis to account for Kant's practice of discussing the three proofs together is that the design argument is thought by him as playing an essential role in rationalist metaphysics, one that is needed to support the mutual link between general and special metaphysics rationalism depends on.

The ontological and cosmological arguments purport to show that there is a self-existent being whose essence guarantees its existence and who further provides a sufficient reason for the existence of all other things. But, for Kant, it is important that the God of natural theology also acts for the sake of ends. It is only this that enables the world to be truly comprehensible. The world is fashioned by a mind of which ours are a reflection and the ends of this mind are visible in the world. This means that the world not merely displays a connected order of things and events in which each item is sufficiently explained, but also that the order of sufficient reasons is comprehensible to us (see Neiman 1994:23–6). The world displays an order put into it by God, a God whose purposes we can discern and thus an order that we can make out. This is the picture at the heart of the teleological argument. Science is the recording of the divinely given order and the link between the divine and the human mind makes the recording possible. Kant's rejection of the principle of sufficient reason as a substantive principle of metaphysics extends to the claim that we cannot infer a designing God and his purposes from the evidence in nature.

Reason's activity in science and morality is not, for Kant, the tracing of a divinely given order. Reason is autonomous, not heteronomous (Neiman 1994:33). For example, it does not, in the course of developing an ever more systematic science of nature, trace out a God-given order. Its picture of the order revealed by science is constructed rather than read off nature. Reason does its constructing under the banner provided by the idea of a designing God whose plan for the world can be discerned in it, but this idea is a postulation, a heuristic device. The principle of sufficient reason plays a vital role in the management of reason's tasks, but it is not an ontological principle – no more is the principle of design an ontological principle. If they were ontological principles, we would have the heteronomy and not the autonomy of reason. This Kantian turn is yet another consequence of the Copernican revolution for philosophy. Rationalist metaphysics, in 'proving' the existence of an all-perfect, all-wise designing creator, thought that it was discovering objective features of the world beyond human cognition. It was instead reading reason's own demands for unity and purpose in nature as if they were objective features of the reality in front of it. As noted in Chapter 1, Kant has his own way of using general metaphysics to support special metaphysics. The Copernican revolution allows reason to be free to make demands on the world – since, while the scope of the deliverances of the understanding is severely limited, they do assure us that any world we can have experience of must have some order to it. Reason demands investigation of the world (and the living of the moral life) under the guidance of the Ideas of Reason, including God, and the Critical Philosophy assures us that those demands can be catered for without fear of contradiction.

We can now see in further detail how the critique of natural theology in Kant is an important offshoot of the Critical Philosophy. The full consequences of the Copernican revolution entail the deontologising of reason and its key notions (such as the principle of sufficient reason, the principle of non-contradiction and the idea of the world as a comprehensible piece of design). They also make room for the autonomy of reason. Nonetheless, the aim of the critique of natural theology must be to show that reason cannot work when ontologised and thus that reason has no apodeictic proofs of the existence of an all-perfect, all-wise supreme reality.

The ontological argument

Kant's discussion of natural theology is famous for affirming that there are three and three only proofs of the existence of God – ontological, cosmological and teleological – and that the cosmological and teleological arguments depend on the ontological. The conjunction of these two theses obviously makes his critique of the ontological argument important.

The affirmation of 'three and three only proofs' is made at A590–91/B618–19. It is very puzzling on both external and internal grounds. This is how Kant makes and supports the claim:

> All paths, which one may follow with this purpose, either begin from determinate experience and the specific constitution of our sensible world known through it, and ascend from it by means of laws of causality to the supreme cause beyond the world; or else they rest on the empirical ground of an indeterminate experience, i.e. on existence in general; or they abstract finally from all experience and argue completely a priori from bare concepts to a supreme cause. The first proof is the *physico-theological*, the second the *cosmological*, and the third the *ontological* proof. There are no more than these and there cannot be any more. (A590–91/B618–19)

The first thing that is odd about this passage is that Kant himself knows about other proofs not his list. In the *Only Possible Ground* he has an a priori argument for God's existence turning around the notion of how something is determined as a possible thing. He distinguishes it from the Cartesian proof from the concept of God, which he later styles the ontological argument (see 2:156–7). The proof from the determination of a possible thing also resurfaces in the first *Critique* in the exposition of the notion of God as an *ens originarium* (from A571/B596 onwards), so Kant has hardly forgotten about it

For Kant in the first *Critique*, the cosmological argument equals the argument from contingency ('something contingent exists, therefore something absolutely necessary must exist'). However, the tradition of natural theology contains more than one argument properly styled 'cosmological'. The Kalam argument starts not from the premise of the argument from contingency, but from the premise that the world had a beginning in time. It then moves to the conclusion that the world must have had a timeless cause via the premise 'that all things that have a beginning of existence must have a cause'. Could Kant really not have been aware of this form of the cosmological argument? The example of the Kalam challenges Kant's initial and highly general way of dividing the proofs. The abstract classification of proofs into those that start from information about the detailed constitution of the world, those that start from 'the empirical ground of an indeterminate experience, i.e. on existence in general', and those that proceed from mere concepts might look plausible, but there are many ways in which a proof in natural theology could start from a fact about things (such as: that they had a beginning in time) that did not deal in the detailed constitution of the world. We can hypothesise that Kant's conviction in the first *Critique* that the ontological argument was central to reason's search for an *ens originarium* led him to be impatient of the variety of proofs in the past and present of natural theology.

Kant's attempted refutation of the ontological argument occupies 14 paragraphs from A592/B620 to A602/B630. Generations of textbooks have taught students of philosophy that these 14 paragraphs comprehensively rebut the argument, but recent, closer examinations have indicated how unclear and tendentious the claims made in them are (see Everitt 1995, Oppy 1995 and Wood 1978 for such critiques of Kant). It must be conceded that there are very unsatisfactory aspects to Kant's attempted refutation. For example, there is no clear statement of the proof given by Kant. And from the outset it is evident (see para. 1) that he is discussing the concept of a most real being, an *ens realissimum* and whether the content of this concept entails that such a being must exist. He has written earlier of the concept of God being that of the most real being, the *ens realissimum* (*Critique$_1$* A576/B604). Yet the ontological argument in the hands of Descartes (reflecting also the tradition established by St Anselm) focuses on God as an absolutely *perfect* being and contends that the divine essence so defined entails the divine existence. It is evident from other places that Kant was acquainted with Descartes' argument and he had some, at least minimal knowledge of Anselm as the author of a proof of God's existence (see the two references to Anselm in the *Nachlass*:18:500 and 20:349), albeit he nowhere discusses Anselm's version of the argument.

Descartes' argument in *Meditation V* begins with the very general reflection that all objects whose natures he clearly and distinctly perceives must have the properties he sees in those natures. He has a clear and distinct perception of the idea of God. God's nature is that of a supremely perfect being and existence is seen to belong to that nature (Descartes 1970:103). The premises that 'a supremely perfect being has all perfections' and that 'existence is a perfection' are spelled out a few paragraphs later (Descartes 1970:104). The first *Critique* presentation seems to ignore these significant details. The outline of the 'Cartesian proof' in the *Only Possible Ground* is both clearer and truer to the original in Descartes:

> In it one thinks of a concept of a possible thing, in which one imagines that all true perfection is united. One then assumes that existence is also a perfection of things; thus one infers the existence of a most perfect being from the possibility of such a being. (2:156)

It is almost as if the treatment in the first *Critique* gives the ontological arguer the premise that existence is part of God's essence, as by definition God is the most real being, with the aim of showing that, even if a definition of God has this element/consequence, it does not follow that there is something corresponding to the definition in actuality.

The most famous part of Kant's refutation of the proof is the statement contained in the opening of the tenth paragraph 'Being is obviously not a real predicate, i.e. a concept of something which could be added to the concept of a thing. It is merely the positing of a thing or of certain determinations in themselves' (A598/B626). This claim could be made to tie in with the details of Descartes' argument. That holds, as we have seen, that existence is perfection. A perfection is a great-making property. If by 'real predicate' Kant means 'a property-denoting word', then his claim entails that existence is not a property and thus not a great-making property.

There are two problems with interpreting the tenth-paragraph claim about being in this fashion. First, the paragraph and its preceding paragraphs give no indication that Kant means to make this argumentative move; there is no indication that his target is the premise 'Existence is a perfection'. Second, the account of 'real predicates' in this part of the discussion is very opaque and does not clearly indicate that Kant has in mind the (apparently) simple idea: real predicates denote properties. Paragraph 9 distinguishes real from logical predicates. We are told that 'anything one likes' can serve as a logical predicate. Real predicates are connected to 'determinations' (*Bestimmungen*) and a determination is something that is added to the concept of a subject and goes beyond and enlarges it. Such a real predicate must not be included in the concept of the subject already (A598/B626). This is most puzzling. It implies that 'unmarried' in 'All bachelors are unmarried' is not a real predicate because it is included in the concept of bachelorhood. Surely it functions just as much as a predicate in that analytic statement as it does in 'All happy men are unmarried'? In both 'unmarried' is a property-denoting word. In the first statement it denotes a property that is included in the subject-term's definition. In the second it denotes a property that is only contingently, albeit universally, connected with the subject term.

Paragraphs 9–10 in the first *Critique* treatment follow a discussion (see para. 8 on A597–8/B625–6) where Kant's opponent wants to put 'exists' into the definition of God as the most real of beings and Kant is trying to convince this ontological reasoner that one cannot get God's actual existence out of this manoeuvre. Yet again, the rebuttal in the *Only Possible Ground* is clearer. The pithy but accurate summary of Descartes noted above is followed by the claim 'that existence is not a predicate at all, and therefore not a predicate of perfection either' (2:156). Kant refers the reader back from these brief statements to a discussion in section 1 of the work entitled 'Existence is not a predicate or a determination of any thing'. Genuine predicates are here linked to determinations of things. Determinations seem to be those qualities that identify something as the thing it is. After noting that 'the term "existence" is used as a predicate in ordinary usage' (2:72), Kant goes on to make a point about the deep logic of the verb 'to be' and its equivalents that is strikingly similar to the essential thought about existence, familiar since Frege and Russell: 'exists' is a second-order predicate, not a direct determinate of objects. On this modern, logical account to say that 'Cows exist' is to say something like 'The concept "cow" has instances', which is to say further that a certain description (one giving the defining properties of cows) is true of something. Existence statements are about objects only indirectly; directly they say something about the relation between language/representations and the world.

This is how Kant makes his point about the logic of 'existence': 'But in those cases where existence is encountered as a predicate in common speech, it is not so much a predicate of the thing itself but more a predicate of the thought which one has of it' (2:72). There is a striking parallel here to the logician's view of existential statements. To say that the sea unicorn or narwhal exists is to say no more than the representation of the narwhal is that of an existing thing and it is along those lines that we explicate 'existence belongs to the sea unicorn but not the land unicorn' (2:72). We do not affirm that a certain determination applies to the one animal but not to the other. A clearer anticipation of the second-order view of existence is this: 'Not: "Regular hexagons exist in nature" but: "There are certain things in nature ... to which belong the predicates which are thought together in thinking of a hexagon"'(2:73).

The *Only Possible Ground* discussion thus has something that directly challenges a key premise in the Cartesian argument. An ontological reasoner will no doubt respond to the challenge. Perhaps the view of existence as a second-order predicate is not true of all uses of 'to be' and its cognates and it thus falls. Let us assume that this response fails. Another response to Kant's challenge might be: there is no proof that the second-order view is true. To this can be added the following thought: the second-order view need not be exclusively true. If it is the case that 'Sea unicorns exist' means in part 'The description of a sea unicorn is true of something', the defender of the ontological proof might claim that this is so only in virtue of the fact that sea unicorns possess a property (existence, reality) which land unicorns lack. The ontological reasoner can thus claim that 'to be' functions both as a second-order predicate and as a first-order predicate (see Oppy 1995:146). These kinds of response lead us to an important point about the refutation of this and other proofs in natural theology. Kant does not need to show the proponent of the ontological proof that existence is not a great-making property. It is up to the ontological reasoner to show that the premises of his argument are true. The burden of proof falls on those advancing the ontological argument. It is enough if Kant shows that alternatives to these premises can reasonably be held and thus that the premises can reasonably be denied. I suggest that the considerations in the *Only Possible Ground* do that for the premise 'Existence is a perfection'.

Kant's explicit concern is with the arguments of natural theology as *Beweisarten*, arguments that prove things. Proofs are more than sound arguments. The following would have to be regarded as a sound argument for God's existence by any theist:

The world exists and God sustains it.
Therefore God sustains the world.
Whatever sustains something must exist.
Therefore God exists.

But of course this argument for God's existence is no proof even if all its premises are true. A proof must have true premises but they must also serve as the means whereby someone not antecedently convinced of the conclusion can be led to that conviction. The conclusion of a proof must follow from its premises or be made highly probable by their truth. And its premises must known to be true and be sufficiently distinct from its conclusion. It is enough therefore to defeat the Cartesian argument *as a proof* to rest on the point that premises such as 'We have a clear and distinct perception of God's nature' and 'Existence is a perfection' are not known to be true or can reasonably be denied by one not previously convinced that there is a God. As Oppy notes, there is a very easy way for the atheist or agnostic to escape the clutches of the ontological proof: it will always be reasonable for such a person to reject one or other key premise (Oppy 1995:11). If this is so, the interest of Kant's discussions should be sought in how well they serve to articulate the dissent the atheist or agnostic registers at steps in the argument.

We have asserted that the way Kant presents the claim that existence is not a property in the first *Critique* does a poor job of articulating the dissent of those who reject the ontological argument. There are, however, two further points of substance he makes in this version of his exposé of the argument. One consists of insisting (in para. 8) that existential statements are all synthetic. This verdict is prepared for from paragraph 4 onwards. In paragraph 4 we are told that 'necessary' properly belongs to judgements rather than things and, as such, is conditional (A593–4/B621–2). Thus the necessity of 'A triangle has three angles' only tells us that *if* something is a triangle, it must have three angles. This leads in the fifth paragraph to the assertion that there can be no contradiction in saying that 'God is not' (A594–5/B622–3). If we posit God and then cancel God's omnipotence, we contradict ourselves, for necessarily if there is a God, God is omnipotent. But if we deny the existence of the subject of God-sentences, no contradiction can result, for thereby all of God's predicates are 'rejected together with the subject' (A595/B623). The sixth paragraph rehearses the conclusion of the last: denying the existence of a subject can never result in contradiction (A595–6/B623–4). The seventh allows the ontological reasoner a reply: there is one special subject, that denoted by the concept of the most real being. This subject has all reality, therefore there is a contradiction in denying its existence (A596/B624). Note that this reply confirms the point that this first *Critique* discussion is not really of the Cartesian argument but of a more direct ontological argument of some such form as: 'God is the most real of things. By definition God therefore has reality as part of his essence, and thus God must exist'. Kant then summarises an argument of just this kind (A596–7/B624–5). He will go on in paragraph 8 to hit the response that there is a special subject whose existence cannot be denied with the thesis that all existential statements are synthetic, but before he does so, he makes the point that the mere fact that we can conceive of the idea of a 'most real of beings' does not prove the real possibility of its object. Real possibility is more than mere coherence in the appropriate concept. Paragraph 8 then wades in with the killer rhetorical question to the ontological reasoner: 'On the other hand, if we admit as every reasonable person must, that all existential propositions are synthetic, then how can we assert that the predicate of existence cannot be rejected without contradiction?' (A598/B626).

This crucial point in Kant's refutation of the argument evidently parallels a similar claim in Hume's *Dialogues*. The ninth *Dialogue* contains the claim that 'There is no being whose non-existence implies a contradiction' (Hume 1976:216). Kant's point is of little value minus an account of the distinction between analytic and synthetic judgements. This is provided at A6–7/B10–11. 'A is B' is analytic or synthetic depending on whether the predicate *B* belongs to the subject as something that is implicitly contained in this concept *A*, or on whether it lies entirely outside the subject concept *A*. The distinction is thus drawn for subject-predicate judgements only. Now since Kant tells us that existence is not a predicate, this will make it trivially true that 'God exists' is not analytic, but also true presumably that it is not synthetic either (since it is not a subject-predicate sentence at all). However, he does at A7/B11 associate the distinction between analytic and synthetic with that between 'judgements of clarification' and 'judgements of amplification'. This suggests that his way of making the distinction may be associated with that customary in modern logic. Analytic judgements are those that can be reduced to logical truths with appropriate definitions; synthetic judgements are those that cannot. More generally: analytic judgements, if true, are somehow linguistic truths; synthetic judgements are true or false in virtue of the way the world is. (This reading of Kant's real point is reinforced at A736/B764.)

If we rescue Kant's point from his initial way of making the analytic/synthetic distinction, a huge problem then faces us. It seems simply question-begging. There is no reason why the ontological reasoner should make the concession invited in paragraph 8 (A598/B626) to the effect that every existential proposition is synthetic, if that means 'no existential proposition is arrived at via the analysis of concepts'. For the proof's supporters, 'God exists' can be seen to be true by analysing the concept of the subject, either in the indirect way of Descartes or via the direct way of Kant's interlocutor's concept of the most real being. And, as noted, Kant has allowed the ontological reasoner to make something like this claim in the seventh paragraph of the discussion. Such a reasoner can support this point by affirming that there are many existential statements that can be established by the mere analysis of concepts. Arithmetic is full of them, for example, 'There is a prime number between 2 and 4'.

Kant can easily turn the force of the arithmetical examples. He might concede the point that such truths as 'There is a prime number between 2 and 4' are analytic – albeit that he has earlier asserted (B14–17) that mathematics deals in synthetic a priori truths – but legitimately counter that ontological reasoners lose their case if they liken God to an arithmetical object. An actual God cannot be causally inert like a number. It is evident in paragraph 8 that he thinks he has supporters of the proof in a destructive dilemma. Suppose that we define God as 'the most real of beings' and then deduce that God exists since existence is included in the concept of that being because it has, by definition, all reality (A596/B624). The consequence, avers Kant, can only be that 'God exists' becomes a miserable tautology (A597/B525). Ontological arguers do not want their conclusion to be a miserable tautology, hence they must make the concession Kant wants from them and admit that we cannot establish God's existence through definition. Imagine we introduce the concept of X and add 'existence' to its definition. It is then necessarily true that X exists, but the truth is a clarificatory only and not substantive. It is a miserable tautology. It is, however, a substantive matter whether X, defined as containing existence, is an actual, and indeed a really possible, entity. To establish that is really possible or actual we have to go beyond the concept of X. This line of thought links nicely with Kant's closing comment on the ontological proof:

> Therefore the famous ontological (Cartesian) proof of the existence of a supreme being from concepts is only so much effort and labour lost, and a human being can no more become richer in insight from mere ideas than a merchant could in assets, if he wanted to better his state by adding a few noughts to his cash account. (A602/B631)

The reworking of Kant's argument in paragraph 8 makes it appear to have greater substance. Yet the ontological reasoner may still object that it is unfair and question-begging. Proponents of the proof such as Descartes, are not, as they see it, introducing a definition of the word 'God' and then tacking on 'exists' to the list of predicates in that definition. They see themselves as having an insight into the essential nature of the divine being and they find existence to be part of that essential nature. It follows indeed from the definition of 'God' that God exists, but the definition is not a nominal or arbitrary one.

We have in the above a point of contention over the proof: does it start from a mere nominal definition (Kant) or a clear and distinct perception of God's nature (Descartes)?

So far Kant's two main points in the first *Critique* (existence is not a predicate and existential statements are one and all synthetic) have produced stalemate. There is one more substantial point. It is contained in the eleventh paragraph.

> If I think a thing through whatever and however many predicates I want (even in its thoroughgoing determination), I do not make the least addition to it when I assert: this thing *is*. For otherwise what would exist would not be the same as what I had thought in the concept, but something more than that, and I could not say that the exact object of my concept exists. (A600/B628)

In this puzzling passage Kant seems to have in view defining a thing by listing its determining qualities. If I define something in this way and subsequently add 'and it exists' to the list of properties I have produced, and if, as the ontological reasoner maintains, 'exists' serves to give a defining quality of this thing, then I have changed the definition of the thing. I am no longer saying that the thing *as first defined* exists. I am extending or changing the definition of this thing. I would not be saying that this concept has instances. Indeed, 'this concept' is now ambiguous. There are two concepts, one with and one without the determining quality of existence.

It is hard to see why a defender of the proof should accept this argument. Ontological reasoners assert that existence is a perfection that is entailed by, or included in, the divine nature. Part of the content of the concept of God is that something answering to this concept must exist. That the divine nature must be actualised is established by inspection of our concept of the divine nature. The property 'the concept of this object is instantiated' is included in or entailed by the list of qualities that make up the concept of God. Of course, Kant denies that 'the concept of this object is instantiated' could be the real property of any object. But the ontological reasoner disagrees. It is hard to see how paragraph 11 could convince him otherwise.

Inspection of the 14 paragraphs of the first *Critique* refutation of the ontological proof reveals that it is rather less than a tour de force. If we view the discussion as intended to show that the proof rests on a series of false premises, it fails. It asserts, rather than proves, that key premises are false. However, it does serve to highlight the fact that the proof is not going to work as a proof just because key premises (such as 'Existence is a perfection') are eminently deniable. Kant helps to show this by providing alternatives to those key premises. However, the discussion in the *Only Possible Ground* is superior in this respect, since it focuses on the Cartesian proof and not on the first *Critique*'s much-truncated version and because it contains a much clearer account of why existence need not be a perfection. As noted, the *Only Possible Ground* discussion contains a striking anticipation of the modern view of existence as a second-order property.

Two further things need to be noted about the first *Critique* refutation. One is that the text is clearly indebted to points Kant thinks he has established previously in the *Critique*. Another is that the discussion need not be read as trying to show that God's nature does not entail his existence.

The first point is shown in the way that Kant has in mind throughout that, for finite knowers such as us, existential claims, and indeed claims about what is really possible, can only be established through experience. This is evident from the end of paragraph 11 (A601/B629) and in the statement in the penultimate paragraph 'the criterion of the possibility of synthetic cognitions always has to be sought only in experience' (A602/B630). The paragraph 10 affirmation that existence is obviously not a real predicate gains its force by reliance on the implicit doctrine that experience is what settles existential questions for us. This is explicit in the *Only Possible Ground*, where we are told that 'existence belongs to the sea unicorn' means that the representation of the narwhal is an empirical concept (2:72). The first *Critique* discussion can then be seen as a way of indicating why the ontological proof fails from the standpoint of the Critical Philosophy.

Perhaps the best way of reading Kant on the ontological argument is not as trying to show the metaphysical truth: God's nature does not guarantee his existence. Rather, he might be read as intending to make the epistemological point that our concept of God does not establish his existence; that is: *our understanding of God's nature* can never be such as to enable us to prove God's existence from that understanding (cf. Everitt 1995). In both the first *Critique* and *Only Possible Ground* discussions Kant makes it clear that his target is the attempt to prove the existence of a most perfect or most real being from some nominal definition of its nature. In the second paragraph of the first *Critique* discussion, we are told that a nominal definition of the concept of an absolutely necessary being is 'quite easy, namely that it is something whose non-existence is impossible; but one becomes through this no richer in insight as to the conditions which make it impossible to view the non-being of a thing as absolutely unthinkable, and it is just these [conditions] which one wants to know' (A592–3/B620–21).

The same point is made in the *Only Possible Ground*: the absolute impossibility of the non-being of a thing can only be established by having its real definition (2:81). The contrast invoked here is between our listing the qualities we use to give sense to the notion of the most real of things and having a true account of the inner nature of that thing. There are places at which he indicates that absolutely necessity of existence can *only* mean existence that can be derived from bare concepts (as at A607/B635). But at other places he is much more guarded. In the *Critique of Judgement* (5:402) he seems content with the thought that our idea of an original being is the idea of something 'existing absolutely necessarily, and in which there is no longer a difference between possibility and actuality at all'. At A641/B669 he declares that the concept of God ('of the supreme being') is a faultless ideal of human reason. It cannot be proved from human cognition, but it cannot be disproved either. He then goes on to list 'necessity' among the attributes of God. Later (at A680/B707) he returns to this theme, stating that we need 'the idea of a *necessary* original being but can never have the least concept of this being and of its absolute *necessity*'. (In the *Critique₃* passage just cited he states that our understanding has absolutely no concept for this idea.) 'Never have the least concept' does not mean that we cannot string a set of words together that define the concept. The phrase picks up what is stated in the previous sentence 'it is a mere something in the idea, of which we have no concept of what it is *in itself*'. Or as he puts it in the third *Critique*, we 'can find no way of representing such a thing or its mode of existence' (5:402). Our concept of it is thus purely nominal.

Kant on 'existence is not a predicate' and like matters can now be seen as attacking the nerve of Descartes' claim that he has a clear and distinct idea of God such that God's nature is evident to his mind. According to Kant, our idea of God corresponds to no more than a nominal definition of God and fails to represent God's nature or way of existing to us. We form the notions of a highest being and a most real being and take them to entail that an absolutely necessary being exists. The underlying mistake in this reasoning is the move from concept to reality. We frame a concept of the highest being not because we derive that concept from acquaintance with the nature of such a being but because of a priori connections amongst our own ideas. (The connections are traced in Kant's account of the Ideal of Pure Reason from A567/B595 onwards, a discussion to which we shall return.) To take these connections as proving the existence of a highest being in actuality is to make the unjustified assumption that God's nature is captured by our nominal definitions. We have no insight into that nature as it is in itself. We do not even know that our concept of a highest being is a concept of something that is really possible. What is thinkable may not be really possible. Actuality and real possibility can only be established via experience, for only experience acquaints us with the natures of things outside our thoughts.

It is in the above context that we can understand Kant's dig at Leibniz in the penultimate paragraph of the *Critique* discussion of the ontological proof:

> the mark of possibility of synthetic cognitions is always to be sought in experience alone, to which, however, the object of an Idea can never belong: thus the famous *Leibniz* was far from having succeeding in accomplishing what he flattered himself he had done, namely, gaining insight a priori into such a sublime ideal being's possibility. (A602/B630)

It is the very mark of an Idea of Reason, such as the concept of God, that it is used to refer to something beyond experience, thus we could not have insight into its real nature if Kantian epistemology is sound. Leibniz offered an argument for the conclusion that the concept of a most perfect being was coherent and thus supplied what he felt was a missing premise in the Cartesian proof (see Leibniz 1956:259–60). Leibniz's argument turns around the definition of a perfection as a simple, positive, absolute quality. Such qualities, asserts Leibniz, cannot be defined or reduced to component parts. In order to demonstrate that two qualities are incompatible, we need to be able to analyse the qualities and show that elements of the one rule out elements of the other. Since simple, positive, absolute qualities cannot be thus analysed, we can never demonstrate that a combination of them yields inconsistency.

Leibniz's proof is open to a number of objections. The sceptic about ontological proofs will question: the initial definition of 'perfection'; the principle that if we cannot demonstrate an incompatibility between two qualities, they must be compatible; the actual existence of any perfections as Leibniz defines them; the claim that indefinable, positive qualities cannot be incompatible. (For discussions of Leibniz's proof of possibility see Oppy 1995:25–6 and Adams 1999:141–56.) As Kant sees it, Leibniz is above all committing the cardinal sin of trying to show what is really possible from the consistency of our ideas. From consistency all that follows is that the idea in question is not of something that is logically impossible.

If we are close to getting the real thrust of Kant's critique of ontological reasoning, then we must acknowledge a striking parallel between that critique and St Thomas Aquinas's well-known objection to the proof. At 1a, 2, 1 of the *Summa Theologiae* Aquinas rejects the argument on the ground that while 'God exists' may be self-evident in itself, it is not self-evident to us 'because what is to be God is not evident to us'. We shall have occasion later to note the similarity between Kant and St Thomas on the crucial point that 'we cannot know what God is' (Aquinas 1964:1a, 2–3).

The cosmological proof

The first *Critique* refutation of the cosmological proof has similarities with the treatment of the ontological proof. It is brief, some 15 paragraphs, and it is like in some respects an exposé previously offered in the *Only Possible Ground*. The heart of the refutation is contained in the fifth to eighth paragraphs. These claim that the pretension of reason to have embarked, via the proof, on a different tack than proving God's existence by mere concepts is an illusion. The cosmological argument depends on the ontological. Before we discuss that central point of Kant, let us weigh the other features in his treatment of the argument.

It is a great failing of Kant's discussion that he states the argument in a highly compressed form. He identifies it with Leibniz's proof *a contingentia mundi* (A604/B632). But when he comes to summarise the proof there is no mention of contingency: 'If something exists, then an absolutely necessary being must also exist. Now I myself, at least, exist: therefore an absolutely necessary being exists' (A604/B632). An argument from the contingency of the world must rather start from the premise that something contingent exists. It must move via a strong version of the principle of sufficient reason to the conclusion that something not contingent, something containing within itself the reason for its existence, must exist. Kant's comments on the argument from contingency do not mention the principle of sufficient reason, but the treatment in the *Only Possible Ground* does manage to note that the argument has to employ the principle of sufficient reason and that the principle is still contested (2:158; cf. the treatment in *Lectures Theology* 28:1006 and 28:1029).

Outside the claim that the proof depends on the ontological, Kant offers two notable criticisms of it in paragraph 10 (I ignore the other two criticisms in that paragraph). The first accuses the argument of misusing the principle that every contingent thing has a cause, an accusation grounded on the assertion that the principle 'has no meaning at all and no criterion for its use, except in the sensible world' (A609/B637). As noted early in this chapter, this criticism presupposes the concept-empiricism at the heart of the Critical Philosophy. The second criticism in this paragraph is deeply puzzling. The argument is accused of ruling out, falsely, the impossibility of an infinite series of causes in order to get to a first cause. While there are, of course, cosmological arguments that do rely on ruling out infinite causal series – notably the first three of Aquinas's Five Ways – the argument as summarised by Kant has no such premise. Moreover, an argument from contingency can be regarded as designed to avoid such matters. Even if the series of causes which explains any given contingent object or event stretches back infinitely in time or spreads infinitely outwards in the present, the proponent of the argument from contingency can still press the question: given that it is a contingent fact that there is such a series, where is the sufficient reason for its existence? Even if each item in such a series is explained in terms of the efficient or sustaining causation of the prior item, there is still an explanatory question to ask once it is conceded that there may not have been such a series at all.

The nub of Kant's rejection of the argument from contingency in the first *Critique* is the assertion that it depends on the ontological. In making this charge Kant takes himself to have diagnosed the deception human reason plays upon itself when it places reliance on the cosmological proof: 'Thus it is really only the ontological proof from pure concepts that contains all the power of a proof in the so-called cosmological proof; and the pretended [appeal to] experience is quite idle' (A607/B635). Kant holds that the cosmological proof must have a second stage. The something that is the absolutely necessary being must be identified as God. A second stage in the proof is therefore needed in order to show that the absolutely necessary being is the most real of beings – the *ens realissimum*. So the second stage of the proof lays down that 'Every absolutely necessary being is at the same time the most real being'. But this proposition yields by conversion 'Some most real beings are at the same time absolutely necessary beings'. Kant then tells us that 'one *ens realissimum* does not differ from another', therefore what holds of some holds of all. Thus the proposition linking absolute necessity in existence with being the most real being must be convertible absolutely. The cosmological proof is then committed to 'Every most real being is a necessary being'. It is then dependent upon the soundness of the ontological argument:

> Now because this proposition ['Every most real being is a necessary being'] is merely determined a priori from its concepts, the bare concept of the most real being must also lead by itself to the absolute necessity of this being; which is just what the ontological proof asserts and the cosmological proof does not recognise. (A608/B636)

So: proponents of the cosmological proof are committed to the claim that any absolutely necessary being is a most real being. That commits them to the converse that any most real being is an absolutely necessary being. That in turn entails that any most real being must exist, for an absolutely necessary being is one whose existence is guaranteed by its very concept. Thus we have the ontological argument by another route, but that has been previously shown to be unsound.

Straightaway we can note an oddity in the above refutation of the cosmological proof. Kant does not need to go through inferences by conversion to get the cosmological arguer committed to the ontological proof. He has previously stated that the only way to make sense of the notion of an absolutely necessary being is by supposing that such a being is one whose very concept entails its existence: 'absolute necessity is an existence from bare concepts' (A607/B635; cf. A613/B640: 'reason recognises as absolutely necessary only what is necessary from its bare concept'). Thus just in getting to the conclusion that there is an absolutely necessary being, the proof has got to the basis for an ontological argument and we did not need to investigate how it then moves on to show that a necessary being is the *ens realissimum*. This point can be reinforced. If the proof rests on the claim that contingent existence needs explanation, it will not be satisfied with anything other than a self-explanatory being to complete the chain of explanation. That will be a being whose nature entails its existence, whose existence is given just in its definition. This is the being described in the ontological argument. Bennett calls this 'the radical criticism' of the cosmological proof, because it makes the second stage of the proof in Kant's presentation redundant (Bennett 1974:253).

The initial oddity in Kant's claim that the cosmological proof rests on the ontological might be deemed to be a defect merely in Kant's presentation of his refutation. There are, however, two major defects of substance in the affirmation that the cosmological proof commits its proponents to the ontological: first, Kant ignores an obvious reply to his affirmation and second, the affirmation reveals him to be grossly inconsistent in his account of necessary existence. Let us call Kant's charge that the cosmological argument depends on the ontological 'the dependence claim'. The reply to the dependence claim that many recent commentators affirm is available is a simple one: the cosmological arguer does not have to accept that 'absolute necessity is an existence from bare concepts'. Perhaps, they suggest, all that the cosmological arguer needs is the premise that *if* an *ens realissimum* exists, then it will have a special kind of existence – non-contingent existence – but this need not involve its existence following from its very concept (see Walsh 1975:227, Vallicella 2000:445–6, Wood 1978:129). This special type of non-contingent existence might involve uncaused, independent, eternal existence. If there is a God, he exists in this special way, but it does not follow that the very concept of God entails his existence and that 'God exists' is an analytic, logically necessary truth. What are necessary truths are such claims as: 'If there is a God, he exists independently of all things', 'If there is no God now, he could not come into existence later'. Thus the dependence claim is false.

It may be thought that Kant has a response to the above: he can claim that the use of the principle of sufficient reason in the cosmological argument commits its proponents to the assumption that 'God exists' is a necessary truth. But we shall see that this response on behalf of Kant will support the dependence claim only at the price of raising the problem of his inconsistency.

The Kantian response immediately above is contained in Bennett's radical criticism of the argument from contingency. If the proof in its guise as the argument from contingency leaves 'God exists' as a contingent truth, then it leaves one brute, contingent fact as without a sufficient explanation. The principle of sufficient reason, which we have seen from the *Only Possible Ground* (2:158) Kant is fully aware is operative in the argument from contingency, will then not be satisfied. We will have just swapped the existence of a contingent, physical cosmos as one brute fact for another: the existence of God. We might claim that God is a better stopping point for explanation on some such grounds as God's simplicity but we will not have met the demands of the principle of sufficient reason. (See Swinburne 2004:148–9 for the difference in the style of cosmological arguments at this juncture.) The only way to meet the demands of the principle of sufficient reason is with a God whose essence entails its existence, whose nature is such that there must be a God. 'God exists' must be a necessary truth and we are back with the dependence claim.

But this is where the inconsistency arises: Kant has asserted things contrary to the substance of the dependence claim. It may be that 'God exists' must be regarded by human reason as a necessary truth without the grounds for this necessity being open to us, in particular without it being the case that 'absolute necessity is an existence from bare concepts', without it being the case that the mere concept of God can be used to demonstrate God's existence. We have noted above that Kant does not consistently hold to 'absolute necessity is an existence from bare concepts'. We have found him admitting the possibility (that is, conceivability not real possibility) that God exists as a necessary being (see A642/B679). We have found a line in his discussions of the ontological proof that has him drawing a distinction between God's nominal definition and real essence. We cannot infer God's existence from some nominal definition. To do so violates the logic of 'to be' and its cognates. It also presumes that our nominal definitions of God give us insight into God's nature as it is in itself. We have seen that at 1a, 2, 1 of the *Summa Theologiae* Aquinas rejects the argument on the ground that while 'God exists' may be self-evident in itself, it is not self-evident to us 'because what it is to be God is not evident to us'. Following Aquinas, we can single out what an ontological argument of a Cartesian kind must claim. It is not merely that there is a God whose nature guarantees his existence. It is further that our insight into God's nature enables us see that and how his nature entails his existence. It may true that if there is a God, then his essence guarantees his existence. It does not follow that we can comprehend God's essence, and thus that our concept of God enables us to demonstrate that he exists.

So it seems that Kant does not consistently hold that 'absolute necessity is an existence from bare concepts' gives the whole truth of the matter. It gives *one* understanding of an absolutely necessary being but he himself acknowledges others. In the *Only Possible Ground* he outlines a proof of God's existence which depends on reflections about the conditions for any thing to be possible. It leads to the conclusion that, necessarily, there is a God, but it is not a proof from the mere definition of God and Kant distinguishes it from the ontological argument. He precisely affirms that we can accept it while rejecting the ontological argument. God is absolutely necessary in this proof in respect of the fact that his existence is required if anything else is to be possible at all. The understanding of God contained in this notion of an absolutely necessary being is repeated in the first *Critique* (from A571/B597 onwards) prior to his consideration of the three traditional proofs. In the third *Critique* Kant clearly states that this concept of an absolutely necessary being is 'an indispensable idea of reason', albeit it is 'an unattainable problematic concept for the human understanding' (5:402). By this he means reason's overarching goals demand the use of this idea of an absolutely necessary being, while it is true that we cannot prove that something real corresponds to the idea. Kant therefore knows that 'absolute necessity is an existence from bare concepts' is not the whole truth even as he writes those words at A607/B635. Moreover, he could not state that 'the supreme being remains ... a faultless ideal' (A641/B669) if he believes that 'absolute necessity is an existence from bare concepts' is the only understanding of 'necessary being' in relation to the concept of God. For he would then have a proof that there could be no highest being. The highest being includes existing necessarily as one of its features. Kant thinks he has shown in his discussion of the ontological proof that the notion of 'an existence from bare concepts' is an incoherent one. It is incoherent because it depends on the logical mistake of taking existence to be a property and it offends against the necessary truth that all existential statements are synthetic. If 'God is a necessary being' meant only that God's existence followed from an appropriate nominal definition of 'God', then Kant has shown there is no necessary being and thus no God. The concept of a highest being would be incoherent (see Vallicella 2000:454). Kant's whole programme would then be in tatters. His Critical Philosophy will not 'cut the very root of materialism, fatalism, atheism' (Bxxxiv). It will have proved atheism to be a priori and necessarily true.

If we grant the cosmological argument a strong form of the principle of sufficient reason (a very big 'if', as Kant himself notes), then it can get to the conclusion that there is a necessary being from the premise that something contingent exists. The conclusion need not be 'There is a being whose existence is entailed by its very concept', provided we distinguish existence being entailed by something's concept from existence being guaranteed by something's nature. We can in turn make this distinction if we can separate God's nominal definition/essence from his real definition/essence. The Critical Philosophy encourages us to make these distinctions. It entails that we cannot know things as they are in themselves but only as they appear to us. It teaches – though we have yet to explore this point – that the nature of a divine being cannot be given in appearance, and thus that there is special force in assertion that we cannot comprehend its nature. The necessary being which the argument from contingency shows to exist will be one whose real definition/essence guarantees its existence. If such a being exists, then reality will be such that it satisfies the principle of sufficient reason where that is understood *as a metaphysical principle*. There will be sufficient cause, reason or ground for all facts and things. Since our concept of the terminus of causes, reasons and grounds does not give us insight into how this terminus exists necessarily, we will not be able to comprehend fully the sufficient reasons lying behind all facts and things. Thus the principle of sufficient reason will not be satisfied *as an epistemological principle*, one that demands that human beings be able to comprehend the therefore behind every wherefore.

The conclusion of the above discussion of Kant's 'refutation' of the cosmological proof is that the chief point he offers against it in the first *Critique* is that it depends on the ontological proof. Further, this chief point fails, and must fail – both if he is to be consistent and if he is to preserve a key element of his own Critical project, namely the unprovability of God's non-existence. This does not mean that the Critical Philosophy must accept the cosmological proof in the form of the argument from contingency. The proof depends on the principle of sufficient reason in a strong form and it will fail if there are merely reasonable grounds for dissenting from the principle. And of course there are. If the principle is true in this strong form, a necessitarian view of things, one denying the existence of any contingent facts, seems to follow. As well as baulking at this high price, one who rejects the proof can easily distinguish between the principle of sufficient reason as a metaphysical claim about what is the case in reality in general and as a heuristic ideal of seeking as full an explanation for as many facts and things as we can. Indeed, the proof can be accused of a subtle form of begging the question in this regard. How could we know that our expectation and hope that we can find a full explanation for every fact was matched by the structure of reality as such? Only, we may reply, if we know that it is the product of the God whom reason seeks in natural theology. Such a view will be seen to be in accord with Kant's account of the use of the notion of God as a regulative ideal.

We are back where we started in this chapter. The principle of sufficient reason and the God of rationalism are in a mutually supporting relationship. The principle enables a priori proofs of God's existence to be provided and thus assures reason of God's existence. God's existence in turn assures reason that the principle of sufficient reason holds throughout finite, mundane reality.

Reflection on this link prompts the highly Kantian thought that, in the argument from contingency, reason misreads a demand it has placed on reality as a fact it has discovered to be true of reality as it is in itself. It has tried to escape from its autonomy into heteronomy but failed.

Chapter 3

Kant on Natural Theology II

The physico-theological proof

Kant's criticism of the physico-theological proof commences at A620/B648 and is similar in length to his treatment of the other two proofs: some 10 pages and 16 paragraphs. It is common for it to be labelled as a critique of the design argument (see, for example, Bennett 1974:255). This is slightly misleading. Kant uses his own title, 'physico-theological proof', to refer to an argument that starts from the determinate experience 'of things within the present world' (A620/B648; cf. *Lectures Religion* 28:1007). Experience of the present world discloses to us 'an immeasurable scene of manifoldness, order, purposiveness and beauty, which one may pursue in the infinity of space or in the unbounded division of it' (A622/B650). Here order and purposiveness in nature are but two examples of the 'immeasurably great wonders' (A622/B650) experience of the present world discloses and which point to a God. It is true that in his step-by-step summary of the proof in the eighth paragraph, Kant cites the facts from which the proof proceeds as amounting to 'purposive order' (A625/B653). So the focus turns out to be on order and purpose in nature. Yet the title Kant gives to the argument is indicative of a concern for a general attempt to argue from natural philosophy to the existence of a wise and powerful creator.

Insofar as Kant is focusing on the teleological argument, his reference to 'purposive order' indicates that he makes no distinction, in this particular discussion of teleology, between arguments *to* and arguments *from* design, that is between arguments from the regular behaviour of the universe over time and arguments from the purposive, adaptive structures and behaviours of living things. A twenty-first-century philosopher might think this odd. An argument from the premise of adaptiveness to the conclusion that there is an intelligent author of nature is open to an empirical objection, namely that non-intelligent causes (as outlined in Darwinian theory) can produce adaptive structures and behaviours. No such empirical objection is possible to the argument from the universe's temporal order. What Kant may have in view is the apparent fact that regularity of the universe over time and the structure of living things combine to reveal the universe as providential whole. This line of thought is hinted at in the presentation of the physico-theological proof in the *Only Possible Ground*: 'The artful nature of the order is then shown by all the purposeful relations it contains, from which is inferred the existence of a wise and benevolent will' (2:117).

The four-step summary of the argument in the first *Critique* at A625–6/B653–4 proceeds from the premise that that there are clear signs of 'an order according to a determinate aim' in the universe. It then claims that this order is quite foreign to the things in the world, which could have it only contingently. Step 3 affirms that there is 'a sublime and wise cause (or several)' responsible for this order and the final step concludes that this cause is a unity from 'the unity of the reciprocal relation of the parts of the world as members of an artful structure'.

A striking feature of Kant's discussion of the proof in the *Critique* is his praise for it. It points to a feature of the world that 'strengthens the belief in a highest author so that it becomes an irresistible conviction' (A624/B652). In the *Only Possible Ground* Kant goes so far as to say that, while the proof lacks 'geometrical rigour', it is rationally convincing (2:159). Many criticisms of it are provided in the 16-paragraph discussion in the first *Critique*, but it is still praised. The clue for solving this conundrum may lie at Bxxxiii (in the preface to the second edition of the *Critique of Pure Reason*). Here Kant describes 'the splendid order, beauty, and providence, which is displayed throughout nature, as alone producing faith in a wise and great *world author*'. In this remark he is documenting a natural human tendency that he does not wish to oppose or ridicule and which, later, he will argue is necessary for the sustenance of both scientific enquiry and moral endeavour. He then tells us at Bxxxiii that the value of his critique of reason is that it demonstrates that 'the schools' can offer 'no higher or fuller insight on any point concerning the universal human concerns [shown in physico-theology] than the insight that is open to the multitude of men'. In other words, the proof works as a piece of popular thought but not as a rigorous or philosophical proof. The tendencies both to see purposive order in the world and to ascribe it to the working out of conscious ends are applauded. What is not is the philosophical attempt to make a proof out of those tendencies. Nothing is added by the so-called proof to a pre-philosophical disposition to see intelligent design behind the world.

No argument drawn from determinate experience of the world will serve to prove the existence of God as philosophy defines God because no experience can be adequate to a transcendental Idea of a necessary, all-sufficient, original being (A621/B649). This general claim is supported by more specific ones. It is not possible by means of the argument to establish that God exists as the creator of the world, rather than as its mere architect. The proof begins from the contingency of certain features of organised matter, not from the contingency of matter itself. So it is compatible with uncreated character of matter (see A626–7/B654–5 and cf. *Only Possible Ground* 2:124–6). The notion that God has 'omni' attributes is not given through the proof. The world as we observe it will not prove that its architect has omnipotence (A628/B656) only that it has great power (*Lectures Theology* 28:1008). It is not even possible to prove 'the absolute unity' of nature's author (A628/B656; see also *Lectures Theology* 28:1008).

These criticisms lead on to Kant's favoured theme: the dependence of both the cosmological and physico-theological proofs on the ontological. In order to get an absolutely necessary and absolutely perfect being, the physico-theological proof 'suddenly jumps in this embarrassment to the cosmological proof, and since this is only a concealed ontological proof, it really fulfils its purpose merely through pure reason' (A629/B657). Toward the close of the discussion, Kant taunts 'the physico-theologians'. They pose as 'clear-sighted students of nature' and look down on abstract, transcendental theologians as dark, brooding weavers of webs (A629/B657). However, their attempt to inform theology with the results of the study of nature is soon forgotten, for they must enter the realm of bare possibilities in order to establish the existence of the God of philosophy, the only one that corresponds to a determinate concept of deity (A630/B658).

At issue in Kant's critique of the proof are the limits and appropriateness of anthropomorphic reasoning to the existence and nature of God. Physico-theologians rely on such reasoning when they move from step two of the argument (there is purposive order in the world that is contingent to matter) to step three (there exists an intelligent cause). They rely, Kant states, on 'the analogy between natural products and those produced by human art' (A626/B654). Yet if they use this analogy and the anthropomorphism behind it to establish the existence of the all-real, all-perfect being, they must at once abandon it. For *this* being and its causality cannot be modelled on the human: 'Reason would not be able to justify to itself, when, from a causality with which it is acquainted, it wants to pass over to obscure and unprovable grounds of explanation, with which it is not acquainted' (A626/B654).

We have noted in Chapter 1, and will have reason to explain in much greater detail in later chapters, that Kant thinks we need to think in anthropomorphic terms about the source of order in the world. Science is guided by the thought that nature is the product of a designing intelligence whose plans we can grasp. But it matters greatly whether this principle is the product of autonomous or heteronomous reason. If it is the product of the latter, then science is guided by the discovery of the existence and plans of a superhuman intelligence. Not the least of the problems which would then be created is that such a being's existence would appear to be incompatible with the existence of the God demanded by other requirements of reason, specifically the God who answers the question 'Why does anything contingent exist at all?' Postulation of a superhuman intelligence will not solve that question, since it is always possible to ask why such an intelligence exists. To answer the question of why anything exists at all, we need to posit a being that is not human-like at all. However, if the idea of a superhuman intelligence is a heuristic one, then it can be employed for pragmatic purposes alongside other concepts of the divine with which it may not be formally compatible.

We have now seen that the nerve of Kant's rejection of the physico-theological argument as a proof rests on the claim that it will not yield any determinate concept of the world's supreme cause (A628/B656), given that the only determinate concept of God is that of an absolutely necessary, all-encompassing reality (A629/B657). That concept belongs to rationalist thought about the *ens realissimum* and there is a huge gulf between it and anything physico-theology might yield.

What the above shows is that Kant's attempt to refute the proof is of limited value. It will not be forceful against those natural theologians whose conception of God is not that of the *ens realissimum*, and whose thought about the divine indeed smacks of anthropomorphism. Richard Swinburne's natural theology is directed toward showing the existence of a God who is defined as a disembodied person, who exists in time, and concerning which it is only a contingent truth that it exists (see Swinburne 2004:7). On a Swinburne-type view, the gulf between what reflection on determinate experience of the present world allows and the defining features of God will not exist. The force of Kant's critique of the physico-theological proof is thus bound to be blunted.

We now have a further pointer to the significance of Kant's discussion of the concept of the *ens realissimum*, the sum of all reality, prior to the treatment of the three traditional proofs. In the *Only Possible Ground* the definition of God as the *ens realissimum*, the sum of all reality, is part of a distinctive proof for God's existence, a proof now referred to as the argument from possibility. The concept of the *ens realissimum* is the concept of God that rational theology must begin with.

The argument from possibility

The argument from possibility presents us with problems. In the *Only Possible Ground* it figures as the hero of the book: it is the only apodeictic proof of God's existence that works. It is reproduced at length in the *Critique of Pure Reason* (A571–83/B579–611). However, it is there presented as merely indicating an ideal, which reason adopts in thinking about reality, but which can have no objective value. Indeed, the proof is said to embody a dialectical illusion, whereby a demand of reason for a certain type of concept is turned into a proof that an object corresponding to this concept exists. The very brief summary of the proof in the *Lectures on Rational Theology* closes with a similar sounding claim to the effect that the proof cannot demonstrate the objective necessity of an original being, but only the subjective necessity of assuming such a being (28:1034).

The proof is notable for indicating that Kant had another notion of an absolutely necessary being than that of a being whose existence is entailed by our very concept of it. This second notion is that of a being who exists of absolute necessity because, if it did not, nothing would be really possible. If anything is really possible, this thing exists (*Only Possible Ground* 2:83). The absolute necessity of the being then rests on the further, and unstated, assumption that if something is possible, then it is necessarily possible (see Adams 2000:433). So, if anything really is possible, there exists, necessarily, a ground of possibility. In the *Only Possible Ground*, after the absolutely necessary being's existence has been established, it acquires the properties of the traditional God of natural theology through further stages of argument: it is unique, simple, immutable, eternal, the supreme reality and a mind. Likewise, the first *Critique* version ends with the conclusion that there is a supreme being 'that is single, simple, all-sufficient, eternal, etc.' (A580/B608).

The route to the above conclusion in the *Critique* is sketchy and reference must be made at certain points to the fuller discussion in the *Only Possible Ground* to fill it out. The first step in the journey is a contrast between the determinable character of concepts and the determinate character of individual, existing things (A571–3/B579–601). My concept of a computer is indeterminate as between laptops versus desktops, white casing versus black casing, and so on. But the particular computer on my desk must have one of these pairs of predicates in order to exist as a concrete individual. This leads to the claim that 'All existing things are thoroughly determined' (A573/B601). This Kant takes to mean that, in order for a concrete particular to exist, it must 'select' from a list of all possible pairs of predicates. A concept of a particular thing must exhibit thoroughgoing determination by exemplifying a selection of predicates (qualities) from the list of all possible predicates. Thus, the existence of any one thing presupposes the existence of 'the sum total of all possibility' (A573/B601).

So far, we might think, so good. If we accept the principle that any particular *is* thoroughly determined, then it can be regarded as embodying a selection from a notional list of all possible pairs of qualities. In the paragraph that introduces the notion of the sum total of all possibility, Kant moves to the much more striking claim that determinate existence in the world takes us to 'an ideal of pure reason', where this is a primordial object – a real thing from whom all possible qualities somehow flow (A573–4/B601–2). A number of moves are necessary to transform the sum of all possibilities into a primordial reality from which the possibilities flow. Kant tells us that this reality would not have both a predicate and its negation; it would not be both mortal and non-mortal. But that is all right, since 'negation ... signifies a mere absence' (A575/B603); negative qualities are not real qualities and thus the ideal of pure reason will be a reality possessing only positive ones. More moves: Kant is aware that not all positive qualities are compatible with one another. If the ideal of reason is a spiritual entity, it cannot exhibit qualities such as extension (*Only Possible Ground* 2:86). The ideal of reason as a primordial object therefore 'excludes a multitude of predicates, which are derived from, and thus already given through, others' (A573/B601). In other words, it must help itself to the thought that many qualities are derivative from fewer, fundamental ones. All these fundamental ones are said to be compatible and thus can be thought of as possessed by the primordial being that is the ground of all possibility. So the highest being is now thought of as embodying the sum total of all positive, non-derivative qualities. Even this is not sufficient to give us an idea that looks like the traditional notion of God. Kant explains:

> The derivation of all other possibility from this original being also cannot, strictly speaking, be regarded as a *limitation* of its supreme reality and as a *division* of it, so to speak; for then the original being would be treated as a mere aggregate of derivative beings, which is impossible according to the above, even though at the beginning of our first rough outline we represented it thus. Rather, the supreme reality supports the possibility of all things as a *ground* and not as an *aggregate* and the manifoldness of the former [i.e. all the derivative beings] *rests not on the limitation of the original being itself, but on its complete consequences.* (A579/B607; closing emphasis mine)

So: the existence of determinate things *cannot* be regarded as a matter of them selecting from a sum total of all reality embodied in one primordial being. Instead, determinate things are the 'consequences' (presumably, effects) of the primordial ground of all things. The next paragraph then takes us to our end-point that there is a supreme being 'that is single, simple, all-sufficient, eternal, etc.' (A580/B608). But we see that there are huge leaps from the original twin ideas (each thing is determinate and can be thought of as selecting from a sum total of possibilities) to the end-point of a being that is the ground of all other things and whose *consequences* enable other things to be really possible. The end-point is a primordial being that is the most real of things in the sense that it is eternal, simple, uncreated, absolutely necessary and the like; it is not most real as containing, in any genuine sense, all qualities in itself, from the array of which determinate things select.

Kant's end-point is not even yet a God. In the *Only Possible Ground* he proceeds to show that the primordial being is a mind, and thus can have traditional properties of divinity. The argument, however, seems to depend on an equivocation. The primordial being is said to embody the greatest possible reality. But, if it does, then it must have understanding and will. For if it lacked these it would be lesser than those beings that did contain understanding and will and thus would not be the greatest possible reality (2:87–8). The argument only works if 'greatest possible reality' is understood to mean 'most perfect possible reality', that is: 'supreme in value'. But the primordial reality need not be that: what it has to contain is all possible, positive qualities. To bring in the notion that it is the first in being in the sense of the *best* being is to introduce an alien consideration into the argument. Indeed, its having mental qualities makes it even more difficult to link it to the sum of all possibilities. For now it is a particular type of being, namely a person, and its particularity in this respect makes it harder still to see how it could be the source of all things in the sense introduced at the start of Kant's reflections.

Two things should now occur to us. We see, first, how right Kant was to admit in his post-1780 philosophy that God's existence as an objective necessity could not be derived from the possibility proof. We see, second, how implausible is his thought that the route from the idea of determinacy in particular things to the notion of the *ens realissimum* shows the necessity of God as an ideal of pure reason. Why not a much simpler argument? Reason seeks and expects a sufficient explanation of all facts and things and therefore is inclined to posit a primordial reality that is the self-explanatory ground of all else.

Matters are even worse for the possibility proof than the above suggests. There is no argument in the first *Critique* account for an initial and major step in this piece of natural theology. Granted that determinate things can exist as such only if there are possible qualities from which to 'select', why do those possible qualities have to be grounded in a really existing object or objects? Kant asserts in the *Only Possible Ground* at 2:83 that 'All possibility presupposes something actual in and through which all that can be thought is given'. The only argument I can find for that claim is the contention that if the predicates delineating a possible, determinate thing are to have meaning they must denote something existing. So, to use Kant's example, if the phrase 'fiery body' denotes a real possibility than a constituent predicate such as 'body' must have meaning and for it to have meaning there must be something it refers to ('the question will be whether space and extension are empty words' – 2:81). Thus the argument appears to rest on the thought that for predicates to mean anything they must denote real things. If the predicates signifying possible qualities did not mean anything by way of referring to something, the possible qualities would not be really possible and thus would not be the ground of determinate things (cf. Adams 2000:432). This has Kant committed to a simple picture of meaning: meaning is reference, so there must be – in some timeless realm – realities corresponding to our concepts for those concepts to have content.

If we abandon Kant's starting reflections about determining particulars from a list of all possible qualities, we might turn to a traditional metaphysical principle much used in natural theology: nothing can come from nothing. The principle is robustly stated by Locke in his proof of the existence of an eternal being: 'Man knows by an intuitive certainty, that bare nothing can no more produce any real Being, than it can be equal to two right angles' (Locke 1975:IV, 10, 3). A similar principle is to be found in Aquinas's 'Third Way' (Aquinas 1964:1a, 2, 3). This principle can be used to show that nothing is really possible unless something is actual. Nothing has the chance of coming to be unless there is something actual with the power of bringing it into being. (Note that this way of reconstructing Kant's argument from possibility involves abandoning the notion that it is independent of traditional cosmological arguments.) Accepting the principle 'nothing comes from nothing', we can reach the conclusion that for anything to be really possible (that is, have a chance of coming into existence) there must be something actual. And if there is eternally the real possibility of things coming into existence, there must eternally be something actual. This takes us some way toward Kant's conclusion in the *Only Possible Ground*, but it is a notorious fallacy to conclude from this that there must be *some one thing* that is eternally actual. If there is eternally the chance of things coming to be, then this can be ensured by the eternal existence of a series of overlapping contingent things, things that themselves come to be and pass away. Call this series 'the universe'. All this piece of traditional metaphysics can show at best is that the eternal possibility of things coming into existence depends on the universe existing eternally. The universe could then be primordial being demanded by the proof from possibility. Kant's conundrum about how things could be really possible, as opposed to notionally so, is then easily solved. That which is really possible is so if it is not self-contradictory and if its qualities are present in, or derivable from, the qualities of the universe. As noted above, Kant seems to have thought that what is possible is necessarily possible (see Adams 2000:43). Accepting that further principle, we would reach the conclusion that there must necessarily be a universe. That means there must be a plurality of grounding things for there to be real possibilities. But the individuals making up the plurality need not be necessary and so, even making generous concessions to Kant, we are nowhere near a proof of God.

In the first *Critique* the answer to the question 'What must be added to formal consistency, to make something really possible?' is no longer 'God, an *ens realissimum*'. It is 'experience'. It is appearance, the totality of things in the empirical world, that grounds real possibility (see A581–2/B608–9). So he is close to the option sketched above: real possibility is dependent on an overlapping series of contingent things.

Our survey shows the wisdom of Kant's abandonment of the possibility proof by 1781. The proof does not lead to God, for the route from something being the 'sum of all possibilities' to its being the simple, infinite and perfect being of classical theism contains too many violent and implausible leaps. It is possible to give sense to the idea of God as the most real of beings, but only by falling back on reasoning typical of the cosmological proof in its form as the argument from contingency. God is most real, and the ground of the real possibility of all else, insofar as he has aseity and necessary existence. But if Kant is right to abandon the proof from possibility as a proof, our analysis shows that he is wrong to retain it because it evinces a necessary ideal of reason. The long quotation from A579/B607 above is sufficient to indicate, ignoring all other problems, that there is no organic connection between reason's alleged ideal of an eternally existing sum of all possibilities and the idea of God as ground of all reality. The notion of the sum of all possibilities does not lead us to the idea of 'the highest reality as a being that is single, simple, all-sufficient, eternal, etc' (A850/B608). It is therefore puzzling to see why Kant thought that the notion of God as the sum total of all possibilities is at the heart of a necessary dialectical illusion. This illusion is held to consist in our moving from the idea that individual things in appearance can only be determined if they are compared 'with all the predicates of experience' to the idea of a transcendental something that as an individual thing contains in itself all empirical reality (see A582–3/B610–11). Thus, a notion we use in thinking about things in experience is transformed into a metaphysical truth that allows us then to infer a metaphysical object.

The reasoning around the proof from possibility does play an important role in Kant's discussion of natural theology. We have seen that it influences Kant's discussion of the ontological proof. In that discussion he introduces God, not as the most perfect being, but as the most real being. Moreover, however invalidly, it is his route into the conception of God as 'the highest reality as a being that is single, simple, all-sufficient, eternal, etc', and this conception is a powerful corrective to the anthropomorphic picture of God we might otherwise have and which dominates the physico-theological proof according to Kant. In the first *Critique* Kant distinguishes theology as it is derived from revelation and as it is derived from pure reason (A631/B659). The latter is divided into transcendental theology and natural theology. Natural theology thinks of God through a concept borrowed from nature. It is further divided into physico-theology and moral theology. In either branch it conceives of God through the concept of that which is the highest intelligence and the source of all natural and all moral perfection. (A632/B660). Natural theology with is concept of a highest intelligence has a latent anthropomorphism. Anthropomorphism represents a particularly dangerous foe of our pure cognition of God for which transcendental theology is the useful counter (*Lectures Theology* 28:1046). Transcendental theology is encountered either as ontotheology – determining God's existence and nature from concepts alone – or as cosmotheology – deriving God's existence from some indeterminate fact about the world (A632/B660). Out of transcendental theology comes the concept of 'the highest reality as a being that is single, simple, all-sufficient, eternal, etc.'.

Arguments from probability

Suppose we accept for the sake of argument that Kant's treatment of the individual proofs of God's existence shows that none of them succeeds as a proof in the sense outlined in the previous chapter. A proof must have true premises but it must also serve as the means whereby someone not antecedently convinced of the conclusion can be led to that conviction. The conclusion of a proof must follow from its premises or be made highly probable by them. And its premises must known to be true and be sufficiently distinct from its conclusion. The admission that the individual proofs do not work as proofs in this sense does not spell the end of natural theology. There is an obvious further option: perhaps each offers some reason to think there is a God and when taken together they collectively offer very good reason so to think.

Could they not work as a cumulative, probable argument? This is a live option in contemporary natural theology, for Richard Swinburne's reconstruction of natural theology is based on the very idea that individual proofs are not probative when taken on their own but work cumulatively.

Kant considers the ontological, cosmological and possibility proofs as deductive arguments. And since success and failure in deductive arguments do not admit of degree, he has a ready-made ground for not considering them as potential parts of a cumulative case for God's existence. We might, however, wonder why he thinks of the physico-theological proof as only a proof and not as suasion that provides *some* reason to think there is a God. We have already observed Kant's high regard for the physico-theological proof. Here he is again praising the argument:

> It suggests ends and purposes where our observation would not have discovered them itself, and extends our information about nature through the guiding thread of a special unity whose principle is outside nature. But this knowledge also reacts upon its cause, namely the idea that directed it, and strengthens the belief in a highest author so that it becomes an irresistible conviction. (A623–4/B651–2)

These statements fit in with other material in the Critical corpus where Kant states that we use the idea of a divine architect to guide us in the study of nature and find that this guidance pays off in new discoveries and new ways of unifying scientific knowledge (as at A687/B715). But what is this other than an admission that the hypothesis of a divine architect is confirmed by experience? Could we not imagine such confirmations building up until we had a cumulative, probabilistic argument for God's existence?

Kant repeatedly insists throughout his Critical discussions of natural theology that there can be no question of using probabilistic arguments for God's existence. For him, it is quite illegitimate to say that some phenomenon or other makes it probable that there is God. He would thus reject the notion that a proof for God's existence might make it highly probable that there is a God. Proofs of God are apodeictic or not proofs at all.

At some places Kant makes this point about metaphysics in the first instance, to which reasoning about God belongs. Metaphysics, he tells us, is an a priori discipline like geometry and as such has no place for probability and conjecture (*Prolegomena* 4:369). It is not a discipline that has hypotheses (*Critique$_1$*:Axiv and cf. A775/B803). Kant also makes the point directly about God (as in *Lectures Theology* 2:1082, *Reflexionen* 18:456–7 and 18:713, *Critique$_1$*:A642/B670). In this connection, he explicitly heaps ridicule on those who offer cumulative arguments for God's existence: we can be sure that the 'dogmatist' who steps forward with ten proofs has none at all (A789/B817).

Just as clear as his rejection of any link between God and probability are the grounds offered for this conclusion. The first ground is the assertion that probability is in place only when making connections within the realm of possible experience and thus cannot be used to reinforce conjectures about realities existing beyond it. Probability is concerned with immanent judgements of causality (*Reflexionen* 18:456–7). As Kant puts it:

Opinions and probable judgements concerning what pertains to things can only occur as explanatory grounds of that which is genuinely given or as consequences of empirical laws of the real grounds of what is genuinely given, and thus they can occur only in the series of objects of experience. (A775/B803)

A second ground is a variation on this theme. It depends on the thought that probability reasoning relies on analogy. I reason from something known to something conjectured and rely on analogy in so doing. The thing known and the thing conjectured must be homogeneous: 'But when we are speaking of a thing that does not belong to this world at all; then no homogeneity and hence no probability obtains' (*Lectures Theology* 28:1082). Note that this point strikes at a key premise of the physico-theological argument as Kant presents it, namely 'the analogy between natural products and those produced by human art' (A626/B654). That analogy is used to convince us that there is a likeness between the causes of human artefacts and the products of nature. But if we respect the messages gleaned from transcendental theology (ontotheology and cosmotheology), we will see there can be no close analogy between God and the human. (In the *Reflexionen* at 18:713 this point about the lack of analogy between God and immanent things is linked to the starker thought that God is incomprehensible.)

Kant argues, thirdly, that probability in God's existence must be out, because what is probable can in principle be known. What is overall probable is backed by reasons that make it more than 0.5 likely and we can conceive of adding to the likelihood until we get the certainty of knowledge. God (and the other Ideas of Reason) are not in principle objects of knowledge, however, and therefore cannot be reached by this kind of additive certainty (see *Progress* 20:299).

Kant's fourth argument against linking probability to God is given in a marginal note of his to the first edition of the first *Critique* at A642 (to be found at 23:43). It concludes: 'Probability in the absolutely necessary is contradictory'. Kant in this argument shows his commitment to the notion that if it is true that there is a God, then it is necessarily true and to the further notion that we cannot have probabilistic arguments for necessary truths.

It will be evident that many of these grounds for rejecting the possibility of probability arguments for God's existence are internal to Kant's Critical system and could easily be rejected without inconsistency by those who favour an inductive approach in natural theology. Thus the first ground (probability judgements are only in place within the realm of possible experience) depends on accepting the Kantian boundary around the limits of thought and knowledge. So does the third ground: non-Kantian natural theologians are unlikely to accept the premise that God cannot in principle be known. The claim that faith and knowledge are not points on a common scale is internal to the Kantian system. The second ground appeals to something that is indeed in broader traditions of philosophical theology, on which indeed Kant is drawing. In Hume's *Dialogues*, Demea, the character who represents the viewpoint of classical theism, objects to the general drift of the design argument on the very ground that to attribute intelligence to the deity is to indulge in anthropomorphism (see Hume 1976:179–80). But there is once more an obvious counter to Hume's and Kant's point. One can reject the God of classical theism and self-consciously adopt a conception of God as a person. The God of Swinburne's natural theology is a person, who exists in time and who is capable of change (see, for example, Swinburne 2004:7). This God can be conceived to have something like intelligence, provided only that we are prepared to accept the coherence of the notion of persons who are incorporeal. Further, Swinburne's reasoning to the existence of this God via probability arguments does not violate the principle 'no probable arguments for the existence of necessary truths' contained in Kant's fourth ground. For it is a contingent fact that Swinburne's God exists and he is a necessary being only in a muted sense of that phrase. Given that he exists, he does not depend on anything else for his existence and cannot conceivably go out of existence (see Swinburne 2004:95–6).

Thus far we can see that Kant's rejection of an inductive, cumulative natural theology is comprehensible but lacks justification independent of his Critical system. Further comparison of Kant and the most important recent defender of inductive, cumulative natural theology, Richard Swinburne, might uncover some deeper Kantian reasoning on this subject.

The point at which to compare Kant and Swinburne is over the autonomy of reason. In Chapter 2 we noted Susan Neiman's argument that Kant sought an autonomous conception of human reason and rejected a heteronomous one. Rejection of natural theology is part of securing reason's autonomy. Of particular importance in this regard is Kant's claim that reason is engaged in an active, constructive task when it produces large-scale scientific theories. For Kant, it is true that any world of which we could have empirical knowledge has to be one in which 'All alterations occur in accordance with the law of the connection of cause and effect' (*Critique$_1$*:B232). That the world is causally ordered is given just with our ability to have experience (where experience is knowledge based on intuition and concept). But *how* the world is causally ordered and, in particular, which large-scale scientific theories are true of it, is not so given. Kant makes this point crystal clear in the first Introduction to the *Critique of Judgement*:

> But it does not follow that nature even in accordance with *empirical laws* is a system that is *comprehensible* to the human faculty of cognition, and that the thoroughgoing systematic interconnection of its appearances in one experience, with that itself as a system, is possible for human beings. For the manifoldness and diversity of empirical laws might be so great that, while it might be possible for us to connect perceptions into one experience to some extent in accordance with contingently discovered particular laws, we may never bring these empirical laws themselves into a unity of relationship under a common principle, if, namely, as is quite possible in itself ... the manifoldness and diversity of these laws being infinitely great, likewise the corresponding natural forms, were to have presented us with a raw aggregate and not the least mark of a system, even though we must presuppose such a system in accordance with transcendental laws. (*Critique$_3$* 20:209)

The discovery of the precise causal order in the world is the work of reason. Reason proceeds in its search for large-scale theories that describe the particular order in the world on the assumption that nature constitutes a systematic unity. Without this assumption of systematic unity in nature, and the search for its precise form, there would be 'no coherent use of the understanding, and, in default of that, no sufficient criterion of empirical truth' (A651/B679). This I take to be the sensible comment that the plausibility of hypotheses about the precise order in nature depends in large measure on their ability to fit into theories.

In searching for systematic unity in nature we are guided by particular ideas such as manifoldness, affinity and unity (A662/B690). Thus, knowing from observation that the orbit of the planets around the Sun is roughly, but only roughly, circular we search for a motion that most approximates to the circular and that is simple and come up with the hypothesis that this motion is elliptical (A662/B690). Reason assumes that, despite the great variety in nature, there lies behind it a unity of fundamental properties, from which the great diversity within nature can be derived (A652/B680). Reason demands that we use principles of simplicity and economy in investigating nature, for otherwise it would not be able to engage in the construction of scientific theories and 'no coherent use of the understanding, and, in default of that, no sufficient criterion of empirical truth'. These demands reason makes upon the world are supported by the Ideas of Reason, and in particular the postulation of the idea of a God as a purposive, intelligent creator. When we investigate nature under the banner of rubrics such as 'nature takes the shortest route', we do so guided by the idea that nature is the product of a supremely wise and powerful architect. We assume that nature is the product of a mind like ours and of whose reason ours is a copy. We 'make possible systematic unity of the manifold in the world-whole and, thereby, the greatest possible empirical use of reason, by seeing all connections *as if* they were ordained by a supreme reason, of which ours is only a faint copy' (A678/B706).

We are now in a position to see the deeper reason Kant has for rejecting probability arguments for God's existence. It is this: probability reasoning depends on rational demands that are in turn dependent on theistic ideas. So such reasoning cannot be used to support theistic ideas.

There is part-confirmation of Kant's objection in the structure of Swinburne's inductive theology itself. For Swinburne, as a good Bayesian, the probability of a hypothesis in relation to a given piece of evidence is a function of the interrelation of three factors. First there is the prior probability of the evidence (in the best case this should be low – the evidence should cry out for explanation). Second there is explanatory power of the hypothesis (in the best case this should be high – the evidence would be very likely if the hypothesis were true). Third there is the prior probability of the hypothesis (in the best case this should be high – minus the evidence and given background information alone, the hypothesis should be likely). The third factor is vital. Even if a hypothesis were to provide, if true, a good explanation of a piece of evidence that cries out for explanation, it does not follow that the evidence renders the hypothesis probable. There is an infinite number of hypotheses capable of explaining any given piece of evidence. So it is always possible that there is one that has greater explanatory power than the hypothesis we wish to confirm. In the case of a piece of evidence such as 'the cosmos contains order', there will be an infinite number of hypotheses that explain it, of which the theistic hypothesis is only one. We need a filter to rule out members of this potentially infinite set and that filter is provided by considerations of prior probability. This is the familiar 'curve fitting problem' (see Swinburne 2004:58–9 and 1997:15). The curve-fitting problem also infects judgements as to which hypotheses fit with background knowledge. A potentially infinite number will be formally consistent with a given body of background knowledge. Which hypothesis fits best with this knowledge is a function of which is the simplest fit.

The prior probability of an hypothesis is usually a function of its fit with background knowledge, but in the case of the hypothesis 'There is a God' all contingent facts about the universe are to be explained by it, so there is no background knowledge in which to fit it. There are only necessary truths (Swinburne 2004:71). Thus in filtering out hypotheses to explain the existence of the universe and its fundamental properties, all we can do is appeal to simplicity. Simplicity plays a two-fold role in Swinburne's inductive theism. There is a general principle linking simplicity and probability (the simple is the sign of the true, the simple is more likely to exist than the complex – 2004:59 and 109) and there is the specific claim that theism is a very simple metaphysical system (2004:96–109). The general principle claiming that the simple is more likely to exist than the complex has to be an objective truth, for inductive theism wishes to produce genuine, that is truth-conducive, arguments for God's existence. 'God exists' is not just a useful hypothesis, but one that has significant verisimilitude. One good way of understanding Swinburne's appeal to the principle of simplicity in his inductive theism (albeit that what follows is not explicit in his texts) depends on our seeing the principle of simplicity as a necessary truth and thus part of the background knowledge with which rival metaphysical accounts of reality have to fit. It could not then be tautological evidence (a phrase Swinburne uses to characterise the necessary truths in background knowledge – 2004:71). If it were, it would obviously have no power to discriminate between hypotheses. Inductive theism in the style of Swinburne must appeal to the principle of simplicity as a synthetic a priori truth. In his *Epistemic Justification*, he describes it as 'a fundamental a priori principle' (2001:102).

If the principle of simplicity is a synthetic a priori proposition, the question then arises: on what can it be based? There is no answer in Swinburne to this question other than 'we need the principle to defeat scepticism about inductive reasoning'. Or, as he himself puts it: 'either science is irrational ... or the principle of simplicity is a fundamental a priori truth' (1997:56). That is, if the principle is not true, then there is no objective prior probability to large-scale theories in science and metaphysics and thus the sceptic who claims that all such theories are arbitrary wins the day.

There is an evident circularity in this justification of principles of economy and simplicity. Their use enables us to make a rational choice between theories, and the choice of theories assists in the choice of hypotheses, but their adoption depends on our insistence that there must be some rational method of theory choice. We have answered the sceptic by putting a foot down and insisting that the sceptic must be answered.

Note that in Swinburne's cumulative, probabilistic natural theology the principle of simplicity comes before the conclusion that there is a God. In Swinburne's system it is a contingent, a posteriori truth that there is a God, but a necessary, a priori truth that the simpler is more likely to be true. In Kant's view the priority should be reversed. Principles such as that of simplicity are given a context of intelligibility by seeing them as grounded in the thought that there is a rational mind not unlike our own that is the ground of all possible reality. If it is true that there is such a ground, then it is necessarily and a priori true. Without the posit of this necessarily existing ground to all reality, the thought that reality is bound to match our desire for an order that is discernible by *our* reason is without foundation. The reason why Kant cannot join in a cumulative, probabilistic natural theology should now be obvious: affirmation of God's existence is for Kant our means of asserting that the world has the rationally discernible structure that enables us to produce large-scale theories about its character. Inductive theism simply puts the cart before the horse. The principles it needs for probabilistic arguments for God's existence to work are, for Kant, dependent on our assuming that reality is grounded in a God.

Swinburne is implicitly agreeing with one of Kant's key claims when he affirms that his principle of simplicity rests on our need to believe that the sceptic is wrong and to have confidence that reason can do its work. For Kant, principles like that of simplicity are maxims that we posit in order to get reason's work done. They are not derived from nature, because without them we could have no theories about nature. We cannot have discovered the rational unity of reality 'from the contingent constitution of nature in accordance with the principles of reason. Since it is necessary for the law of reason to seek unity, since without it we would have no reason at all' (A651/B679). And, as we have seen, without reason, we would have 'no coherent use of the understanding, and, in default of that, no sufficient criterion of empirical truth' (A651/B679). Principles like that of simplicity are expressions of autonomous reason. As demands we make on nature, they inevitably give rise to illusion. We cannot but think that reality has a rational structure in it discernible by our kind of intelligence. By analogy, standing on the beach and looking at the ocean, we cannot but prevent the sea appearing higher in the middle than at the shore, since we see the former through higher rays of light than the latter (A298/B354). For that perception not to produce the conviction that the sea is actually lower at its edges, we need to remind ourselves continually of the facts that explain the perception as an illusion. Something similar applies in the case of theism. We have the subjectively necessary idea that the world is rationally ordered according to principles of simplicity and economy. We are bound to see it so. That fact lends subjective necessity to the idea of God as the supremely rational ground of all possible reality. Unless we have materials provided by the criticism of reason continually to hand, we will assume that these subjectively necessary ideas rest on objective facts and inferences. It is in this assumption that transcendental illusion arises: taking how things cannot but appear to us as reflecting how they objectively are in themselves (see A298/B354 and Grier 2001:250). The failure to struggle against the subjectively necessary appearance of things in case of theism shows itself in the readiness to produce and embrace rational proofs of God's existence. It just must be the case that the idea of a rational ground of all things is objectively based:

> Hence there is a natural and unavoidable dialectic of pure reason, not one in which a bungler might embroil himself through lack of knowledge, or one that some sophist has artfully invented in order to confuse rational people, but one that is inseparably attached to human reason, so that even after we have uncovered the delusion it will still not cease

to trick our reason, continually trapping it in momentary confusions that always need to be removed. (A298/B354–5)

It might be objected to the foregoing that we are not faced with a stark choice between the autonomy and heteronomy of reason. Granted that we must bring assumptions like the principle of simplicity to the study of reality, can we not find them inductively confirmed once the study of reality has got underway? Suppose we choose between hypotheses and theories on grounds such as simplicity and thereby build up an empirical science. It is surely down to reality, and not to us, that this project succeeds. A science constructed by the use of such principles either works or it does not. If it works, then it enables us to predict phenomena and create taxonomies of natural substances into which the things we encounter can be fitted. That humanly constructed science works is surely inductive evidence of a strong kind that reality is indeed ordered according to principles of economy and order that human beings can grasp, and thus evidence for the existence of a human-like intelligence behind reality. Science shows this to be an intelligible universe and an intelligible universe is strong a posteriori evidence for God's existence (see Meynell 1982:64ff.).

There are two replies on behalf of Kant to this final attempt to free inductive natural theology from the charge of transcendental illusion. One consists in pointing out that the argument from the success of science has not appreciated Swinburne's curve-fitting problem. That science has succeeded by using transcendental principles of simplicity and economy is just another datum. As such, a potentially infinite number of hypotheses will fit and explain this datum. For example, it comports with the Epicurean hypothesis that humanly comprehensible order is the local and temporally limited product of the random movements of eternally enduring matter. Natural theologians who select the hypothesis that reality is the product of a mind like the human are influenced by principles of simplicity and economy. And then we are back at our Kantian starting-point. A second reply to the pragmatic inductive argument can come straight from Kant's texts. For Kant it is one thing that reality has a source of humanly comprehensible order in it, but quite another that the source of this order is pictured by the traditional concept of God. That it is so pictured is down to *us*. It reflects what pictures beings like us find natural and sustaining. The principle of unity in reality is in fact entirely inscrutable and the notion of a divine intelligence as the source of that unity is determined anthropomorphically (A692/B720).

There is thus a double dose of transcendental illusion in natural theology for Kant. First the subjective necessity in reality's being ordered is taken to correspond to an objective fact we have discerned. Second the subjective necessity we as human creatures are under to see the putatively objective source of this order as an intelligence, a mind, is taken to correspond to what objectively exists. To pursue this latter point further would take us into Kant's account of religious language, and particularly his doctrine of analogy. This is something we must postpone to the next chapter.

God as an object of intuition

This chapter and the preceding one have explored Kant's case for saying that thought about God lies beyond the boundary separating knowledge from speculations that have no chance of attaining to knowledge. In a number of places, Kant distinguishes between opining, knowing and believing: *meinen*, *wissen* and *glauben* (see *Critique₁* A820–29/B848–57, *Lectures Logic* 24:850–59, *Kant's Logic* 9:66–70). All three states of mind are forms of 'holding something to be true' (*das Fürwahrhalten*). Opining is holding-to-be-true that is both objectively and subjectively insufficient. An opinion is not held with conviction by the subject and lacks objective certainty. That which is known is held with conviction and possesses objective certainty. That is which is the object of *glauben* is held with conviction but lacks objective certainty.

That which is the object of opinion can become knowledge. It is on a scale of subjective and objective certainty/uncertainty that can see both types of certainty increase with the acquisition of evidence to the point where knowledge is attained. Belief in God, however, involves a commitment beyond the boundaries of knowledge that are fixed and determined a priori. Kant's rejection of probabilistic natural theology is a clear indication of this fact. We are not to imagine that that which makes us believe in God could be added to until knowledge is attained. This is because the holding-to-be-true in the case of 'God exists' is founded upon needs of the autonomous human reason and not upon evidence that derives from the putative object of the belief, and thus not upon evidence that could be added to. The exploration of the distinctively moral needs of autonomous reason that fuel belief in God awaits later chapters of this study, but it is in relation to these that Kant states in the first *Critique* discussion of opining, believing and knowing that I must not say '*It is* morally certain that there is a God' but rather '*I am* morally certain' (A829/B857). The holding-to-be-true that is opinion is based on evidence that is seen to be insufficient for full conviction, but which might be added to the point where knowledge is attained. *Glaube* in God is not based on evidence. The conviction thus produced has an irredeemably subjective aspect; not being based on evidence, it lacks a conviction that can be communicated so as to command universal agreement (*Kant's Logic* 9:70).

The exploration of why Kant thinks God can never be an object of theoretical knowledge needs to be completed by describing his treatment of one further possibility. This is the possibility that 'God exists' may be established directly by intuition. From our summary of Kant's theory of knowledge in Chapter 1 it is obvious that and why Kant must reject this possibility. It is, however, worth pausing to review his reasoning, given that philosophy of religion in our own day contains a number of extensive defences of the idea that God is an object of perception (see Alston 1991 and Swinburne 2004, for examples).

If there is anything Kant is consistent on in his Critical period it is that God cannot be an object of experience. This message is proclaimed in the *Conflict of the Faculties*. The general doctrine that supersensible experience is impossible is there (7:47). Experience as an encounter with specific things is via the forms of intuition in combination with the organising work of understanding and its categories. For something to be given to intuition it must be in space and time. None of the Ideas of

Reason is of an item that is in space and time. Reason has no objects in the sensible world; therefore nothing in the sensible world can correspond to them (*Conflict* 7:72). Even the claim to feel God's influence on one is self-contradictory because the idea of God lies wholly in reason (*Conflict* 7:58).

This message is repeated in other places in the Critical corpus: *Critique*$_1$ A327/B384, A567/B596, A621/B649; *Lectures Ethics* 27:723; *Orientation* 8:142–3; *Religion* 6:174. It flows from the fact that, as we have seen, the notion of God reason requires is the notion of a timeless, simple, absolutely necessary reality. God could not be one thing amongst other things. He could not be a discriminable item in the list of possible objects of experience. Moreover, if we reflect on the key attributes of God that arise from Kant's discussion of the ontological argument, we see that these identifying properties of the divine could never be phenomenally given. For example, God's identifying property as the source of all reality could not be given in experience. A number of contemporary writers have used the argument that nothing could be phenomenally identified as God to counter the resurgent appeal to religious experience (see, for example, Forgie 1994, Kenny 1992).

Kant's own system rules out experiential encounter with God. In general, he is allied to those whose 'high' view of the divine nature and attributes mean that God cannot be an object of experience. Thus, independently of his system, he can be seen to be a participant in contemporary debates about the possibility of religious experience. Kant's 'high' view of the divine nature stresses metaphysical attributes, remote from what is perceptible, as identifying something as God: simplicity, absolute necessity, being the source of all reality, etc. Proponents of religious experience might counter with a stress on other attributes of God that look as if they could be phenomenally given. These would be God's personal attributes, such as his love. Something we shall see in Chapter 4 is that Kant thinks we cannot take such descriptions of God at face value and literally. Points already made in this chapter prepare us for Kant's thought that this would be an unwarranted reliance on our anthropomorphic picture preferences.

A further reason for Kant's dismissal of experientially encountering God is that to admit alleged encounters with God as grounds for believing this or that in religion amounts to opening the door to superstition, fanaticism and enthusiasm. This point is made in the *Religion* (6:174) and is a theme running through the Critical works (see *Orientation* 8:143, *Reflexionen* 19:644). The theme is standard Enlightenment fare, and founded on discussions such as Locke's in Book IV, Chapter 19 of *An Essay concerning Human Understanding*. For Kant the appeal to religious experience as a ground for beliefs about God must entail the abandonment of reason in religion and the substitution of private fantasies for publicly grounded judgements. As we have seen by reference to *Kant's Logic* above, Kant takes a rational ground for a proposition to be something that can be communicated to others and that can command universal agreement. Religious experience as a ground of assent fails this test, for Kant, and hence ushers in rampant subjectivity. It is on this ground, amongst others, that Kant rejects Jacobi's attempt to separate faith from reason in *What Does it Mean: to Orient Oneself in Thinking?* (see 8:143).

It is an essential feature of Kant's account of experience (as empirical knowledge) that it be rule-governed. It has the unity that comes from possessing a rule-governed character. Unity and rule comes from the fact that genuine experience is such that the categories can be applied to it. Though Kant does not make this point directly for himself, there is an argument that alleged perceptions of God violate a fundamental feature of the rule-governed character of experience that amounts to empirical knowledge. Perception is of objects and their properties. Perceptible objects exist in a public space, such that if an object is genuinely given to me then I can expect other people similarly situated to be able to share in this perception. This fact grounds the inter-subjectively testable character of genuine perceptual claims. My claim to have perceived X is open to doubt just in that case where no one else can verify the claim that X is present for themselves (see Gale 1994). This feature of the rule-governed character of experience is violated in the case of alleged perceptions of God. There is no expectation that others similarly situated will have the same (or any) experiences of God as oneself. Those who claim to encounter God in experience precisely do not think it a reason for withdrawing their claims about what God has said to them, or what he has revealed about himself, that others did not hear the divine voice or did not have the divine revelation. To be sure, in established religious traditions there are tests for veridical experiences of God insofar as the upshot of such experiences must conform to existing doctrinal patterns. But religious traditions are notoriously given to schism and to the growth of sects. Who is to say that some alleged encounter with the divine is spurious because its doctrinal upshot is inconsistent with orthodoxy, or genuine because its upshot indicates the receipt of new revelation?

Communicability and checkability are the marks of reason for Kant. Reason seeks universal agreement. Religious experience as the basis for beliefs about God simply lacks these marks and is fundamentally different from experience of things in space and time. Kant's complaints about superstition, fanaticism and enthusiasm are thus integrally related to his own account of rational belief and empirical knowledge and latch on to a real problem with religious experience. (See Wood 1970:204 for further exploration of this point.)

The above is not to say that Kant's system excludes all experiences that may count as religious. It is possible to see his remarks on the sublime as leaving open the door to religious experience as a form of *experiencing-as*. We can experience some things as possessing the majesty and mystery we associate with divinity. Some experiences can thus take on a 'tone' that is religious. In the *Critique of Judgement* Kant discusses at length the experience of the sublime in nature and how it can be associated with divinity (5:244ff.). Sublimity is marked in the sense of greatness or overwhelming power. Kant's examples include: bold, overhanging cliffs, the boundless ocean set into a rage, crashes of thunder (5:261). This sense of greatness is the result of the interplay between perceptions of mighty things in nature and the human mind. The sublime object has this character insofar as limitlessness is represented in it (5:244). The experience of greatness in nature, interacting with our minds, 'awakens the feeling of a supersensible faculty in us' and '*shows a faculty of mind, which exceeds every measure of the senses*' (5:250). Sublimity is thus easily associated with the idea of God. In the right circumstances, awareness of great and powerful things in nature awakens in us 'the idea of the sublimity of this being' (5:263). It is not only natural objects and scenes that will awaken in us the idea of the sublimity of God. There is a famous passage at the end of the *Critique of Practical*

Reason in which Kant says that there are two things which fill the mind with awe: 'the starry heavens above me and the moral law within me' (5:161). Awareness of both gives rise to a sense of sublimity (5:164; the third *Critique* also associates sublimity and morality, see 5:271).

In the light of Kant's recognition of the sublime in our experience of nature and of the demands of morality, it is not outrageous to say that there is a mystical strand in Kant's thought (see Lawrence 2001 for an example of a commentator who makes much of this). Experiences of an accessible kind give rise to a sense of God. This is connected to something we must discuss at much greater length in following chapters: Kant's definition of religion as the awareness of all moral duties as divine commands. This must be taken to include (amongst other things) an association between awareness of moral duties and awareness of the sublime.

Thus there is religious experience in Kant but it is not perception of God. The sense of the sublime is anchored in us and in our minds' reaction to those things that give rise to the sense of the supersensible. This is not experience that feeds into cognitions or gives rise to beliefs. It is not the source of information about God or evidence for his existence. It is a tone or aspect attaching to awareness of natural scenes through the five senses or to awareness of moral duties through conscience.

Chapter 4

Religious Language and the Boundaries of Sense

Kant the positivist?

We have noted the central aim of the Critical Philosophy: to set boundaries to the use of human reason. In the previous two chapters we have explored the grounds Kant offers for the contention that religious faith cannot cross over the boundaries set for knowledge in the Critical system. Religious faith is possible but it cannot in principle amount to knowledge. It is not even on the scale that includes opinion at one end and knowledge at the other. But for faith to be possible, God – and the other Ideas of Reason – must surely be thinkable.

The boundary around knowledge is created because Kant ties the possibility of knowledge to the possibility of experience. The limits of experience provide the limits of knowledge. If he ties the possibility of sense to those same limits, then he is a proto-positivist and he must adhere to some late eighteenth-century version of the verification principle. Contemporary commentators of Kant who wish to reclaim him for Christian orthodoxy are therefore keen to contend that he is not a proto-positivist. It will be important for any attempt to reconcile Kantian philosophy of religion with Christian orthodoxy to argue that Kant's boundaries around knowledge of God are not boundaries around meaningful talk about God. Kant may be agnostic about doctrinal claims, but he accepts their meaningfulness (see, for example, Hare 1996:274). Kant does, however, extend his claims about knowledge to claims about meaningfulness. He certainly appears in places to deny the possibility of meaningful language about God.

The proto-positivism in Kant is signalled by Strawson's well-known documentation of a 'principle of significance' in Kant's Critical Philosophy:

> This is the principle that there can be no legitimate, or even meaningful, employment of ideas or concepts which does not relate them to empirical or experiential conditions of their application. If we wish to use a concept in a certain way, but are unable to specify the kind of experience-situation to which the concept, used in that way, would apply, then we are not really envisaging any legitimate use of that concept at all. In so using it, we shall not merely be saying what we do not know; we shall not really know what we are saying. (Strawson 1966:16)

Many passages from the first *Critique* can be cited to show that the attribution of a quasi-empiricist principle of significance to Kant is amply justified. The thought is implicit in the famous statement that 'Thoughts without content are empty, intuitions without concepts are blind' (A51/B75) and explicit in such statements as 'concepts are completely impossible, and cannot have any meaning, where an object is not given either for themselves or at least for the elements of which they are composed' (A139/B178). The principle of significance is also endorsed in the *Prolegomena* (4:312) and in his *Correspondence* (as at 13:463).

The underlying source of this doctrine is Kant's account of the interconnected roles of understanding, the faculty of concepts, and sensibility, the faculty of intuition, in the production of human thought. Understanding's role is an ordering one, but it must have something to order. There must be material, provided by intuition, for the understanding's concepts to work on so as to generate thought that has any content. The fundamental concepts, the categories, only yield cognition of things insofar as things are taken as objects of possible experience (*Critique$_1$*:B147-8) and thus 'Our sensible and empirical intuition can alone give them sense and meaning' (B149).

Kant's principle of significance looks as if it must culminate in making him the all-destroying Robespierre of the world of thought that Heine accuses him of being. There is an obvious tension in his work between the principle and his desire to curb once and for all the claims of materialism, between the principle and his desire to leave room for faith. We find that, at the same time as he declares use of the categories beyond the bounds of experience to be impossible, he makes room for us to *think* through concepts that cannot denote anything empirical (as at Bxxvi). For all that he states that the categories are empty minus experience, he distinguishes two uses or forms of them: schematised and unschematised. A category needs a schema because it needs something to mediate between its pure, abstract form and the temporally bound experience of human subjects. So the pure concept of substance (something in which properties can inhere) becomes, in its schematised form, the notion of an enduring thing in time. The category of cause when schematised becomes the concept of successive events linked by a rule such that, given that the first happens, the second event will always follow (see A144/B183). When we divorce the category of cause from its schema all we get is a purely logical relation between propositions ('from something's existence we can infer the existence of something else', A243/B301). In other words, the category of cause unschematised is little more than the idea that one fact can be linked to another by an 'if, then', the idea of one thing as the ground of another. This is obviously inadequate as a representation of the concept of cause, since it will not account for the direction of causality. If p is a ground for q in this sense, then q is also a ground for p in respect of it being a necessary condition for p. The notion of the direction of causality is lost if it is simply the logical relation between ground and consequent. 'God is the first cause of the universe' must mean more than 'God is the sufficient condition for the universe's existence'. For that proposition entails 'The universe is the necessary condition for God' and the sense of dependence that comes with causality is lost.

The distinction between schematised and unschematised categories surely underpins Kant's claims throughout his critique of natural theology that the principle that everything must have a cause cannot be used to infer a transcendent cause of the cosmos. For such a cause could not be a cause in the schematised sense of the category of causality. Thus Kant states that 'the principle of causality has no meaning at all and no criterion for its use, except in the sensible world' (A609/B637).

Disabled though categories like substance and causality are when divorced from their schema, it is the case that Kant's discussion allows unschematised categories to have some formal or merely logical meaning. This notion of a merely logical meaning to the categories when applied beyond experience connects with others: with the categories so used we can think but cannot cognise anything (Bxxv–Bxxvi); only with the categories used in application to possible experience do we grasp real possibilities (A219–20/B267–8); only with the categories used in relation to possible experience is thought about objects possible (A147/B186–7). These connecting notions are themselves interlinked. Cognition (*Erkenntniss/erkennen*) is thought that is not mere idle speculation but capable of extending what we know or can reliably believe. It is thus thought that relates to possible objects of human enquiry. It is thus thought that deals in what is really possible, as opposed to what is notionally so.

Some of these interconnections are displayed in a passage in the first *Critique* at A147/B186–7. Kant writes:

> In fact, there remains a meaning in the pure concepts of the understanding even after removal of every sensible condition, but it is only a logical significance of the bare unity of representations, but no object is given, and with that no meaning that could yield a concept of the object. Thus, to take the example of substance, if one leaves out the sensible determination of persistence, it would mean nothing more than a something that can be thought as a subject (without being a predicate of something else). Now I can make nothing from this representation, as it shows me nothing at all about what determinations the thing that is to be considered as such a first subject is to have. Therefore, without schemata, the categories are only functions of the understanding for concepts, but do not represent any object. This meaning comes to them from sensibility, which realises the understanding, while it at the same time it restricts it.

Since 'meaning' in the above passage translates *Bedeuting*, it is tempting to read Kant as stating that unschematised categories have *Sinn* (sense), but lack reference. However, Kant draws no consistent distinction between *Sinn* and *Bedeuting* in making such comments about meaning. At A239/B298 he states of a concept that lacks relation to a possible object: *Ohne diesen letztern hat er keinen Sinn*.

The key to the A147/B186–7 passage is the claim that concepts minus a schema that connects them with possible experience cannot represent any object. Kant is taking it, surely, that concepts which have full, substantive meaning must be capable of representing things, events, qualities and the like. But concepts that (see above) lack a connection with a 'sensible determination' leave us in the dark about what determinations the thing they allegedly denote might have. Thinking becomes cognition where it has representative force. Kant defines a cognition as 'an objective perception', having informed us that perceptions are a species of the genus 'representation' (A320/B376). Concepts wholly divorced from any application to possible experience lack representative force and thus are 'empty' or 'mere play'. They are empty because without representative force they cannot point to really possible objects and thus have no possibility of reference. (For more on Kant's theory of judgement and the role of representations in giving thought the possibility of objective truth see Hanna 2004.)

At this point we need to look at Kant's account of how real possibility is established as this is presented at A218–22/B265–9. The governing principle of this account is the claim that 'Whatever agrees with the formal conditions of experience (in accordance with intuitions and concepts) is *possible*' (A218/B265). The formal conditions of experience go beyond the mere coherence of the concept that we use to frame a putative real possibility: 'That in such a concept no contradiction must be contained is indeed a necessary logical condition; but for the objective reality of the concept, i.e. for the possibility of such an object as is thought through the concept, it is far and away not sufficient' (A220/B267–8). Absence of contradiction suffices for mere notional possibility. Real possibility arrives when we have a concept that could represent an object. And for that, the concept must be conceived in accordance with the categories and in accordance with the forms of intuition. A concept, Kant explains, embodies a synthesis (presumably: of determinations – features that enable us to recognise something). But the synthesis included in a concept is 'to be regarded as empty, and as not relating to any object, if this synthesis does not belong to experience' (A220/B267) in some manner or other. It is in this context that Kant affirms his point that for the categories to have more than a mere logical significance, and 'to concern *things* and their possibility, actuality, and necessity', they must pertain to possible experience and its synthetic unity 'in which alone objects of cognition are given' (A219/B267). Kant wants to draw the distinction between notional and real definitions of objects that we have seen crop up in the context of discussion of the ontological argument. A concept framed by uniting determinations of a putative object is merely empty, notional, if it remains the case that it has no power to represent an object to us, if the determinations are not sensible. It lacks such power because there is nothing in it that could help us to recognise what would fall under it.

Though we can form concepts of things prior to ever discovering them in the advance of science and empirical knowledge, such anticipation of experience is governed by a fundamental restriction:

> One can, however, also cognise the existence of the thing prior to the perception of it, and therefore cognise it *comparatively* a priori, if only it is connected with some perceptions in accordance with the principles of their empirical connection (the analogies). For then the existence of the thing is still bound up with our perceptions in a possible experience, and we can proceed from our actual perceptions with the guiding thread of the analogies to the thing in a series of possible perceptions. (A225–6/B273)

Kant then gives the example of the concept of a magnetic field. That concept is not derived from experience where that means our direct intuition of something. Our senses are not fit to enable us to perceive a magnetic matter pervading bodies. Talk about such matter is nonetheless meaningful. Kant then seems to offer two suggestions as to how it is meaningful in the absence of a direct experience of magnetism. One is that we could imagine, 'if our senses … were more refined', having direct experience of magnetism. The other is inference 'in accordance with the laws of empirical connection of appearances' to the existence of the thing. Mention of such laws connects with the reference to the analogies of experience referred to in the above quotation. Empirical laws of causality enable us to connect talk of magnetic matter to something that we can recognise in experience. The second suggestion is much more sophisticated than the first. It cannot be right to suppose that the concept of magnetic field was introduced into scientific discourse and given meaning only after satisfying the condition that we could imagine what it would be like to have direct experience of its referent via finer senses. Kant's view of the logic of scientific discourse is much more subtle than that which states that all talk of theoretical entities must be translatable into talk about what we might directly observe. (See Allison 1983:30ff. for a full discussion of this point.)

Where Strawson sees a 'principle of significance' in Kant, Bennett sees 'concept empiricism'. This is something he defines as stating that 'I cannot articulate a judgement at all, even to consider it as a possible candidate for acceptance, unless I know something about what intuitions of mine *would*, if they occurred, be relevant to its truth or falsity' (Bennett 1974:27). We have seen that there is a principle of significance and a form of concept empiricism in Kant, but that it is a little more subtle then Bennett's statement of it. Judgements are indeed not *possible candidates for acceptance* unless I know something about what intuitions (not necessarily mine) *would*, if they occurred, be relevant to their truth or falsity. That condition enables us to distinguish mere thought from cognition. But the very distinction between thought and cognition means that Kant allows that we can articulate judgements that do not meet the condition enshrined within concept empiricism. These judgements are 'formal' or 'empty' insofar as they have no representational power, since a judgement only has that if the concepts within it contain some determinations that can be correlated (albeit via the medium of the laws of empirical advance) with something we can recognise.

All this may look as if Kant's principle of significance and concept empiricism is an eighteenth-century version of the verification principle: a sentence has cognitive meaning if and only if it is verifiable by sense experience. But this is not quite right. The alternatives to cognitive meaning for verificationists were such things as emotive or prescriptive meaning. Kant's more nuanced position wants to allow talk about putative entities beyond any possible empirical verification to have a meaning that is other than that of merely expressing our emotions or than merely declaring how we will act. Entities beyond experience remain conceivable, but not as possible objects of knowledge or recognition. Our thought about them is indeed seriously defective. Such thought has no power to represent something as a possible object of recognition or discernment. It deals in formal, non-substantive possibilities only. But it is thought nonetheless. Perhaps the best way to get clear (or: clearer) about what Kant has in mind is to look closely at his account of the meaning of religious language.

Kant on God-talk: the fundamentals

While we shall note later in this chapter some 'wobbles' by Kant on the subject of the sense to be attached to talk about God, there should be no real dispute as to the nature of his overall account. Two substantial paragraphs in the first *Critique* running from A695/B723 to A698/B726 spell out his considered position with great clarity and we can find many passages in other parts of the Critical corpus that tell a similar tale.

In the first of these two first *Critique* paragraphs Kant asks three key questions about the concept of God. The first is 'whether there is anything distinct from the world which contains the ground of the order of the world and its connection according to universal laws?' The second question is stated in cryptic form: 'whether this being is substance, of the greatest reality, necessary, etc.?' The third question is 'whether we may not at least think this being, which is distinct from the world, by means of an analogy with objects of experience?'

The answer to the first question is an unequivocal 'yes'. The world is 'the sum of appearances, and so there must be some transcendental ground for it, i.e. one that is thinkable only by the pure understanding'. Kant's answer indicates that by the 'world' in his question he has in mind the world *qua* phenomenon. His unequivocal answer to the question arises from his conviction that the use of reason, and, we have seen, understanding, in application to phenomenal reality depends on our supposing that reality is grounded upon an ordering principle.

By his second question about this transcendental ground of order that reason forces us to posit ('whether this being is substance, of the greatest reality, necessary, etc.?'), Kant evidently has in mind whether this being is the being of transcendental theology (to which the ontological and cosmological proofs, in the guise of the argument from contingency, belong). Is this being the necessarily existing *ens realissimum*? His reply to this question, printed in the text with emphasis added, is '*that this question has no meaning at all*'. The reason why it has no meaning at all is:

> For all the categories through which I attempt to form a concept of such an object have only an empirical use, and they have no meaning whatsoever when they are not applied to objects of possible experience, i.e. to the sensible world. Outside this field they are mere titles for concepts, which one might permit, but through which one can understand nothing. (A696/B724)

The message in this passage has to be interpreted in the light of our exposition in the previous section. The concept of a necessary, perfect being that is the first cause of all things can be allowed, but it does not for us signify a real possibility or an object of cognition.

The third question in the paragraph ('whether we may not at least think this being different from the world in accordance with an analogy with objects of experience?') introduces the descriptions of God contained in natural theology (to which physico-theological and moral proofs of God's existence belong). '*To be sure*', replies Kant, 'but only as an object in the idea and not in reality' (A696–7/B724–5). The reply means: we can form an idea of the first cause on the basis of analogies with agents in the world of experience, but we cannot suppose that the conception thus constructed represents something in reality that is as our idea presents it to be. All that we can suppose to exist in reality is an unknown substratum of the world's systematic unity, order and apparent purposiveness (A697/B725). The analogies between this unknown substratum and empirical things can be taken further. We can think of the substratum in anthropomorphic terms, so long as we are clear that the anthropomorphisms are not attempts to represent what it is like, but merely a way of making the regulative use of the idea easier and more potent for us. Kant spells this point out with crystal clarity:

> Still more, we admit certain anthropomorphisms in this idea, which are useful for the regulative principle in question, without fear or censure. For it is always only an idea, which is not at all directly related to a being distinct from the world, but rather to the regulative principle of the world's systematic unity, and only by means of a schema of this unity, namely of a supreme intelligence that acts as its author by means of wise purposes. What this primordial ground of the world's unity is in itself ought not to have been thought through this, but rather only how we ought to use it, or much more its idea, relative to the systematic employment of reason in regard to things in the world. (A697/B725)

We now have a clear account of the function of religious language in front of us. Given the vital need of autonomous reason to proceed as if the world of appearances is the embodiment of a rational order that we can comprehend, we suppose that there is some source or other of such order behind the world. We flesh out the thought of this transcendent ground with language belonging to transcendental theology: it is the sum of all reality, the absolutely simple first cause of all, and so on. But this language introduces no cognition of an object and presents us with no real possibility. For key concepts in it, such as that of cause, remain unschematised. The ends of reason require us to enrich further the picture associated with the thought of transcendent ground of order. We do this through analogies drawn upon things in the world of experience. In particular, we draw upon analogies with human intelligent agents. The picture of the world-orderer as like a wise and powerful intelligence is a natural, indeed inescapable, model for us to employ if we are to make the regulative posit of a ground of order both vivid and the supplier of an 'answer' to the question of why the order in things should be comprehensible to creatures like us. But the resultant picture does not represent anything in reality. The question of whether God is really like this is seen to have no sense once we realise how we got to the concept of God and what its role is.

In the second of the two paragraphs in this part of the first *Critique* Kant tells us that we can assume (*annehmen*) that there is a wise and all-powerful author of the world. But in doing so we do not by any means extend our cognition of things beyond possible experience:

> For we have only presupposed a something, of which we have no concept at all of what it is in itself (a merely transcendental object); but, in relation to the systematic and purposive order of the world's construction, which we must presuppose when we study nature, we have thought this unknown being *by means of the analogy* with an intelligence (an empirical concept), i.e. in regard to the ends and the perfection, which are grounded on themselves, we have endowed it with just those properties that could contain the ground for such a systematic unity in accordance *with the conditions of our reason*. (A697–8/B725–6; last emphasis mine)

Note Kant's statement that we produce the idea of a wise and powerful world-author in accordance 'with the conditions of our reason'. It is our human reason that constrains us to think of the unknown something as being like a human agent (thus the presence of 'wise' and the like in our descriptions of it). Hence the filling in the concept of God is 'completely grounded *with respect to the this-worldly use* our reason makes of it' (A698/B726). The filling we put into the concept of God in no way derives from any awareness of what the referent of 'God' is like in itself. But that does not matter. The purpose of the concept is to regulate our thinking, not to represent an object whose nature we might want to investigate. Thus there is no need to worry about the relation between the concept and any object it might pick out.

Without using the terminology of 'sense' and 'reference', Kant has in effect given us an account of the meaning of 'God' that sharply distinguishes the sense and reference of that name. The Critical Philosopher's reconstruction of the meaning of 'God' takes it that the word is used to refer to the whatever-it-is that is the transcendent ground of the order in the world as it appears to us. How that thing is then portrayed is through a series of analogies that culminate in a picture of this ground as a human-like intelligence. But the manner in which the transcendent ground of order is thus presented to us need not, and *cannot*, be relied on as a genuine portrayal of its character. Its actual character lies beyond the boundary of what we can conceive. We have to assume that there is some transcendent ground or other of order and we have to have a picture of that thing's nature if the assumption is to play the required heuristic role in human thought. But the content of the picture is wholly down to us and our needs. So the bare sense of 'God' as picking out the unknowable source of order is objective or realist in its intent, but the full sense of 'God' is not. So we cannot say that, for Kant, God is in all respects a useful fiction, though we can say that much of the concept of God (all the positive, substantive content of the concept) is a useful fiction.

Thus far we have got the fundamentals of Kant's account of religious language from two paragraphs in the *Critique of Pure Reason* at A695–8/B723–6. The discussion continues in the same vein to the end of the relevant section at A704/B732. What must now be emphasised is the extent to which this same fundamental account dominates Kant's treatment of the concept of God throughout the Critical corpus. As already noted, we will have occasion toward the end of this chapter to note some characteristic Kantian 'wobbles' on this topic, but if we leave those aside there is a remarkable and uniform adherence to the fundamental account throughout the 1780s and 1790s.

In proof of the above point, we can cite the discussions of religious language in the *Critique of Judgement* of 1790. Kant here distinguishes expressions that contain 'the true schema for a concept' (that is, something that will mediate between a concept and a real object and thus connect the two) from that which is 'only a symbol for reflection' (5:352). He affirms the picture element in our concept of God through his statement that all our cognition of God is merely symbolic (*so ist alle unsere Erkenntniß von Gott bloß symbolisch*, 5:353). Anyone who takes it otherwise (as 'schematic') and thinks that properties like understanding and will are in the object 'lapses into anthropomorphism'. The non-schematic nature of the symbol 'God' is reinforced through the claim that our assumption of an intelligent cause of organic life in the universe depends on the 'constitution of the human understanding' (5:413), that is on how beings like us are able to picture such causality. In reiterating his moral theology in the third *Critique*, Kant makes it plain that the idea of God as a moral, intelligent being is produced 'only by means of analogy' (5:456). By means of this analogy 'we only think this being, and thereby do not cognise it theoretically'. To cognise it theoretically we would have to have some insight 'into what the supreme world-cause is in itself'. Such insight is lacking to us and is, in any event, irrelevant. For the reason why we conceive of God as an intelligent, moral being is rooted in our subjectivity: '*in accordance with the constitution of our faculty of reason* we could not make at all intelligible the kind of purposiveness connected *to the moral law* and its object that there is in this final end without a world author and ruler who is at the same time a moral legislator' (5:455).

As Kant puts it, what is at issue when we frame a picture of God's nature is 'only which concept we are to form of it in accordance with the constitution of our cognitive faculty' (5:456). To be sure, that reflection is linked to the question of whether we have to assume God's existence, but the question of God's existence is immediately separated from the question of what God may be like. What we need to assume as existing is something defined only as producing a certain effect: a moral, teleological order in reality ('only to be able to think of an intended effect as possible', 5:456). The core of the assumption of God's existence is thus the assumption that there is some source of a moral, teleological order in the world. We surround the core reference to this cause with anthropomorphisms, 'the purpose behind our using them is not that of determining its for-us-inaccessible nature, but of determining ourselves and our will in accordance with them' (5:457). Kant here rams home the point made in the first *Critique* discussions to the effect that, beyond the bare reference to the unknown source of order, the point of talk about God is not to represent something. This talk is there for a heuristic purpose and its substantive content is determined by that heuristic purpose. The purpose does indeed entail that we take the language to refer to something or other, but it does not at all entail that the sense of the word 'God' represents the referent. It cannot be taken as so representing it and there is no need for it to represent it.

At the close of the third *Critique* Kant confronts the dilemma posed by juxtaposition of the first *Critique*'s principle of significance and his positive use for the concept of God as a transcendent entity. He makes it plain that he has not abandoned the empiricist-type thoughts about meaning of 1781 and 1787. He refers to the 'apparent contradiction between the possibility of a theology that is asserted here and what was said about the categories in the critique of speculative reason' (5:482). The contradiction is removed by noting that theological talk serves a practical purpose only and does not function so as to extend theoretical cognition. As the discussion proceeds Kant makes it plain that it is not merely the anthropomorphic language about God, contained in such concepts as intelligence, which fails of representational power. If we think of God as the prime mover, and thus employ the category of causality, our language about God becomes problematic in the manner argued for in the first *Critique*. A mover is in space and time. The prime mover would not be in space and time:

> Accordingly I do not have any determinations at all that could make the condition of the possibility of motion comprehensible through this being. Consequently, I do not

cognise it at all through the predicate of cause (as prime mover): but rather, I have only the representation of a something which contains the ground of motions in the world; and the relation of these motions to this something, as their cause, since it yields me nothing else about the constitution of this thing, which is the cause, leaves the concept of it wholly empty. (5:483)

The reason why the concept of the first cause is left 'wholly empty' as a representation of something is straight out of the *Critique of Pure Reason*: the predicates that we use to fill out the concept 'find their object only in the sensible world' and thus cannot determine the concept of a supersensible being. We have not left concept empiricism behind. What Kant does in the closing page of the *Critique of Judgement* is in effect tell us that the point of predicates like 'intelligence' used of God is not to describe him. I use this and other predicates not to attribute corresponding properties in God, thus not to 'determine' him, that is not to provide identifying marks of God's nature. Rather:

> It is in no way permitted to attribute an understanding to it, and thereby flatter myself that I am able to *cognise* it by means of its property: because in this case I must omit all those conditions under which alone I recognise an understanding, and thereby the predicate, which serves only for the determination of the human being, cannot be related to a supersensible object at all, and thus, through a causality so determined [i.e. for the human case], what God is cannot be cognised at all. (5:484)

Thus: we try to specify what kind of cause the transcendent ground of order is by affirming that it is an intelligent cause. But 'intelligent' turns out to be incapable of doing that, since it cannot in this context be understood as naming a property of the object it is putatively qualifying. 'Intelligent' turns out only to be an apt analogy for conceiving of the first cause's nature because it serves our practical purposes to use the traditional God-symbol containing the notion of an intelligent agent to refer to the unknowable nature of that cause.

Kant's steady adherence to this account of religious language can be further confirmed by the brief references to the topic in his essay of 1794 *What Real Progress Has Metaphysics Made in Germany since the Time of Leibniz and Wolff?* Here Kant affirms that the concept of God produced by transcendental theology – that of a necessary, absolutely simple being – leaves us without any real concept of an object. Nothing is identified by this concept: 'if, I say, things go so badly with the attempt to construct a concept of it, then the concept of this metaphysical God remains always an empty one' (20:304). We can know nothing whatever of the nature of supersensible objects, such as God (20:296). I use symbols to refer to the object of an idea of pure reason, such as God, that are constructed by analogy with things and relations within the world. But these analogy-based symbols do not yield knowledge of their referents 'because they do not by themselves determine any object' (20:280).

It is important to note that these restrictive doctrines about the meaning of religious language are present in those works in practical philosophy and theology in which Kant seems to have many positive things to say about God. If the restrictive doctrines govern these apparently positive accounts of the divine nature and activities, then these accounts must be understand as ways in which we flesh out a picture of the divine that is fit for our purposes. They are not in any sense intended to have descriptive force. The accounts will give us a picture of God (say, as the legislator of the moral law) concerning which it is inappropriate to ask 'Is God really like this?' The picture's validity is a function of its heuristic value in guiding our thought and action. Early on in the *Critique of Practical Reason* Kant affirms that he will remain consistent with the teaching of the first *Critique*. The use of the Ideas of Reason by pure practical reason will not violate the condition that there is to be no 'extension of cognition to the supersensible' (5:5). The postulates of pure practical reason does not enable or require us to cognise 'the nature of our souls, nor the intelligible world, nor the supreme being as to what they are in themselves', for the possibility of these things 'no human understanding will ever fathom' (5:133). The tacit 'sense versus reference' theme in Kant's account of religious language identified above surfaces in an extended discussion of the precise extension of our cognition yielded by the postulates of practical reason in the Dialectic of the second *Critique*. Here Kant tells us that the requirements of practical reason he has disclosed in the earlier arguments of the second *Critique* convince us that the Ideas of Reason have objects 'although we are not able to show how their concept refers to an object, and this is not yet cognition of these objects' (5:135). Objects are given to the Ideas of Reason by Kant's appeals to the requirements of practical reason but thereby there is no 'extension of the cognition of *given supersensible objects*' (5:135). Kant states that, in relation to the ideas, our concern is not with theoretical cognition of their objects, but with whether they have objects at all (5:136). He affirms the view we found in the third *Critique*. Practical reason leads to a God pictured in a certain way. However, the predicates we use to fill out the picture we have of that God do not function to pick out attributes which God might actually have. Instead, they fill out the picture we must have of God if our practical purposes are to be served:

> These are attributes, of which we can frame no concept that serves for cognition of the object, and through this we learn that they can never be used for a theory of supersensible beings, and therefore that on this side they are not at all able to ground a speculative cognition, but their use is, instead, *restricted solely to the practice of the moral law*. (5:137; my emphasis)

The force of 'restricted solely to the practice of the moral law' is surely to re-affirm the conviction that the question 'Might God really be like our picture of him?' is illegitimate. It is not our purpose in picturing God to give a description of God's nature. Our purpose is rather to make the concept of God fit for our practical purposes. Those practical ends require only the assurance *that* there is a source of moral teleology in the world, not a true description of *what* this source is like. The substantive picture we have of this God is irredeemably anthropomorphic and thus irredeemably fails as a picture of what a supersensible source of order might be like. At 5:137–8 Kant challenges natural theologians to

> name (over and above the merely ontological predicates) even one determinative property, perhaps of the understanding or will, of this object of theirs, of which one could not irrefutably show that if *one removes everything anthropomorphic from it nothing would remain to us but the mere word*. (my emphasis)

Kant's practical philosophy is thus perfectly consistent with the first *Critique*'s concept empiricism in its teaching that rich descriptions of God as omnipotent, omniscient and so forth are not representational (see *Critique$_2$* 5:140). He is consistent because he carries forward the account of religious language advanced at A696/B724ff. Our filling out of the concept of God beyond the mere reference to a supersensible source of order and teleology serves no descriptive purpose but only a heuristic one.

It finally behoves us to note that Kant's account of religious language must be taken as covering the manifold positive things said about God in *Religion within the Boundaries of Bare Reason*. There is, to be sure, no very extensive treatment of religious language in the text, but Kant gives us sufficient indications that the views we have thus far traced through to 1794 are present in this work of the early 1790s. There are four places in the *Religion* where Kant discusses matters relating to religious language: 6:64$_n$, 6:139, 6:142, 6:182–3. The message of the four passages is internally consistent and consistent with the doctrines outlined above. 6:64$_n$ provides the most extensive discussion. It focuses in particular on our talk about God being analogical (of which more in the following section). We need note for the moment only that Kant states that our analogies for describing God are drawn from the human but do not serve the purpose of 'object-determination'. This we can gloss as: do not serve to present properties of God that might serve to characterise God's nature. We can 'in no way conclude by means of analogy that what befits the former [the sensible] must also be attributed to the latter [the supersensible] (thus *expanding* its concept)'. This is the third *Critique*'s teaching that predicates used of God do not serve to ascribe attributes to him. 6:64$_n$ presents the clear cost of taking these predicates to be attribute-ascribing: anthropomorphism (which is, of course, out). He also clearly distinguishes between two ways of making God comprehensible. I can make the idea of God as, say, the cause of living things, comprehensible *to me* by thinking of God after the model of an intelligent agent with understanding. Or, in addition, I can try to make God himself comprehensible by affirming that God truly has understanding ('to attribute understanding to it not merely as the condition of my ability to comprehend but of the possibility of the cause itself'). Only the first mode of making something comprehensible works in the case of God. For if I attribute understanding directly to God I undertake 'a formidable leap ... which leads straight into anthropomorphism'. Once again, Kant has affirmed that the point of God-talk is to fill out certain ideas and possibilities so as to serve our practical purposes and that the descriptive content of this talk is heuristic and not cognitive in function.

The remaining passages in the *Religion* harmonise with 6:64$_n$. They tell us: that God is a mystery, concerning whom we have no need to know what he is in himself (139); that our accounts of God (the example discussed is Trinitarian descriptions of God) are not true of God as he is in himself (142); and that, if we go beyond thinking of God in terms of his moral relation to us, beyond what is required for our self-subsistent determination to duty, and try to conceive of his nature, we fall into the trap of anthropomorphism (182–3).

Analogy

The notion of analogy plays an important role in Kant's many attempts to address the problem of the meaning of talk about God. The notion is to be found in what I have presented as Kant's key discussion in the *Critique of Pure Reason*. At A696/B724 we are assured that we can speak of the unknown, transcendent source of order by analogy with objects of experience. There are mentions of analogy as tool for talking about God at: *Critique*$_2$ 5:56–7, *Critique*$_3$ 5:546–7, *Prolegomena* 4:355–8, *Progress* 20:280, *Religion* 6:65$_n$. The main point to be made about Kant's use of the doctrine that we can speak about God analogically is that it does not in any way mark a departure from his account of religious language given above, and in particular from the key claim that talk about God does not serve to ascribe properties to God.

Textbook accounts of analogy in religious language divide analogical talk about God into two kinds: attribution and proper proportionality. According to the former, we can ascribe, say, intelligence to God on the grounds that God is the cause of intelligence in our world and, since effects betray a likeness to their cause, God must have something similar to human intelligence. According to proper proportionality, we can ascribe intelligence to God insofar as we presume there must be a property in God that plays the same role in his nature and activities that intelligence plays in human nature and its activities. Both kinds of analogy are meant to enable us to work out a sense for a word like 'intelligent' when it is applied to God. He will be said to be intelligent in some extended, but related sense of 'intelligent' when that word is used of us. There is no need to go over the general problems that beset this textbook account of analogical language about God. Suffice it to note that Kant does not use analogy to determine the nature of God or to provide a precise sense for the names of divine attributes. It is evident that both analogy of attribution and of proper proportionality are out for Kant. Analogy of attribution will not work because causal reasoning fails when extended beyond the world of sense because causal principles lose their meaning. This, as noted in Chapter 2 above, is one of the main planks in Kant's rejection of the cosmological proof (see also Stroble 1993:70). Analogy of proper proportionality is out because Kant's drastic agnosticism about the divine nature forbids us giving an account of it such that we could then understand the role alleged properties like intelligence play in it.

Analogy in Kant is another way of making his point that talk about God is not a means of describing God as such, but a way of providing us with a notion that works for us. This is the point behind the distinction in *Religion* 6:64$_n$ between a 'schematism of analogy' and 'schematism of object-determination'. Analogical language about God is not a way of bringing together a list of qualities that determines (that is: picks out, characterises) God. What then is such language for? The answer in the texts we have listed is clear: analogical language serves the purpose of characterising God's relation to the world or how he exists *for us*. That answer is a further variation of the theme that talk of God serves a heuristic and human purpose, not a descriptive one.

The real point of analogical talk of God for Kant is not to ascribe properties to God but rather to characterise the relation between God and the world. To say that God is an intelligent author of nature is to say that the unknown something or other that is God acts on the world as an intelligent human engineer or artificer acts within it. We note and make comprehensible a feature of our world (in this case, the presence in it of what appears to be intelligent design) by conceiving of the supra-sensible cause of all *as if* it were like an intelligent artificer. We thereby do not characterise it, but rather characterise only the effects we ascribe to its causality. The point of so doing is to further our practical purposes (by, say, encouraging the unification and simplification of our scientific theories). This indirect use of analogy is clearly set out in the *Prolegomena* at 4:357:

> If I say we are forced to look upon the world *as if* it were the work of a supreme understanding and will, I say indeed nothing more than: as a watch, a ship, and a regiment are related to an artisan, a builder, and a commander, so the sensible world ... is related to the unknown, which I do not then cognise according to what it is in itself, but only according to what it is for me, that is, in respect to the world of which I am a part.

Kant precedes this passage with the affirmation that his doctrine of talk about God amounts to 'a symbolic anthropomorphism'. He continues his account in the *Prolegomena* by telling us that this 'cognition according to analogy'

> does not signify ... an imperfect similarity between two things, but rather a perfect similarity in two relations between wholly dissimilar things. By means of this analogy there still remains *for us* a determinate concept of the supreme being, though we have removed everything that could have *determined* this concept absolutely and *in itself*; for we determine the concept only with respect to the world and hence with respect to us, and nothing more is necessary for us. (4:357–8)

A footnote to this passage illustrates the point with reference to the concept of love in God. We conceive of God's love through the schema of proper proportionality. There is something in God (labelled by us 'love') that stands to the welfare of humankind as the happiness of children stands to the love of their parents. 'Love' then refers to the 'unknown' something in God thus conceived. But it is not as if this unknown had the least similarity with any human drive or attribute. Thus: analogical language used of God is not a way of finding similarities between God and us and thus not a way of identifying qualities that God has. That would be to transform a merely symbolic anthropomorphism into what we must avoid: a dogmatic anthropomorphism (5:347).

At this juncture it is worth pointing out that Kant's account of positive talk of God as 'symbolic anthropomorphism' is not new. He stands in a long tradition of Western thinkers who have denied that there can be direct, univocal property ascriptions to God. Many thinkers have reached the same conclusion as Kant: direct talk about God, as opposed to talk about God's acts or his relations to the world, comes up against a boundary of sense. Kant's own, unique way of drawing the boundary of sense is dependent on the precise claims of his critique of reason. Others have had the thought that our understanding of terms is limited by our experience, and that 'God' is used to refer to something that lies beyond experience and therefore cannot be comprehended and delimited by our attempted descriptions of him. There is a form of concept empiricism behind and within Aquinas's discussion of the divine names in question 13 of the *prima pars* of the *Summa Theologiae*. Reading from article 1 through to 4, we glean that words can be used to signify things by virtue of them being immediately associated in our minds with a concept that has been formed in confrontation with things we experience. This concept gives the mode of signification of a term, in virtue of which the thing it signifies is picked out for us. But the mode of signification of the positive descriptions we frame of God (such as wisdom, life, knowledge, goodness and the like) is fundamentally creaturely, since our experience of the relevant qualities is of their manifestation in creatures. Thus these descriptions used of God are not ways by which we can comprehend God's essence, or what he is in himself. Thus 1a, 13, 1: 'It is the knowledge we have of creatures that enables us to use words to refer to God, and so these words do not express the divine essence in itself'.

A clearer, fuller parallel for Kant's ideas about religious language can be found in Moses Maimonides *The Guide of the Perplexed*, Book 1, 50ff. Central to Maimonides' account is the recognition that our way of filling out the positive picture of God relies on anthropomorphisms: 'The Torah speaketh in the language of the sons of man' (Maimonides 1963:120). So we ascribe to God attributes that we regard as perfections in human beings: wisdom, knowledge, power and the like. But none of the predicates in sentences such as 'God is wise' are to be truly taken as ascribing attributes to God. For Maimonides this is so because God is an absolutely simple being and therefore possessed of no attributes. Some of the sense of these attribute terms is negative. To say that God is wise truly signifies that God is not foolish. But Maimonides also allows that we can name God from his actions: 'A thing has its action predicated of it' (1963:118). We can thus say that God is merciful, gracious and long-suffering, because these are 'simply pure attributes of action' (1963:124). God acts in these ways upon us. His operations to this effect are seen in the world and therefore he is named by these names. But this does not mean that the use of 'attributes of action' involves ascribing attributes to God. We know that 'the acts in question need not be carried out by means of differing notions subsisting within the essence of the agent' (1963:119). All these different acts are carried out by means of the essence of God, which is both absolutely simple and unknowable by us. Thus Maimonides has a very similar doctrine to that found in Kant's account of analogical discourse about God. We speak of God by analogy with human beings, but only in order to signify something about his relation to us, specifically how the effects of his actions upon us can be marked. The analogies with the human we employ do not carry over to the nature of the incomprehensible cause of those actions. Moreover, Maimonides hints at a further, Kantian-like pragmatic, heuristic justification of using human perfection terms of God. In order to sustain an appropriate faith and attitude of worship to the divine, the multitude need to be given a way of indicating that God is perfect in every respect. This can be done by allowing God to be described as if he has human perfections: 'if people imagined that this human perfection was lacking in Him, may He be exalted, this would constitute, in their opinion, a deficiency in Him' (1963:162). Thus: speaking as if God has attributes (specifically, anthropomorphic ones), serves our practical interests for Maimonides as it does for Kant. Maimonides has with a Kant a 'symbolic anthropomorphism', since he too sees anthropomorphic language about God as necessary but as non-descriptive in nature. It does not refer to anything in the divine nature.

The notion that there is a boundary of sense separating human language about the divine from the nature of the divine is obviously not new to Kant. Nor is the notion that the boundary leaves us with no comprehension of what God positively is. Aquinas is famous for stating in the introduction to question three of the *Summa, prima pars* that 'we cannot know what God is, only what God is not'. Analogical discourse does not get us over that fact. For Maimonides and Aquinas the boundary of sense is created by the fact that the language we use is devised for compound and finite reality and thus constitutionally disabled for describing an absolutely simple and infinite reality. Kant's boundary is in part built on these same foundations, but, as we have seen, rises still higher on the building blocks provided by transcendental idealism and its attendant concept empiricism. No more than for his predecessors in the tradition of apophatic theology is he forced to the unqualified conclusion that we speak as if there is a God. We assume that there is a transcendent ground of order. To that assumption we are committed. But we speak as if this ground has the positive qualities of the God of traditional theism. As to what qualities it has independent of our symbolic accounts of its nature, we can neither know nor say.

Wobbles?

I have claimed that there is a consistent account of the function and logic of religious language in the Critical Philosophy that respects the boundaries of sense provided by that philosophy and that leaves open a positive, albeit symbolic, non-descriptive, use for that language. Kant would not be Kant if his post-1780 works did not contain some passages not quite fitting into this account.

Notable in this regard is the discussion of the divine attributes in the *Lectures on Rational Theology*. From 28:1048ff. Kant discusses the attributes that a theistic, as opposed to a deistic, God must have. His lecture makes frequent reference to the text of Baumgarten's *Metaphysica*. He contends that God must have a faculty of cognition and founds this conclusion on appeal to the analogy of attribution: 'We cannot have the least idea of how a reality could exist in an effect without already existing in its cause – how beings with understanding could stem from an original source which is lifeless and lacking a faculty of cognition' (28:1050). Not the least of the problems in this supporting argumentative principle is that it uses a Scholastic maxim ('There must be as least as much reality in the cause as is in the effect') to infer what properties must exist in a transcendent cause of all things from properties that obtain in the sensible world. As we have seen in the previous section of this chapter, operating with the analogy of attribution in this way violates a firmly stated Critical rule to the effect that causal principles lose validity and meaning when taken from a mundane context to make inferences about the transcendent. This is not an incidental rule. It is bound up with the distinction between schematised and unschematised concepts. It is appealed to in the critique of natural theology.

In the pages that follow, Kant does make the point that understanding in God will be very different from understanding in human creatures. It will be pure (not sensible), intuitive and wholly a priori. Nonetheless, the discussion assumes that we can ascribe the property of having an understanding to God.

This discussion in *Lectures Theology* is wholly at variance with the clear messages gleaned from other Critical writings earlier in this chapter. In them it is made plain that, though we can speak as if God had human-like attributes, to suppose that he actually does have them is to make an illegitimate leap beyond the Critical boundaries of sense. Kant has been quoted from the second *Critique* telling us that, if we take all that is anthropomorphic from properties like understanding and will which natural theologians apply to God 'nothing would remain to us but the mere word' (5:138). We have also made use of a passage from the *Prolegomena* that clearly states that, though we can talk as if God had the property of causality through reason, we don't attribute this reason to the being itself (4:358). The *Religion* at 6:64$_n$ also contains the same message. More generally, the discussion of God possessing understanding in *Lectures Theology* goes clean against the thrust of the *symbolic* anthropomorphism Kant expounds across a variety of texts in the 1780s and is still committed to in the *Progress* essay of 1794.

There is nothing to be done, in my opinion, with the *Lectures Theology* discussion of God as having understanding other than set it down as an aberration. Kant is, after all, not expounding the Critical doctrine of God in this passage but rather working through a textbook in rationalist metaphysics with his students. We must give the decisive weight to Kant's words when he is expounding the Critical system. There is indeed something in the *Lectures* discussion that harmonises with elements in the Critical account of God. The discussion of God as possessed of cognition/understanding is preceded by a distinction between a deistic and theistic idea of God. The deist, says Kant, conceives of a world-cause, but it is a blind, non-personal source of all. By contrast, the theist conceives of a world-cause who acts through freedom, who is a living God and thus possessed of some human-like traits (20:1047). This way of characterising the difference between deism and theism is typical of Kant's treatment of the topic (see *Critique*$_1$:A631/B659 for an example). Kant makes it plain that he wishes to espouse theism not deism. We need to describe God using the resources of natural and moral theology as well as those provided by onto-theology.

We shall have occasion to return to Kant's apparent rejection of deism later in this study. Two points about it suffice now. The first is that Kant's espousal of what he styles the theistic account of God is perfectly consistent with the stance on religious language described in this chapter. Kant does want to take over and endorse the rich vocabulary for describing God that comes from traditional theological discourse. We have seen how he can do this: the rich description of God that comes from natural and moral theology is necessary and valid for the heuristic purposes of human reason, but it does not enable us to represent or recognise God. The second point about Kant's discussion is that his account of deism is fictional – but more of that in a later chapter.

If the discussion in the *Lectures* just seems odd, there is a more substantial strand in Kant's writings that *appears* to be at outs with what I have given as his canonical account of religious language. A first hint of this strand is seen in the preface to the second edition of the first *Critique*. In the text at Bxxvi Kant introduces a now familiar distinction between the boundaries of cognition and those of thought: cognition is limited to objects of experience but we can think 'these same objects as things in themselves'. A footnote to Bxxvi expands on this distinction by telling us that more is required for real possibility than mere lack of contradiction, but he does not specify, as we might assume he must, that only possible experience can provide the basis for real possibility: 'This "more", however, need not be sought in theoretical sources of cognition, it can also lie in practical [sources]'. How can Kant imply that something other than possible experience is the ground of real possibility? We have seen in the above that such is the consistent teaching of 'The postulates of empirical thought in general' (A218–22/B265–9), a teaching that can be supported by many other passages in the *Critique of Pure Reason* (such as A581–2/B609–10).

The answer to the question about real possibility is perhaps best given by taking it with another puzzle: why does Kant affirm that cognition *can* be extended to God on the back of practical reason? I take it that these two puzzles are related. That a synthesis of ideas in a concept enables us to grasp its putative object as a real possibility is connected with the thought that the concept enables us to cognise that object, as opposed to merely think it. We have seen that it is Kant's consistent teaching that we cannot cognise God. But it is not his consistent teaching. In Section VI, Chapter 2 of the Dialectic of the *Critique of Practical Reason* Kant is commenting on what, in precise terms, has been shown in the preceding moral proofs of the existence of God and of the immortality of the soul. He asks early on in the section whether our cognition has really been extended by these so-called proofs. The answer – in apparent defiance of his statement earlier in the work (see $5:11_n$) that the postulates give us no cognition of objects – is 'yes', with the rider 'but only *for a practical purpose*' (5:133). Later passages in the second *Critique* speak in a similar vein of the extension of cognition through practical reason (as: 5:134–5, 137). Connecting with Bxxvi$_n$, Kant also writes of practical reason showing 'that those concepts are real and really have their (possible) objects' (5:134).

We are entitled to ask what is going on here and what happened to the nice distinction between cognising a transcendent object and thinking it. The reassuring answer is: do not panic; all can be explained. We have already quoted at length from the pages of the second *Critique* (5:133–9) that contain these references to cognising God and that also contain the 'official' message that we cannot cognise God. The apparent inconsistency in adjacent passages is really not such when we realise that Kant here distinguishes two things: practical reason instructing us *that* ideas like God have objects and instructing us *how* God is to be cognised. He affirms: 'we are taught through this *that they have objects*, without indeed being able to show how their concept refers to an object, and this is not yet cognition *of these objects*' (5:135). Thus the teaching that cognition is extended by reference to the work of practical reason is precisely not the teaching that practical reason gives us the means to cognise the object it must postulate via the concept of God. Practical reason gives us cognition of God only in giving us the right to assume that 'God' has a reference. We may blame Kant for his looseness of language, but I submit that the message of 5:133–9 is consistent with the fundamental distinction that governs Kant's account of religious language and that is to be seen most clearly in *Critique*$_1$: A696–8/B724–6. Practical interests of human reason give us the right to assume that there is something corresponding to the idea of God, but neither they nor theoretical deductions give us a picture of what God is really like. And so toward the end of the discussion in which Kant has said that we can extend cognition through practical reason, he informs us that by going through the attributes of God that arise from natural and moral theology 'we can frame no concept suitable for *cognition* of the object' (5:137).

My suggestion, then, is that Kant does not really violate the parameters he lays down for religious language by the references to practical reason assuring us of concepts representing real possibilities and extending our cognition. Practical reason is not able to show how God refers to an object.

Chapter 5

The Positive Case for God

Teleology

We have now established the boundaries of knowledge and meaning in the Critical Philosophy that separate us from a positive, assertoric and traditional belief in God. Beyond those boundaries thought about God is not only possible but also necessary. The previous chapter has shown that the content of this thought is severely restricted. Its positive meaning does not represent the nature of its putative object. That object cannot be truly represented, though it can be referred to via relational and negative characterisations.

We know already (from Chapter 3) that the necessity for us to think about God beyond the boundaries of cognition rests upon teleology. A multifaceted teleology is in question. Human reason has ends. It seeks the goal of unity in science. It also seeks the goal of the completion of the moral life. Its ends cannot be pursued unless it has some belief that the world is teleological in character. It must suppose that its ends are matched (at least potentially) in the reality it seeks to comprehend. In order for that supposition to be plausible, it must further assume that something like the being pictured in traditional philosophical theology exists.

What impels us beyond the boundaries of knowledge and meaning is something subjective but also objective. It is subjective insofar as it is grounded in us, specifically our needs. It is objective insofar as those needs are universal among human beings and rational. Belief in God (or at least, in the possibility of God) is thus rationally required of all, but the requirement reflects facts about us as human thinkers and not facts about reality. Belief in God exists for the Critical philosopher as a result of human reason's need to orient itself. That is a universal need and it points one way. But it is still a need and not a fact about reality independent of us.

The theme of orientation is spelled out in Kant's 1786 essay *What Does it Mean: to Orient Oneself in Thinking?* This essay is a response to an argument about the role of reason and faith in religion between F. H. Jacobi and Moses Mendelssohn that centred on the intellectual legacy of Lessing (who had died in 1781). Jacobi claimed that Lessing had confessed to belief in Spinozism before his death. Further, Jacobi maintained, Spinozism, with its view of reality as a thoroughly rational and determined system, was the inevitable outcome of the rationalism of his day. The only alternative to Spinozism was traditional Christianity and faith therein. Mendelssohn tried to argue that it was perfectly possible to marry an orthodox, non-pantheistic, non-deterministic theism with a commitment to reason as a guide to truth. *Orientation* devotes most of its commentary on the debate to rebutting Mendelssohn's claims that reason can lead us to the God of philosophical theology via metaphysics. Such claims are of course contrary to the whole thrust of the Critical Philosophy. But Kant makes plain his attitude to Jacobi's insistence on the need to return to faith from reason when he comments on the baleful resort to enthusiasm and superstition that results from the abandonment of reason's autonomy and its subjection to external masters (8:145).

Orientation has a simple answer to the question of why reason needs to postulate the existence of God: it needs to orient itself. It needs to plot the direction in which its investigations and tasks are to proceed. If we are orienting ourselves at the start of a physical journey, we can rely on objective pointers. The sun at midday is in the south (if you are in Königsberg). But objective orientation depends on subjective orientation. If the sun is southward at its highest point, I can work out east and west only if I know my left hand from my right and nothing out there will yield me that knowledge (8:134–5). This message about the subjective basis of orientation extends to orientation in human thinking. Especially in the case where reason seeks direction in thought about the transcendent, it cannot rely on objective principles of cognition but must fall back on 'a subjective ground of differentiation' (8:136):

> But now there enters *the right of the need* of reason, as a subjective ground to presuppose and assume something which reason may not pretend to know through objective grounds; and consequently for *orienting* itself in thinking, solely through reason's own need, in that immeasurable space of the supersensible that is filled for us with dark night. (8:137)

The supersensible, being filled with dark night, has no external landmarks to guide human enquirers. They must rely on internal pointers. Kant's thesis that belief in God properly arises out of reason's need to orient itself thus finds truth in both Jacobi's and Mendelssohn's positions. Jacobi is right that reason cannot prove the existence and nature of the traditional theistic God and that something subjective must take us to it. Mendelssohn is right in thinking that it is reason, not a faith that is understood as opposed to reason, which gets us to God.

Orientation briefly rehearses the needs of reason that require thought to orient itself through the idea of God. In theoretical reason, orientation requires the idea of an unlimited ground for all things and a source of the purposiveness and order we see in the cosmos (8:138–9). But 'Far more important is the need of reason in its practical use' (8:139). This is the need to assume that the highest good, which we seek in the moral life, is possible and to imagine a mechanism by which it can come about.

It is the subjective character of the impulse that forces us across the boundaries of knowledge and sense that explains why, in *Orientation*, Kant offers us his now familiar characterisation of religious assent as rational faith. This is a mode of assent not on the scale 'opinion-knowledge'. It is subjectively certain but not on the road toward knowledge because it does not rest on any considerations of an objective kind (8:141).

Teleology in nature

From the discussion in Chapter 3, we know that Kant thinks that reason has important ends controlling its use in natural science. These are principally to seek the highest possible unity in scientific theorising. This end is not an optional one, for it is by reference to incorporation into larger-scale theories unifying our knowledge of nature that specific hypotheses as to nature's laws are deemed to be valid. We know that this search for unity involves, according to Kant, the assumption that nature is the product of a purposeful intelligence conceived by analogy with human intelligence. The teaching of the essay *What Does it Mean: to Orient Oneself in Thinking?* reinforces the point made while discussing probabilistic arguments for God's existence in Chapter 3: Kant thinks only an initial move by human reason itself enables us to see nature as the product of such an intelligence. Minus that move on our behalf, there is no basis for such an interpretation of nature.

Our earlier discussion was largely based on Kant's account of the concept of God as a regulative principle in science in the first *Critique*, A644–62/B672–90. There is no need to elaborate a great deal further on this aspect of Kant's teleological use of God. Mention should made, however, of the treatment of this theme in the *Critique of Judgement*. There is a terminological change in the third *Critique*'s treatment of these issues. The 'maxim' (see, for example, 5:385 for this much-used term in the third *Critique*) that the world is a product of a purposive intelligence modelled on the human is said to be the product of the reflective judgement, rather than of reason *per se*. Judgement is the faculty of being able to think some particular thing or fact under a universal law, rule or principle. It is determinative when the universal is given and I then subsume some particular under it. It is reflective when the particular is given and I seek, through reflection, some universal under which it might fall (*Critique$_3$* 5:179). Kant now places the problem described in Chapter 3 above into the lap of reflective judgement. A myriad of particular facts may be given me that may in turn be subsumed (in the manner of Swinburne) under an infinite number of natural 'laws'. Reflective judgement seeks the best set of laws that might fit these particulars. It can only do so by helping itself to a thought that is not given by determinative judgement at all and is not borrowed from experience. This is the thought that nature is the product of an understanding like ours. The ends of reflective judgement can be pursued only if we assume nature has a teleological order in it placed there by a mind that thinks like ours:

> Now this principle can be no other than this: that, because universal laws of nature have their ground in our understanding, which prescribes them to nature (albeit only in accordance with the universal concept of it as nature), particular empirical laws, in respect of that which is left undetermined in them by the former [the universal laws of nature], must be considered in the light of such unity they would have if an understanding (even though not ours) had likewise supplied them on behalf of our faculty of cognition, in order to make possible a system of experience in accordance with particular laws of nature. (5:180)

As in the *Critique of Pure Reason*, the postulation of a cosmic understanding as the author of laws of nature is heuristic only, a fact shown in the continuation of the above quotation: 'Not as if in this way such an understanding must actually be assumed (for it is only for reflective judgement that this serves as a principle, for reflecting, not determining); rather this faculty through this gives a law to itself alone, and not to nature' (5:180).

It has to be said that the attempts in the first and third *Critiques* to argue for God as a necessary but merely regulative postulate/maxim of scientific thought meet with considerable scepticism in contemporary commentary. Jonathan Bennett's dismissal of Kant's reasoning can be taken as typical:

> A principle which was guaranteed to be permanently regulative would have to be necessarily incapable of (dis)confirmation. That privilege might belong to a principle which was somehow presupposed by scientific endeavour as such, so that its confirmation would be question begging and its disconfirmation self-refuting. I doubt if there are any such principles. (1974:275)

Kant can be presented with a dilemma: if the postulation of a cosmic intelligence is really necessary for scientific reasoning, it must be confirmed as that reasoning progresses and succeeds. In this case it will no longer be a regulative principle, but a constitutive one. If the postulation is not confirmed by the success of science, then it cannot really be necessary for science and will not be a valid regulative principle. The first horn of the dilemma is accepted by the likes of Meynell (1982:68–83) and Wood (1978:142–5). These authors think the success of science is some kind of objective evidence for the truth of theism. The second horn is represented by Bennett above and by Strawson (1966:223). These authors think that science has no need of God as a regulative principle.

As noted in Chapter 3, Kant does have an answer to this dilemma. His essential point can be put in this way. Scientific reasoning proceeds by means of ampliative reasoning. That is to say, it relies on data to establish hypotheses, where the data do not entail those hypotheses – in fact the data will be formally compatible with an infinite number of hypotheses. The filters used to guide this ampliative reasoning depend upon assuming that nature conforms to laws that are simple and economical when judged from the standpoint of our understanding. The use of those filters presupposes an assumption of a harmony between nature and our understanding. The postulation of God is no more than one way of articulating that assumption (of a humanly intelligible universe). But this postulation and its underlying assumption cannot be confirmed because its confirmation would involve just that use of ampliative reasoning that the assumption of intelligibility was designed to support. In other words, Kant has a reasonable case for saying that this regulative maxim precisely fits the bill outlined by Bennett. It is presupposed both in any attempt to confirm it or disconfirm it and it articulates an assumption that does appear to be presupposed by science.

In the third *Critique* the motif of a humanly intelligible universe is conjoined with another ground for the heuristic postulation of teleology in nature. This second ground relates to the understanding of living things. Kant's exploration of this ground for the postulate of God covers some 25 pages of the third *Critique* (5:375–400). I will just give an outline of Kant's reasoning.

Kant draws attention to the manner in which living things exist as 'organised beings' (5:375–6) and as 'natural ends' (5:375). Such things exhibit purposiveness in and through their internal forms. We naturally tend to understand such purposive things through the thought that they are intentional products. Kant notes that some philosophers wish to resist this tendency and adopt an 'idealism of purposiveness' (5:391). This means regarding purposiveness as not really present in living things and supposing that some wholly mechanical causal process produces the appearance of purposiveness. Spinozism and Epicureanism are cited as two forms such 'idealism of purposiveness' can take. The alternative is a 'realism of purposiveness' (5:392). This also comes in two forms. Hylozoism explains organised beings/natural ends by supposing that they are made from a special type of 'living matter'. Hyloz0ism fails because of an alleged, fundamental incoherence: matter is in its essence lifeless. (This looks suspiciously like Kant trying to win a point through verbal legislation.) This leaves the second form of 'realism of purposiveness': theism. The theistic postulate 'has the advantage that, by means of attributing understanding to the primordial being, it can best save the purposiveness of nature from idealism and introduce an intentional causality for its generation' (5:395).

One point about this 'argument' needs to be noted straight away. Kant indicates that the conclusion is massively restricted. Though he states that 'for us there is no other means of judging the formation of its [nature's] products as natural ends than through a supreme understanding as the world cause' (5:395), this is a maxim for reflective judgement, not determinative. That is, it is a purely heuristic assumption flowing from the impossibility of someone with *'the specific constitution of my cognitive faculties'* (5:397) understanding organised, living things save through the notion of external, intentional causality. To convert this heuristic assumption into a determinative judgement we would need to demonstrate the impossibility of a non-intentional, mechanical cause of natural purposiveness. And we cannot do that owing to 'the constitution and limits of our cognitive faculties' (5:395). Kant declares that we are bound to seek a mechanical explanation of things in nature so far as this is possible. He is also not averse to the idea that, once we have living forms in existence, evolutionary mechanisms will generate the variety of, and differentiations amongst, the species we now see around us (5:419).

What resists a complete mechanical explanation of the living world according to Kant is the possibility of 'the purposive form of the products of the animal and vegetable kingdoms' (5:419). These products exhibit internal purposiveness. This internal purposiveness is described as follows: *'An organised product of nature is that in which everything is an end and reciprocally a means as well'* (5:376). Kant had earlier provided an illustration of what is meant by 'internal purposiveness' via the example of a tree. Here is one of his central points about the tree as a natural end:

> one part of this creature also generates itself thus: so that the preservation of the one [part] is reciprocally dependent on the preservation of the other. An eye from the leaf of a tree grafted into the twig of another generates a growth of its own species in an alien stock, and similarly a scion attached to another trunk. Hence even in the case of the same tree, one can view every twig or leaf as merely grafted or inoculated into it, hence as a tree existing in itself, which only depends on the other and nourishes itself parasitically. At the same time the leaves are certainly products of the tree, yet they maintain it in turn, for repeated defoliation would kill it, and its growth depends upon their action on the trunk. (5:371–2)

This passage continues with ruminations on the way in which the tree will repair itself when injured. Self-organised living things are thus ones in which there is a peculiarly intimate part–whole relation. Parts can only exist because they are 'grafted' onto the whole; the whole can only exist because these parts nourish and sustain it.

Clear and striking though this understanding of living things is, it does raise a serious question about Kant's case that we need theism as a heuristic maxim for understanding natural ends. What Kant is *not* doing is running the old analogy behind the argument from design:

Living things exhibit a purposiveness that is like that displayed by machines.
Machines are the result of designing intelligence.
Therefore, living things are the result of designing intelligence.

Kant is not running this analogy because the purposiveness he has described in living things is not like the purposiveness exhibited by machines. He makes this point crystal clear himself: 'In a watch one part is the instrument for the movement of the other, but one wheel is not the efficient cause for the production of the other' (5:374). The cogs in a watch are not related to the whole that is the watch in the way in which the leaves of a tree are related to the whole that is the tree. The cogs can exist while not a part of the watch. Kant then draws an interesting moral: given that the producing cause of both the watch and of its form is not contained in the nature of its matter, but outside it, we mark the obvious truth that the cause of the existence and form of the watch is external to it. The mechanically ordered thing must have an external cause. An organised being like a tree is not 'a mere machine'. In contrast to the machine, the tree contains an internal '*formative* power'; the machine merely has an internal '*motive* power'. How then, we must ask, does it help to understand the self-organised being by adopting the heuristic maxim of an intelligent, purposive creator?

The problem here is that the kind of internal purposiveness Kant is describing is quite other than that found in a made thing. It is precisely a property of living things, and not of machines, and therefore not a property of things intelligent agents construct. So how can bringing in the idea of an intelligent divine agent help in understanding this peculiar kind of purposiveness? Kant himself states 'Strictly speaking, the organisation of nature has therefore no analogy with any causality with which we are acquainted' (5:375). So why then the reference to an imagined intelligent cause of this organisation? Kant does qualify the above point in a note to 5:375. The organisation of natural things is like the organisation of elements in a human commonwealth, for here too the members of the whole could not survive without the whole, but the whole exists only insofar as it has functioning members. In response to this, it may be conceded that we can illuminate the nature of a human community through understanding it as an organic whole, but that does not entail that we can understand an organism better through thinking it as like a commonwealth. It is the organic model that is doing the work here.

I suggest, in the light of the above, that, while Kant has a case for linking the assumption of the intelligibility of the universe with a heuristic, theistic maxim, his case for linking the understanding of living things with such a maxim is weak.

Moral teleology

The discussion of the link between natural teleology and God in the *Critique of Judgement* moves into a discussion of the link between moral teleology and God. The transition is mediated by the introduction of the notion that the highest end of nature is the human being. Humanity can be considered by reflective judgement to be the end of nature because only human beings have the concept of ends (5:429). But it is not human happiness that can be heuristically considered as the unconditioned end of nature. It is rather our flowering as free and moral beings that may be viewed as the final end of nature (5:435–6). Humanity as the locus of the Good Will embodies absolute value and nature can thus be considered to have humanity as its final end (5:443). Thus is the ground prepared for the so-called moral proof of the existence of God. (We will see that this is not the best label for Kant's attempt to link God and the ends of practical reason.) In morality lies the highest flowering and perfection of the human being. For the moral ends of humanity to be thought of as possible certain conditions must be assumed to obtain and God is the guarantor of those conditions.

The moral proof reflects the multifaceted teleology discerned thus far. Human beings, in their capacity as moral agents, seek certain goals and to conceive of how this search may be possible they assume an answering teleology in reality. Students of Kant have sometimes puzzled over the question of how Kant can insist on the rational necessity of the pursuit of ends in the moral life when he has so clear a deontological understanding of ethics. He does have such an understanding. In the *Groundwork* and the second *Critique* he prioritises the right over the good. He offers us a choice: either the moral law immediately determines the will, or the will is determined by some object. If we embrace the latter alternative, we do not end up with true practical laws. The concept of which ends are worthy of pursuit – the concept of the good – is to be determined after and not before we have worked out what the moral law demands of us, that is after we have determined what ends are morally worthy of pursuit. If we started with some determinate conception of the good and tried to derive moral laws from it, these would lack universality and in the end would rest merely on experience and the feeling of pleasure. If we place the good first, we end up with heteronomous moral willing and the autonomy of the moral will is destroyed (see *Critique$_2$* 5:62–4). But none of these familiar assertions in Kantian ethics entails that the rational human being does not have ends, does not seek the good in its various guises. In fact, Kant acknowledges the obvious truth that it is impossible to act without seeking ends. All that Kant's ethics entails is that the worthwhileness of an act does not derive from the end it pursues, but rather from conformity of the maxim behind the act with the principles of right, that is with the demands of universal, impartial and rational legislation.

The moral proof proceeds from two overarching and interacting ends that Kant thinks that any finite, rational agent (such as a human being) must pursue. They are happiness and virtue, linked together in the concept of the highest good. The moral proof works by arguing that the goal of pursuing the highest good is impossible of attainment unless something like a traditional God exists. There are versions of the moral proof in all three *Critiques*. It is also referred to in *Lectures Ethics*, *Lectures Theology* and the *Religion*. My strategy for exposition and discussion of it will be based on summarising the account of it in the *Critique of Practical Reason* and then listing the points of interpretation and criticism that arise out of that version, points which can be pursued by reference to other works of Kant.

The moral proof in the second *Critique*

The moral proof is contained in Section 5 of Chapter 2 of the Dialectic of the *Critique of Practical Reason*. It is placed therein because, together with a parallel argument for the rational postulation of the immortality of the soul, it is the means of solving an antinomy in practical reason. It is thus a solution to an example of the dialectical character of human thinking. Reason seeks the highest good, but faces an apparent contradiction when conceiving how the highest good is possible.

The notion of the highest good is introduced at the start of Chapter 2 and is said to consist of two elements: virtue, which is moral perfection and thus the worthiness to be happy, and happiness itself. Both elements are necessary ends because they represent two applications of reason's standard requirement for completeness in the pursuit of its ends. The finite agent seeks completeness in the pursuit of its non-moral needs (happiness). The finite moral agent seeks completeness in the pursuit of its moral ends, that is: complete harmony between its actions and the moral law (virtue). Reason everywhere seeks the 'unconditioned for everything conditioned' (5:107). We are told that 'the furthering of the highest good ... is an a priori necessary object of our will and inseparably connected with the moral law' (5:114). So the attainment of this conjoint good must be possible. The antinomy of practical reason is then set up through an argument that rules out the assumption that these two parts of the highest good are internally or analytically connected. If that were the case, then the maxims of happiness and of virtue would always and automatically coincide. But they do not. Classical moralists who analytically link virtue and happiness are castigated. The Stoics affirm that virtue is a state that produces a consciousness of right acting and then wrongly claim that such a state in turn constitutes 'real' happiness. The Epicureans are similarly criticised for making happiness out to be the chief good and the maxims of virtue to be the only rational route to happiness. The highest good must, in contrast, be a synthesis of concepts (5:113). We cannot keep the synthesis of virtue and happiness stable by supposing that the desire for happiness is the motive to virtuous action, for that would destroy virtuous action. Its motive must be respect for the moral law alone. Nor can we suppose that acting out of respect for the moral law is the reliable, efficient cause of our becoming happy. This is because the order of events in nature is not dependent on our moral will. It is, rather, dependent upon natural causes:

> all practical connections of causes and effects in the world as a consequence of the will's determination do not depend upon the moral dispositions of the will, but upon acquaintance with the laws of nature and the physical ability to use them for one's purposes, consequently, no necessary connection of happiness with virtue in the world, sufficient for the highest good, can be expected from the most meticulous observance of moral laws. (5:113–14)

The above passage introduces a crucial thought behind Kant's moral teleology. Kant views the moral agent as acting in accordance with rational and necessary moral laws. But the world in which these actions take place, the space-time world of physical objects, is not, as it appears to us, a moral world. Moral laws should govern our actions and they mandate us to pursue certain ends but they do not appear to govern the world in which those actions take place and in which the ends might be realised. The moral teleology Kant seeks to secure via the postulate of God is meant to assure us that, behind the appearances, the world is a moral world. The moral realm and the natural realm will come to coincide. Something outside both the desire for happiness and respect for the moral law must therefore secure the interconnection of the elements of the highest good, and this third thing is God.

The second paragraph of Section 5, Chapter 2 of the Dialectic brings these threads together in the classic statement of the so-called moral proof (5:124–5). First Kant restates the antinomy arising out of joint pursuit of the two parts of the highest good:

> *Happiness* is the state of a rational being in the world, in whose whole existence *everything goes according to his wish and will*, and rests therefore, on the agreement of nature with his whole end, and likewise with the essential determining ground of his will. Now the moral law as a law of freedom commands through determining grounds that will be completely independent of nature and of its agreement with our faculty of desire (as incentives). (5:124)

Because finite rational beings are not the cause of nature, they cannot by their own powers make it harmonise thoroughly with their practical principles. So 'there is not the slightest ground in the moral law for a necessary connection between the morality and the proportionate happiness of a being who belongs to the world as part of it and is thus dependent upon it' (5:124). The antinomy thus established, Kant then wheels out his claim that our obligation to pursue the highest good falls if it is not possible to attain it: 'Nevertheless, in the practical task of pure reason, i.e. in the necessary cultivation of the highest good, such a connection is postulated as necessary: we *ought* to strive to further the highest good (which therefore must be possible)' (5:125). If 'ought' implies 'can' and we ought to pursue the highest good, then we must postulate a moral agency of a non-human kind to ensure the coincidence of the parts of the good: 'Therefore the existence of a cause of the whole of nature, distinct from nature, which contains the ground of this connection, namely of the exact agreement of happiness with morality, is also *postulated*' (5:125). This causality will, more precisely, ensure a correspondence not merely between happiness and our moral conduct outwardly considered, but between happiness and our inward moral disposition: 'Therefore, the highest good in the world is only possible insofar as a supreme cause of nature is assumed, which has a causality corresponding to the moral disposition' (5:125). For the supreme cause to match our inward disposition and the flow of external events it must have intelligence and understanding, for it must be capable of representing the moral law to itself. It must combine intelligence and understanding with the necessary powers of will, and thus it must be God as traditionally conceived. The 'proof' finishes with the claim 'it is morally necessary to assume the existence of God'. More precisely, we have to assume the existence of a *highest original good* (that is, an intelligent being with completeness of power and a pure, holy moral will) in order to make conceivable our end of pursuing the *highest derived good*, which is 'the best world' wherein moral virtue is crowned with happiness.

The argument thus set out in detail looks simple in outline and can indeed be summarised in a few steps:

1. It is rationally and morally necessary to attain the highest good (happiness arising out of complete virtue).
2. What we are obliged to attain, it must be possible for us to attain.
3. Attaining the highest good is only possible if natural order and causality are part of an overarching moral order and causality.
4. Moral order and causality are only possible if we postulate a God as their source.

Simplicity, as is usual, hides problems. There are five key areas of discussion that Kant's second *Critique* version of the moral proof throws up. Entry into each of these areas reveals manifold complexities in Kant's moral teleology. Over this and the next chapter we will consider the following matters:

1. What is the force of the postulate of God Kant arrives at through moral teleology? What kind of certainty is it meant to produce? Does it entail postulating God's actual or merely possible existence?
2. That leads to a linked issue: What happens to the moral law and the moral agent if the highest good is not deemed possible of attainment? Is the agent left without a belief in the validity of the moral law?
3. What is happiness? Why is it a necessary object of our wills? Is it attainable even if there is a God?
4. What is virtue? Does Kant mean virtue or holiness to be the moral part of the highest good? Is either attainable even with God's help?
5. Depending on our treatment of the previous two sets of issues, is the highest good an immanent or transcendent end? That is to say: is it attainable in the world of appearance or some temporal continuation thereof? Or can it only be a state reached after temporal existence is left behind?

The force of the postulate

Here we turn to the first set of questions listed above. In Kant's statements of the moral proof in his major works he makes it plain that it is not really a proof. It does not lead to the conclusion that there is a God, but only to the conclusion that *I* am certain that there is a God (*Critique$_1$*:A829/B857). It is specifically characterised as 'a subjective argument' in the third *Critique* a verdict that follows this account of its force:

> This moral argument is not meant to offer any *objectively* valid proof of the existence of God, nor meant to prove to the sceptic that there is a God; rather it is meant to show him

that he *must adopt* the assumption of this proposition among the maxims of his practical reason if his moral thinking is to be consistent. – Thus it is also not intended to affirm: it is necessary *for morality* that the happiness of all rational beings in the world in accordance with their morality be assumed; but rather it is necessary *through it* [morality]. Thereby it is a sufficient, *subjective* argument for moral beings. (5:450$_n$)

The force of the proof, then, is bound up with its subjective nature. It is not an argument from a fact about the world to God or from a piece of evidence that discloses God's existence. It is an argument attempting to show for each of us in turn that, given that we must have a certain end, then we must adopt a certain 'assumption' to make our pursuit of that end rational.

The subjective force of the argument is highlighted further through comments Kant offers on it in the third paragraph of Section 5 of Dialectic Chapter 2 in the *Critique of Practical Reason* (5:125–6). Here Kant declares that the argument does not show that we have a duty to assume the existence of God. The only duty we have in connection with the moral argument is 'the attempt to produce and further the highest good in the world'. We must in consequence postulate the possibility of the highest good. Significantly, Kant states that '*our reason* finds this thinkable in no other way than on the presupposition of a supreme intelligence' (my emphasis). This hint is expanded upon in the eighth section of Chapter 2, were we are told that the impossibility of conceiving how virtue and happiness can be interconnected in the highest good by means of natural causality is

> *merely subjective*, i.e. our reason finds it *impossible for it* to conceive, in the mere course of nature, a connection between events, so exactly proportioned and so thoroughly purposive, occurring in the world in accordance with such heterogeneous laws, although, as with every other purposive thing in nature, it nevertheless cannot prove the impossibility of it in accordance with universal laws of nature, that is show it sufficiently on objective grounds. (5:145)

What these passages indicate is that the argument operates throughout in the spirit of an exercise in orientation in human thinking. Human agents seek the highest good and need to orient themselves in the right direction for that task. Orientation involves helping themselves to the belief that there is an intelligent, creator God with the traditional attributes. Such a belief can provide orientation in pursuit of this end *for beings with intellects like ours*. We have not discovered that nature on its own is not the source of the purposiveness in reality that practical reason requires. We have not discovered that only a God could provide this purposiveness. The result is a faith that there is a God that is motivated by reason in its end-seeking guise, but that is not even on the scale that is flanked by opinion at one end and knowledge at the other. Kant explains how reason will help itself to the assumption that the God who makes the highest good possible will be omniscient, omnipotent, omnipresent, eternal 'and so forth' (5:140). But it should be clear from our discussion of religious language in Chapter 4 and from the points immediately above, that this picture is not meant to represent in an accurate manner what an objectively existing God must be really like. Rather it is the necessary filling out of an orienting assumption for beings like us.

Kant is aware that, for all the careful qualifications he has made about the force of the moral argument, he is open to the charge of wishful thinking. The charge can be put in this way: how can anything as subjective as Kant describes in his moral argument be a reason for holding that something is true? In a lengthy footnote in the Dialectic of the second *Critique* (at 5:143), Kant considers this charge as it was put to him by Thomas Wizenmann in an article in the *Deutsches Museum* of 1787. Wizenmann was commenting on Kant's *Orientation* of the previous year and raised the following puzzle about Kant's conception of rational faith: how can our needs give rational authority for the belief in the objective reality of God? Wizenmann gives a parallel: a man who felt he needed to believe in the existence of a beautiful beloved would be irrational in concluding from his wish that such a person really existed somewhere. Kant's response to this charge that he has merely dressed up a piece of wishful thinking in his moral argument turns around distinguishing between beliefs based on mere 'inclinations' and beliefs based on 'needs of reason'. That is why we can agree with the implied judgement on the deluded lover without rejecting the moral argument. In the case of the moral argument, we are dealing with a belief based on a '*need of reason* arising from an *objective* determining ground of the will, namely the moral law, which necessarily binds every rational being, and therefore justifies a priori the presupposition of suitable conditions in nature and makes the latter inseparable from the complete practical use of reason'. Kant then repeats essential steps in the moral argument. It is our duty to realise the highest good. The highest good must therefore be possible. Hence it is unavoidable for every rational being in the world to assume what is necessary for its objective possibility.

Kant's response to Wizenmann is too hasty. Further reflection shows that Kant faces a crucial dilemma in presenting the argumentative force of his case for the postulate of God. The dilemma's horns are: if the moral argument is capable of producing belief it must rest on evidence for God's existence; if the argument does not present evidence for God's existence, it cannot produce belief. At the heart of this dilemma are questions concerning the cognitive character of rational faith and the nature of an orienting assumption.

Let us assume that a non-theist will accept the general premise that we ought, as a matter of universal practical reason, to seek the highest good. Let the non-theist accept the further premise that we cannot see how this good is achievable unless we believe in a divine source of moral order. Kant can still be charged with arguing from premises about what we need or would like to be true to conclusions about the likelihood of reality being thus and so. That our rational goals could not be obtained if there is no God provides no reason to think it is true that there is a God. That it would be good if a claim is true is no reason to believe that claim. These conclusions follow from the transparency of belief. Believing p is transparent in the first person case (see Edgley 1969:90ff.). The following three questions are equivalent when I ask them – that is, a yes or no answer to any one entails the same answer to any of the other two:

(1) *p*? [Is there a God?]
(2) Do I believe that *p*? [Do I believe that there is a God?]
(3) Ought I believe that *p*? [Ought I to believe that there is a God?]

In particular there cannot be reasons for giving a 'yes' answer to (3) that are not reasons for giving a 'yes' answer to (1), and thus that are not reasons for thinking that there is a God. The transparency of belief creates a problem because, when Kant tells us that we have *Glaube* that there is a God, he takes *glauben* (along with the contrasting *meinen* and *wissen*) to be forms of 'holding something to be true' (*das Fürwahrhalten*, see *Critique₁* A820–29/B848–57, *Lectures Logic* 24:850–59, *Kant's Logic* 9:66–70). Thus to have rational faith that there is a God seems to amount to holding 'There is a God' to be true. If the considerations in the moral argument provide grounds for concluding that I ought to believe that there is a God, they provide grounds for my thinking that it is indeed true that there is a God. The grounds must therefore be indicative of the truth that there is a God.

Our dilemma can now be pressed on Kant. The considerations in the moral argument are either truth-indicative or not. If they are truth-indicative, they can lead to genuine belief but belong to theoretical reason and are not based on our needs. If they are not truth-indicative, they can belong to practical reason, but they will not lead to genuine belief.

It is hard to think how the existence of a rational, universal need to conceive the highest good as genuinely possible provides good reason for thinking that there is a God. It would only provide such reasons if we thought it probable that reality is such as to meet our rational needs. This is something the atheist might well deny just in denying that there is a human-like intelligent power behind reality. If there is no God, we have precisely no ground to suppose that the world dances to the tune of human needs. Supposing that we do think our rational needs in connection with the highest good provide good reason for believing that there is a God, then they provide reason for thinking 'There is a God' is true. They are thus truth-indicative. They are thus evidence for God's existence. And now the distinctively practical character of a postulate or maxim arising out of reason's attempts at orientation has been lost. Practical reason has transformed into theoretical reason.

There is a way of taking Kant to be embracing the first horn of the dilemma I have posed for him: the moral argument is based on evidence for God's existence. In the reply to Wizenmann Kant states that the assumption of what is necessary for the objective possibility of the highest good 'is as necessary as the moral law' (5:143ₙ). We have already quoted him affirming in this passage that the moral law is an objective determining ground of the will which necessarily binds every rational being and which 'therefore justifies him a priori in presupposing in nature the conditions befitting it'. Kant has much earlier in the second *Critique* argued that our awareness of the moral law gives us a cognition that we are free (5:30). He could then be taken to be affirming that we have in our awareness of moral demands evidence that we are part of a moral-cum-teleological realm as well as of a natural one. The moral argument is then a further teasing out of what this insight into the moral realm reveals. So to interpret Kant makes it difficult to make out the distinction between theoretical belief and practical faith and generally places great strain on the Critical boundaries around knowledge and sense. For example, what would then become of the attempt to keep practical faith out of the scale that has opinion and knowledge at its extremes? This reading is in fundamental conflict with his thoughts about faith in God being the result of an exercise in orientation in thinking.

There is one clear way in which Kant might embrace the second horn of our dilemma. This is to characterise rational faith that there is a God, postulating God and adopting 'There is a God' as an assumption as all consisting in acting as if there is a God. That is to say, what is variously described as faith, postulation and maxim is a matter of accepting as a working assumption that there is a God. I can accept something as a working assumption even though I do not positively believe it to be true. I can treat the assumption as true for the sake of planning and acting while not actually believing it. I can do all this while, Kant-like, I admit that whether or not this assumption really is true is something I cannot determine. Perhaps this is all that *Fürwahrhalten* amounts to in the case of a *Glaube* in God. As Ferreira puts it, *practical* belief in God might simply amount to following imperatives to act in ways appropriate to the existence of a God without a theoretical belief in his existence (Ferreira 1983:80). Kant's references to the conviction that accompanies rational faith would then refer to the unhesitating spirit in which I plan and act as if the assumption that there is a God is true.

The 'acting as if' solution fits in very neatly with the references in Kant noted thus far to the heuristic character of reason's assumption of God's reality. There are in contemporary philosophy of religion developed accounts of religious faith that are non-doxastic and that can be cited in support of Kant thus read (see Audi 1991). Moreover, there is the odd passage in Kant supporting this interpretation. In *Kant's Logic* we find the following statement: 'The reality of the idea of God can only be proved through this [the idea of freedom/the moral law], and hence only with a practical purpose, i.e. to act *as if there is a God* [*als ob ein Gott sei*], and hence only for this purpose' (9:93). In an account of the *Credo* that constitutes moral faith in the *Progress* essay, Kant writes that we must take the postulates to be subjectively and practically valid, and, in the light of the sufficient guidance our purposes supply, 'so to act, as if we knew that these objects were real' (*zu handeln, als ob wir wüßten, daß diese Gegenstände wirklich wären*, 20:298).

The fact that Kant does not use the 'as if' formulation very often stands in the way of regarding it as the solution to the problem. And indeed, it must be noted that the *Progress* passage has the *als ob* qualifying the knowledge we have of God and not his existence. In places he affirms the opposite of the 'as if' view. His account of faith in the first *Critique* tells us that the object of *glauben* is held with conviction but lacks objective certainty (see A820–29/B848–57). In *Lectures Theology* he states that morality demands a firm belief in the presupposition of God (28:1084). Moreover, his accounts of religious language seem to place an 'as if' at a different point in belief in God. If we recall the passage on religious language that I have said is central to Kant's account of the divine, namely A696–7/B724–5, we note that Kant distinguishes the reference in talk about God to some ground or other of the world's order and the clothing we give to that reference. It appears right to conclude that the conception of this entity as an intelligent and all-powerful personal God is a matter of 'as if', but the reference behind this representation is not. It is 'without a doubt' that some referent or other exists, even while it is true that our clothing for the reference represents what we as human beings find natural and intelligible by way of conceptions of its nature.

The 'as if' interpretation provides a radical gloss on the word 'assume' (*anzunehmen*) in the conclusion of the moral argument in the Dialectic: 'it is morally necessary to assume the existence of God' (5:125). The conclusion would amount to: 'it is morally necessary to act in ways appropriate to God's existence without believing that he actually does exist'. That all Kant needs is a suasion in favour of taking it to be possible that there is a God is argued by Ferreira. She notes that the structure of the moral argument requires no more than that God is possible. If we have an obligation to promote the highest good, the 'ought' implies 'can' principle merely shows that the highest good must be possible of attainment. It will be so possible if it is possible that there is a source of moral teleology in reality. All the moral agent needs is the inward assurance that the highest good can be attained through moral effort. It can be so attained if it is possible that there is a God with the traditional attributes (Ferreira 1983:79). Ferreira also notes a number of places in the second *Critique* where Kant explicitly refers to the need for the conditions behind the highest good to be *possible*. In his preface Kant states that *the possibility* of God and immortality must be assumed (5:4). Ferreira also cites 5:11$_n$ as referring to the postulates of practical reason postulating the *possibility* of an object (God and the immortality of the soul).

It might help us if we consider what Kant thinks the atheist or the person without rational faith in the postulate of God does not believe. What this person denies is, presumably, what the person with rational faith accepts. At one point in the *Lectures on Rational Theology* Kant gives us some detail on this score. He distinguishes dogmatic atheism from sceptical atheism and declares that it is to the former type of atheist that moral theism stands opposed (28:1010). Dogmatic atheists cannot practice morality. They must be the most evil of human beings if they are genuine in their atheism. They are dogmatic in 'directly' denying the existence of God and in declaring it impossible that there is God at all. Sceptical atheists, in contrast, find no proof that there is a God but acknowledge that there is a real possibility that God exists. Kant offers a significant comment on this kind of atheism:

> Now indeed the belief in a merely possible God as world ruler is obviously the minimum of theology; but is of great enough influence, that for a human being, who already recognises the necessity of his duties with apodeictic certainty, it can call forth his morality. It is quite otherwise with the dogmatic atheist, who directly denies the existence of a God, and who declares it impossible that there is a God at all. Such dogmatic atheists have either never existed, or they are the most evil of human beings. In them all the incentives of morality have fallen away; and it is to these atheists that moral theism stands opposed. (28:1010)

There are other places where Kant states that acknowledgement of the mere possibility that there might be a God will provide the minimum of theology that morality needs to work (see *Progress* 20:305, *Reflexionen* 18:315, *Religion* 6:153$_n$). His acknowledgement of this as a viable, minimal faith coheres with the 'as if' interpretation of practical faith. So long as someone takes 'There is a God' to be possibly true, he or she can use it as a working hypothesis in guiding the pursuit of ends without positive belief that there is a God.

So Kant's remarks on the force of the moral argument point in two ways. In the main, he contends that the argument is productive of faith in God, where this is a firm conviction based on non-evidential grounds. In some places, he appears to imply that all that respect for the goal of the highest good needs is belief in the possibility of God's existence.

It may be objected on Kant's behalf at this point that he has grounds for demanding more from the atheist than 'it is possible, in some way or other, that the highest good is attainable'. To give substance to the underlying 'ought implies can' principle, we need to be assured that highest good is really possible, and not merely notionally possible. We have already seen in Chapter 2 how this distinction was of vital importance in Kant's pre-Critical natural theology and the source of his long-standing argument that there must be a first being if anything is to be really possible at all. How can we be assured that there is a real possibility that we are members of a teleological order unless we believe in some ground for that possibility? That entails we must have a positive belief in some ground of teleology. God as the ground of moral teleology makes that teleology really possible.

This defence of Kant is undermined by two crucial points of Kant's own making. In the first place, and as noted in Chapter 3 above, Kant's critical teaching on what must be added to formal consistency to make something really possible is no longer 'God, an *ens realissimum*'. It is 'experience'. It is appearance, the totality of things in the empirical world that grounds real possibility (see A581–2/B608–9). That is to say, in his Critical phase he consistently rejects the notion that appeal to supersensible realities can give us insight into the grounds of real possibility. His account of religious language, documented in Chapter 4, confirms that thought. Talk about the supersensible gives us no insight into its character; it is not representative in its function. Thus it can furnish no insight into how the supersensible might ground actualities and possibilities. It cannot answer our questions about what makes things really possible. As we have seen, the 'Proof from Possibility' comes to have merely subjective significance. In the second place, there is the fact that Kant states that the moral argument works solely at the level of human psychology. We have already quoted the significant passage from 5:145 where Kant states that the ground of the moral argument is *merely subjective*, depending on what our reason finds it *impossible for it* to conceive. So: the argument as presented by Kant claims no insight into what makes the highest good really possible. The Critical theist has no comprehension of its real possibility. (For further discussion of these points see Guyer 2000:355ff.)

Regardless of Kant's own 'final' conclusion (if he reached one), there is thus a real question of whether atheists must abandon the belief that the highest good is possible of attainment if the moral argument is sound. Sceptical atheists, admitting the possibility that there is God, definitely need not abandon the possibility of the highest good. They acknowledge the possibility of a God whose existence would entail that the highest good would come about, and thus they can acknowledge the possibility of the highest good. Dogmatic atheists might appear to be in a hopeless position with regard to the possibility of the highest good. However, Kant's concession that reason 'nevertheless cannot prove the impossibility of it [the agreement of morality and nature] in accordance with universal laws of nature, that is show it sufficiently on objective grounds' at 5:145 might give dogmatic atheists some room for manoeuvre. Why can they not say that, though they are convinced that is not possible that the God of theism exists, the fact of the authority of the drive to the highest good indicates that there must be *some* non-theistic way in which moral worth is connected to happiness in the long run? There appear to be two distinct issues here. One is whether such a moral teleology can only be thought of as obtaining through the effect of an intelligence, that is a reality that conceives of goals and is aware of such things as someone's moral worth. The second issue concerns whether such an intelligence need be thought of as a transcendent creator. On the first issue, we can note that in Eastern thought the concept of karma is precisely that of a moral mechanism in reality that, in at least some systems (such as Theravadin Buddhism), operates independently of gods or a God. On the second issue, we can note that pantheistic systems such as Stoicism have a central place for an intelligent principle that rules the world of nature while yet conceiving of that intelligence as immanent and embodied in nature. Why can there not be room then for dogmatic atheists to rule out theism while leaving the highest good's possibility to be grounded on some unknown moral mechanism? It might be thought that dogmatic atheists are on slippery ground at this point. A position that rules out, with certainty, the truth of theism seems to be badly situated to hold open the thought that all manner of metaphysical systems may be true for all we know. Whence the source of the dogmatism in dogmatic atheism? On the other hand, Kant's easy assumption in central places in his corpus (see, e.g., *Critique$_3$* 5:540–41) that only theism will ground belief in the highest good seems contrary to the spirit of the Critical Philosophy. The concession from the *Critique of Practical Reason* 5:145 quoted above appears, in contrast, to be much more in keeping with a philosophy that tells us we cannot know things as they are in themselves. We can ask what is wrong with the stance of someone who, reading 5:145 simply states: it is incumbent on me to pursue the highest good; this end must therefore be realisable; but I do not know enough to speculate on how it might be realisable; it must be realisable some way or other (see Denis 2003:216). This criticism of Kant can accept that rational agents need to orient themselves in relation to the moral life. It can accept that part of the orientation consists in setting the highest good as a goal of moral striving. All it then needs is the assumption that there is some mechanism, either immanent or transcendent, whereby the highest good will come about through such striving. Successful orientation in regard to these matters simply consists in avoiding dogmatic rejection of the possible truth of a variety of metaphysical schemes that would serve to flesh out the possibility of the highest good. It might even be argued that this avoidance of any commitment to the actual truth of metaphysical assumptions containing rich pictures of the possible mechanism behind moral teleology is more 'Critical' than Kant's own apparatus of postulates.

I think Kant's answer to the last suggestion would consist in appealing to the naturalness of the assumption that something like us is in control of things and the advantages for our successful orientation of running with this picture. And on his account nothing is risked intellectually, and nothing is lost, by running with the picture – provided that its use is kept within the Critical boundaries. But, given his favourable, albeit brief, comments on the sceptical atheist, he might concede that if someone's orientation works without the picture of the God of theism, then all is well with that person.

Wizenmann's critical comments on the arguments in *Orientation* point to a deep problem in Kant's moral argument, and indeed in the entire Kantian appeal to orienting assumptions as the basis for theological claims. The 'as-if' route accompanied by the concession that we only need it to be possible that there is a God provides a solution to this deep problem, I have suggested, but it has to be said that it opens up Kant's argument to further questions. The route stresses the subjective, non-evidential character of the argument. In this connection, I have concluded, Kant is much too swift in his contention that only a conception of the God of theism answers to our need to envision how a moral teleology in nature is possible. Some Eastern religions, it may be argued, have very different portraits of the ultimate principle from that found in standard theism, but they are just as firmly productive of a belief in a moral teleology that connects actions and character to outcomes for personal happiness. There can be surely many ways of clothing Kant's reference to a transcendent ground of moral teleology. (For this argument see Green 1978:100ff.).

Doing without the highest good

In the final part of this chapter we turn to the second of the five sets of questions about the status and meaning of the moral argument. What happens to the moral law and the moral agent if the highest good is not deemed possible of attainment? Is the agent left without a belief in the validity of the moral law? In discussing these matters we will assume for the sake of the argument that 'the atheist' is one who rejects any source of moral teleology and thus abandons the highest good.

There are apparent tensions in Kant's account of the dependence of morality upon the highest good. An unequivocal statement that morality is finished if the highest good is deemed impossible is found in the Dialectic of second *Critique*:

> Now, since the furthering of the highest good ... is an a priori necessary object of our will and inextricably connected with the moral law, the impossibility of the first must prove the falsity of the second. Should, therefore, the highest good be impossible in accordance with practical rules, then the moral law, which commands us to further it, must be fantastic and directed to empty imaginary ends, and must thereby be false in itself [*an sich falsch sein*]. (5:114)

This seems clear enough: no possibility of highest good, then no moral law. Yet in the third *Critique* Kant is equally clear when discussing the import of moral teleology that the moral law continues to bind regardless of the highest good: 'The moral law as the formal rational condition of the use of our freedom binds us by itself alone, without depending on any kind of end as a material condition' (5:450). This clear message is fully consistent with the main teaching on the bindingness of moral law in the *Groundwork* and the Analytic of the second *Critique*. That message is of course that, as categorical imperatives, moral laws bind immediately and unconditionally.

To think that they bind only if certain ends of the agent would be met by following them is to deny their intrinsic authority and the fact that they are rooted in practical reason. One of the central messages of these accounts is that reason is practical. Reason of itself binds the moral will and thus does not rely on anything outside of its own demands to do the job. Respect for the impartial, universal demands of reason of itself gives moral law authority.

If atheism (as stipulatively defined in this section) meant that the moral law ceased to be binding, then atheists would thereby free themselves of moral obligations. But, says Kant in the third *Critique*: 'No! only the *goal* of realising the final end in the world would have to be surrendered in that case ... Each rational being would still have to recognise himself as strongly bound forever to the precept of morals; for its laws are formal and command unconditionally, without regard to ends (as the material of the will)' (5:451; the same message is in the Preface to the *Religion*, 6:3ff.).

Kant's claim that, minus a belief in the possibility of the highest good, morality must be 'directed to empty imaginary ends' cannot be allowed to pass without comment. Even if the atheist has given up on the highest good, it is still surely the case that specific acts of virtue may have worthwhile ends for this person. Suppose Byrne performs an act under the category of justice: he repays a long-owed debt to a friend. He is motivated so to do sufficiently and solely be his respect for the relevant moral rules. His act, though motivated out of respect for the form of universal moral legislation, will nonetheless have a material end: to repay this individual. Even if there is no possibility of the highest good, the material end of this, and of other moral acts, may still be accomplished. Morality can thus make a difference in the world. Kant's dire warning about 'empty imaginary ends' would only seem to be in place if the atheist's universe is one in which the material ends of moral acts always, or perhaps mostly, misfired. If acting morally v. acting immorally never, or rarely ever, made a difference to the material state of human beings, then morality would appear to be false – amounting to no more than a series of gestures. A separate argument, however, is needed for reading the atheist's universe in that light (see Zagzebski 1987 for such an argument).

Another point can be entered on behalf of the atheist who denies the real possibility of the highest good. Kant himself recognises that reason can seek ends that it views at the same time as impossible of attainment. This recognition casts doubt on his 'ought implies can' principle. Concerning the principles which guide reason in the pursuit of completeness in scientific endeavour Kant states:

> they seem to be transcendental, and even though they contain mere ideas for the guidance of the empirical use of reason, which reason can follow only *asymptotically, as it were, i.e. merely approaching, without ever reaching them*, yet they nonetheless possess, as synthetic propositions a priori, objective, but indeterminate validity, and serve as a rule of possible experience, and can even be used, in the treatment of the same, with good success, as heuristic principles. (*Critique*, A663/B691; my emphasis)

Why can we not seek the highest good through moral endeavour believing that it cannot be attained, but using the notion of the highest good as a regulative principle and an asymptotic goal? Readers may be assured that the writing of this volume is governed by the goal of producing an error-free book. I know that this goal cannot be achieved, but it is a necessary goal to have. The value of the goal lies in the fact that there is always something I can do in the light of it that improves the book, even while the perfect book always lies beyond possible attainment. So might the atheist view the regulative value of the highest good, provided that there is always something that can be done that takes us further in moral endeavour. There are things we can do to foster the highest good. Systems of human justice, for example, seek to create communities in which virtue and happiness are correlated even while their authors know that human justice will never be perfect.

The question of whether the highest good could function as an asymptotic goal is connected with that of the precise nature of our duty in regard to it. Do moral agents have a duty to bring it about? If they do, then their failure to bring it about it is a failure to do their duty. It seems difficult to interpret Kant as meaning this, given (as will be shown in the next chapter) that he recognises that neither happiness nor holiness/virtue is attainable by human effort alone. There is the odd passage in Kant's discussions of these matters where he describes our duty as being to *seek* for the realisation of the highest good. At 5:125 (*Critique*$_2$) he writes: 'we ought to seek to further the highest good (which must therefore be possible)' (*wir sollen das höchste Gut (welches also doch möglich sein muß) zu befördern suchen*; cf. also *Progress* 20:298). Strictly speaking, all that the duty to seek for the promotion of the highest good entails is that it must be possible to seek its realisation, not that it must be possible to realise it. In the case of asymptotic goals, I precisely engage in activities that seek to realise an end, while knowing that the end lies forever beyond attainment.

Some kind of consistency can be found in Kant on the falsity of the moral law in the absence of the highest good if we interpret him as contrasting atheists' responses to individual categorical imperatives with their long-term moral attitudes. The 'falsity' of the moral law may be established for atheists in this sense: in taking a long-term view of the moral life, they would have to concede that it led to utter despair with existence. Such despair would then disable their commitment to morality. This line is suggested by the continuation of Kant's discussion of morality without God in the third *Critique*. At 5:452 he imagines what would happen to 'a righteous man (like Spinoza)' who does his moral duty but has no belief in a law-like connection between the performance of duty and what happens to himself and others. This individual is said to seek unselfishly the good to which the moral law directs his powers. He gets some assistance here and there from external events. But he faces a world that appears to be wholly indifferent to the moral demands driving his conduct:

> Deceit, violence, and envy will always be rife around him, even though he himself is honest, peaceable, and benevolent; and the righteous ones around himself that he meets will, irrespective of their worthiness to be happy, be subject through nature, which takes no account of that, to all the evils of deprivation, diseases, and untimely death like all the other animals on earth, and will always remain thus, until one wide grave engulfs them all (whether honest or dishonest, it counts the same here) and hurls them, who had the ability to believe themselves to be the final end of creation, back into the abyss of the purposeless chaos of matter from which they were taken.

Faced with this bleak vision of a universe without a controlling moral author, the righteous atheist, Kant continues, must assume the existence of God, 'if he is to stay committed to the call of his moral inner destiny and not weaken the respect, through which the moral law immediately influences him to obedience'. Thus: individual moral acts are possible for this atheist, but in the long term only disabling moral despair awaits.

It is notable that the powerful rhetoric of the above passage refuses to accept that we can maintain our respect for ourselves as moral agents if we think that we are subject to chance and contingency 'just like all the other animals on earth'. Each of us must have an eternal destiny taking us beyond chance and contingency for this respect to be maintained. But must Kant's atheist despair in this way? If Kant means to be predicting what atheists will come to think about themselves and others, he appears to be plain wrong. He must be claiming that the long-term, non-despairing atheist is guilty of some kind of inconsistency. But where is this inconsistency? The atheist, having read Kant's *Groundwork*, believes that virtuous acts are inherently valuable and give worth to those who perform them. The inherent value of something need not be lost if it is not eternal. As Aristotle noted 'But it will not be good any the more for being eternal, since that which lasts long is no whiter than that which perishes in a day' (1941:1097^b). Moral acts can have extrinsic value – as noted above they can bring about goods that are beyond them and contribute to the long-term betterment of the race. But they also have a value that is internal to them. The reflection that we are destined for dust 'just like all the other animals on earth' may strengthen, rather than weaken, the thought that while we are here we had better act decently. Can it really be the case that moral acts have worth in the long run only if we are guaranteed an escape from mortality and contingency? (For further critique of Kant's 'despair' argument see Denis 2003:211ff.)

In some presentations of the moral argument, Kant suggests that doing without the highest good significantly weakens the incentives behind the moral law. The first *Critique*'s version of the moral argument is notable for the presence of this thought. In summing up how the ideas of God and the future life are the underpinnings of moral hope, Kant states: 'Without a God and a world not now not visible to us but hoped for, the glorious ideas of morality are, indeed, objects of approval and admiration but not incentives for resolution and practice' (A813/B841). This verdict suggests that only with the incentives provided by hope for the highest good will moral principles be able to engage human action. It follows a passage in which Kant makes explicit the connection between morality and the idea of divine reward and punishment embodied in the highest good:

> everyone regards the moral laws as *commands*, which, however they could not be if they did not connect a priori suitable consequences with their rule, and thus carry with them *promises* and *threats*. But this they could not do if they did not rest in a necessary being as the highest good, which such a purposive unity can alone make possible. (A811–12/B839–40)

The commentator may be tempted to cry 'Foul!' at this point. All this talk of morality being associated with reward and punishment must be a throwback to the pre-Critical moral philosophy that had to appeal to non-rational incentives to get us from the apprehension of our moral duties to acting in accordance with them. But this would be too hasty a dismissal. Why would Kant leave such passages in the 1787, second edition of the *Critique* if they did not correspond to something in his mature thinking? What they might correspond to is Kant's perception that we are moral beings but not holy beings. We are aware of the moral law but encounter it as an imperative, that is: something to which we do not give automatic, unresisting obedience. Other things than perception of the demands of moral reason move us to act. So being moral is a struggle for us. The thought about the highest good as an incentive fits in with the portrait of the evil in human nature that Kant diagnoses as radical in the *Religion*. This evil manifests itself in the frailty, impurity and depravity of human nature. At this point we need only concern ourselves with our frailty and impurity. Our frailty is indicated in the way in which the good – the law – is objectively or ideally an irresistible incentive, but in reality weaker in us than non-moral motives, such as are provided by our inclinations (6:29). Our impurity manifests itself in the way in which the motive of respect for law 'needs still other incentives besides it in order to determine the power of choice for what duty requires' (6:30).

So the frail and impure human being needs the incentives given by the thought that morality leads to the highest good (which includes happiness) and immorality leads away from happiness. These incentives may buttress respect for the moral law. Such thoughts as these, embedded in a belief in a moral teleology to reality, might be part of a discipline that can help us move toward a purity of moral disposition in which we would do right acts simply out of respect for the moral law.

The best reply on behalf of the atheist to this view that morality minus belief in moral teleology lacks incentives is drawn from Kant. In a number of places he distinguishes theological morality from moral theology (as in *Lectures Theology* 28:1002). The latter begins with the idea of morality and with respect for duty as its principle and interprets God in the light of that principle. He tells us that if, as happens in theological morality, we *begin* with the idea of a rewarding and punishing God, then this will generate fear in us and destroy morality by moving us to follow moral laws from coercion, or to avoid punishment (28:1002). To be sure, he states in the same passage that, having passed to theology via the starting point of morality, 'our morality will obtain more incentives and a morally moving power'. But he has provided the denier of moral teleology in reality with a powerful *tu quoque*: if we try to encourage active respect for moral law through the route of associating morality with rewards and punishments, we risk destroying that which we are trying to support. Such a reply can, of course, draw sustenance from Kant's own affirmation in the *Groundwork* that an action has no moral worth unless it is sufficiently motivated by respect for the moral law alone, so motivated that the agent would do it in the absence of all other inclinations (4:398). Moreover, in the *Critique of Practical Reason*, in the very context of discussing the idea that we must regard the moral law as if it came from a morally perfect and all-powerful will, Kant warns us not to take this as licensing any connection between obedience to the moral law and the rewards and sanctions such a being might associate with the law: 'Here again, then, everything remains disinterested and grounded merely on duty; without being required to base it on fear and hope as incentives, which, if they became principles, would destroy the entire moral worth of actions' (5:129).

There is more to be said about God *qua* commander of the moral law, particularly in relation to Kant's standard definition of religion as the recognition of our duties as divine commands. But that is matter for a later chapter.

Chapter 6

Kant on the Elements of the Highest Good

Happiness

We now turn our attention to the third set of questions to be asked about Kant's moral argument. What is happiness? Why is it the necessary object of our wills? Is it attainable even if there is a God?

Kant's moral argument is based on the premise that we are under a duty to seek the highest good. The duty is compounded of a duty to become morally perfect and a rational necessity to seek happiness. Kant tells us that, though we have no direct duty to seek happiness, we are bound by our character as finite, natural beings to seek happiness as a goal (see, e.g., *Groundwork* 4:415 and *Critique*$_2$ 5:25). There are also connections between the goal of happiness and our duties that can be summed up as follows: we have a direct duty to seek the happiness of others and an indirect duty to seek our own happiness.

Let us consider the relation between happiness and our duties first. Kant tells us that human persons constitute objective ends. We are to treat humanity as an end in itself (*Groundwork* 4:429). As part of that we have negative duties. We are not to use human beings as mere means to our own ends; we are not to interfere with the legitimate exercise of their own freedom. But we also have a positive duty of benevolence toward them. We are to promote their welfare, so far as this lies within our power. The other person's end (happiness) must become my end as well (*Morals* 6:388). The happiness of others is an end of mine that is also a duty (*Morals* 6:393). In addition, I have an indirect duty to my own happiness that arises out of the direct duty to become morally perfect. The duty to seek our perfection, natural and moral, is affirmed at a number of places in Kant's ethics (see *Morals* 6:386ff. for an extended treatment). From that obligation it follows that we must remove obstacles that stand in the way of our pursuit of moral perfection. One of these obstacles is unhappiness: 'Adversity, pain, and deprivation are great temptations to violate one's duty' (*Morals* 6:388). It follows, says Kant, that things which check the influence of temptations can be considered as ends which are duties. Such ends as prosperity, strength, health and well-being in general are thus to be considered as duties. On this basis, one has a duty to further one's own happiness and not just that of others (*Morals* 6:388; see also *Groundwork* 4:399).

The main reason Kant gives for denying that my own happiness can be a direct duty is linked to his account of duty as involving an imperative and with that a sense of constraint. Since, as noted above, he considers that all pursue their own happiness as a matter of natural, rational necessity, then all are unavoidably committed to that end. We thus feel no constraint in pursuing it: 'What everyone unavoidably and from himself wants, does not belong to the concept of *duty*; for that involves *compulsion* to a reluctantly adopted end. It is therefore self-contradictory to say: one is *under obligation* to promote one's own happiness with all power' (*Morals* 6:386). Why is Kant so adamant that everyone is under a necessity to seek his or her own happiness? It is surely a plain fact of experience that many people give up the prospect of happiness in the light of other goods they seek, perhaps for large parts of their lives. Many people are placed in circumstances in which they feel they have no choice but to forego the pursuit of personal happiness. Thus people who give up career, leisure pursuits and the like so that they can care for a disabled or sick relative may (if reflective enough) agree that they have given up on happiness. *Contra* Kant, many of them seem able to remain fully committed to fulfilling their obligations even while they give up on happiness. Kant appears to be saying one, or perhaps both, of two things about these individuals: they cannot really be sincere in disavowing the goal of happiness, and/or they would be involved in some kind of irrationality (with their goal of caring clashing with their necessary of goal of happiness). I submit that it is hard to see, independently of our prior commitment to the theory that all must seek their happiness, why these descriptions should be forced upon us.

Perhaps the answer to this line of questioning lies in Kant's account of happiness. Alas we find that he defines happiness in at least three different ways. These have been summed up by Allen Wood as pleasure, contentment and desire satisfaction (Wood 2001: 266; a much more detailed survey of Kant's various notions of happiness can be found in Wike 1994). The notion of happiness as pleasure is found early on in the second *Critique*. Happiness is there identified with the consciousness that life is accompanied by 'agreeableness' (5:22) and is linked to an account of the manner in which people, when they act on their desires, seek pleasure and the agreeableness of life, satisfactions that can be measured in terms of duration and magnitude (5:23). The contentment notion of happiness comes in when Kant defines happiness as 'satisfaction with one's state' (*Morals* 6:387). In the *Groundwork* it is similarly defined as 'that complete well-being and satisfaction with one's condition' (4:393). The happy life as the contented, satisfied life is obviously not to be identified with the life full of agreeable sensations. A life full of such sensations might be found, upon reflection or after a while, not to give rise to content and satisfaction; it might seem cloying after a short while. A life found satisfying might be like a satisfying day on the fells: something accompanied by pain and struggle. The third account of happiness comes in with this statement, from the second *Critique*: '*Happiness* is the state of a rational being in the world, in whose whole existence *everything goes according his wish and will*' (5:124). Happiness is thus getting what you want, fully and completely: the satisfaction of all one's desires. As desire satisfaction, happiness is clearly not the same as having life accompanied by agreeable sensations, since people can, and frequently do, have many desires for things that do not yield agreeable sensations upon their possession. It is self-evidently a mistake to think that all desires are desires for pleasurable sensations, or that they all produce agreeable sensations when satisfied, albeit the mere satisfaction of desire may yield a degree of pleasure. Nor is desire satisfaction the same thing as living a contented, satisfied life. It depends on what one desires. All of us some of the time have desires which, upon being satisfied, leave us feeling discontented and dissatisfied with life.

There is an important ambiguity in the notion of an 'existence [in which] everything goes according his wish and will'. What I 'wish and will' may refer to my felt desires, what Kant would call my 'inclinations' (*Neigungen*). Included in my desires in this sense are those for a cappuccino each morning and a largish glass of malt whisky each evening. But 'my desires' might also refer to my ends, the things I seek in intentional actions. There is a massive non-overlap between these two classes of 'things I desire' in the lives of all normal people. We seek in action many things for which we have no felt desires (I set out one morning to mark 25 undergraduate essays) and we choose not to let many felt desires shape the ends we intentionally pursue. I might have a very strong felt desire for a very large glass of malt, but realise that it would be foolish to satisfy it tonight (I have a headache). If we ignore this distinction between notions of desire, we (Kant?) might think we have an easy proof of the theory that all necessarily seek their happiness. It is obviously irrational not to seek maximal satisfaction of one's intentions (that is just a requirement of consistency in rationally planned action). And it is at least initially plausible (though false, as we have seen above) to suppose that happiness consists in satisfying one's felt desires. Mix up these two notions of desire and you might think it obvious that all finite agents are under a rational necessity to seek their happiness.

The above criticisms of Kant appear to point to obvious distinctions between notions of happiness of the kind listed by Wood. Alas, there are places where Kant seems to have no awareness of these distinctions whatsoever. In the Catechism at the end of the *Metaphysics of Morals* Kant's Teacher puts two questions to the Pupil: 'What is your greatest, in fact your whole, desire in life?' 'What does one call such a state?' The answer to the first question is 'That *everything* should *always* go according to wish and will'. The answer to the second question is 'One calls it *happiness* (continuous well-being, enjoyment of life, complete satisfaction with one's state)' (6:480). But, we want to counter, everything might go as someone would like it to and that person be without enjoyment (because they sought the wrong things) and even if they had enjoyment, they might still judge their state not to be satisfying.

Kant is, it must be said, more sophisticated about the notion of happiness and about how it can be attained on other occasions. His deeper reflections on the subject indicate a preference for the contentment notion of happiness. Happiness is an assured, long-term satisfaction with one's lot. He is fully aware of the point that only experience can teach us which of our desires, when satisfied, bring such contentment:

> For however likely it may sound: that reason even prior to experience, could understand the means for achieving a lasting enjoyment of the true joys of life, yet everything, that is taught a priori about this, is either tautological, or assumed quite groundlessly. Only experience can teach what brings us joy. The natural drives for nourishment, for sex, for rest, and for movement, and (as our natural tendencies develop) the drives for honour, for enlarging our cognition and so forth, can alone make each of us aware, and only

in his particular way, in what we he will *place* those joys, in just this same way, can it [experience] teach him the means by which to *seek* them. (*Morals* 6:215)

Kant continues by condemning all 'apparently a priori reasoning' on the topic of what brings happiness to individual human beings. All we can do is make the most tenuous generalisations about what will bring individuals happiness: 'everyone must be allowed endlessly many exceptions, in order to adapt the choice of his way of life to his particular inclinations and susceptibility to enjoyment and in the end become prudent only through his own or others' injuries' (*Morals* 6:216). This is surely a condemnation of one of his definitions of happiness as the state of a rational being in the world in the whole of whose existence everything goes according his wish and will. 'Satisfy all your desires' is just another a priori rule for attaining happiness that Kant's more mature reflections must condemn.

Kant is also aware of the need for any agent who seeks happiness to produce an *order* in his or her desires. Not all the desires of a finite rational agent will be jointly satisfiable and thus the agent must choose which desires to satisfy and which to forego. The agent has to create a system of desires. Kant states that our natural inclinations must be brought 'into a harmony in a whole, called happiness. Now the reason which achieves this is called *prudence*' (*Religion* 6:58). Again, reflection shows that prudence cannot produce an ordered whole out of desires according to an a priori rule. A maximising rule such as 'satisfy as many desires as are compatible' will run up against Kant's own point about experience: some of the desires that such a project would jettison might be just those whose satisfaction brings lasting contentment and some of those retained in a maximising strategy might be ones that leave us with a nasty taste in the mouth when acted upon. The same point will apply if the rule 'give priority to the strongest desires' is adopted. That desire A is stronger than desire B is no guarantee that acting on A will bring more satisfaction than acting on B.

What the above points indicate is that we must pause before accepting Kant's claim that we have a duty to make others happy. By his own 'ought implies can' principle, I cannot be duty-bound to seek the happiness of others if that end is not capable of being realised by my conduct. I can do things such as promote the material well-being of others, foster their security and promote their self-respect. But altruistic forms of behaviour such as these may have no tendency to make others happy if their systems of desires are badly ordered or if they simply desire things that, once attained, will not bring them satisfaction. There is a conceptual problem here: whether and how human beings can be happy is a function of something that is down to them. It is a function of how they order, promote and select between desires and projects in their own lives. It is a function of the construction of their own self-hoods. It seems to be conceptually impossible that someone could give them happiness while allowing them to be free, autonomous human beings. This means that not even God could guarantee a free, autonomous human being happiness – once we reflect on what it is for a finite rational creature to be happy.

We must therefore ask the question 'what is gained through the postulate of God in the moral argument?' Kant's account of the highest good is telling us that the complete good for a finite rational creature cannot consist wholly in a state of complete virtue. Granted that such a state brings about a form of self-contentment, which consists in being conscious that one has fulfilled all one's moral obligations, complete virtue does not equal happiness. One may be virtuous but not living a life that is overall satisfying, because many of one's most central non-moral desires and ends are frustrated. While it seems that an all-powerful, all-knowing moral agency may ensure that virtuous individuals are not subject to misfortune, serious illness or handicap, it still cannot ensure that they are happy. For even if it protects virtuous individuals from these external harms, and even if it arranges nature so that their most heart-felt, non-moral desires are satisfied, it cannot for certain bring it about that they live lives that are suffused with contentment and felt satisfying. For only the individuals concerned can acquire the 'prudence' needed to work out a set of non-moral desires whose satisfaction will bring a satisfied life. Only they, for example, can do the necessary learning from experience that means they invest in those desires and projects that bring lasting and secure contentment.

We are edging toward a conclusion that threatens the fundamental premise of the moral argument. Happiness cannot be given to someone (no matter whose agency is invoked). Perhaps, happiness is unattainable. It is a deep problem in Kantian interpretation that Kant himself seems to come this latter conclusion. Before exploring Kant's own thoughts on the unattainability of happiness, we need to see more clearly how Kant relates the pursuit of happiness to the pursuit of virtue. We need to grasp the point that Kant holds the pursuit of happiness to be integrally related to, and dependent on, the pursuit of virtue. We need to avoid that interpretation of the highest good which holds that its two component parts are wholly externally related. In his lectures on philosophical theology Kant speaks of the moral argument as being based on an *absurdum practicum*, an absurdity in practical reason (28:1083). It is tempting to think that the absurdity practical reason faces is this: minus God, two parts of practical reason conflict with one another. Prudence – practical reason devoted to the attainment of happiness – places us under one set of injunctions; and morality – practical reason devoted to the attainment of virtue – places us under another set of injunctions. We need the thought of a divine agency and an eternal life to envisage circumstances in which both the goal of prudence and the goal of morality are conjointly attainable. The force behind the moral argument is then: in the absence of the postulates of God and immortality, practical reason faces a contradiction between its two modes, prudential and moral. Contrary to this reading of Kant, we must see that, for him, only the individual who is pursuing the end of virtue has a chance of happiness. It is impossible to pursue happiness via prudence unless one is also pursuing virtue. Though there is a synthesis of two elements in the highest good, the two elements in the synthesis are not wholly alien to one another. Happiness is other than virtue but the two things are not antagonistic goals.

Kant is perfectly clear on the point that happiness is not a good unless it is achieved by the virtuous. Kant's thought here seems on the surface paradoxical: happiness adds something to the supreme good, virtue, to produce the highest good, but it would not itself be a good unless it comes on top of virtuous conduct: 'happiness is always something that … is not of itself alone absolutely and in all respects good, but at all times presupposes morally lawful conduct as its condition' (*Critique$_2$* 5:111). The happiness of a scoundrel is not a good that reason can endorse (see *Groundwork* 4:393). Thus it is a necessary condition of happiness being a good that it be pursued by the person who is also on the way to becoming virtuous. Kant is also clear that being a moral individual, or at least being a participating member of a moral community, is a necessary condition of the attainment of happiness at all. In a community in which morality does not hold sway, people act in a manner that does not respect the right of others to pursue their own ends in their own way. A nonmoral community is thus inevitably characterised by conflict: my pursuit of my ends conflicts with your pursuit of yours. Moreover, in such a community people to do not generally recognise that the well-being of others is a necessary end of theirs. They will tend not to give aid to others in distress, tend not to support other people's self-esteem and self-development and the like. In such a society, any happiness achieved by me will be at the expense of other's happiness. Thus happiness will be hard to come by and be decidedly precarious if attained at all. This is why pursuing the goal of morality – a society in which all act according to the principles of impartial right – is a necessary condition for the individual pursuit of happiness. The goal of moral reason and prudential reason are thus not in fundamental conflict.

Kant wants to go further than the above, at least in some of his writings. In places he suggests that creating the perfect moral community will be the means of establishing the happiness of each and all. In the first *Critique* he describes an 'intelligible world', that is a human society in which morality holds sway:

> Now in an intelligible world, i.e. the moral world, in whose concept we have abstracted from all the hindrances to morality (of the inclinations), such a system of proportional happiness combined with morality can also be thought of as necessary, because, partly moved by and partly restricted by moral laws, freedom would itself be the cause of the general happiness, and rational beings, under the direction of such principles would themselves be the authors of their own and at the same time others' enduring welfare. (A809/B837)

This system of self-rewarding morality is deemed to be 'only an idea' because it rests on all being virtuous, and that is not an empirically attainable objective. It is true that Kant speaks of a form of the highest good being realisable on earth in the shape of a future human community that is through and through moral. This community would be ethical in respect of that fact its members would need no external laws and sanctions to make them obey the moral law. It would be 'a universal republic based on the laws of virtue' (*Religion* 6:98). This ethical community looks as though it might be an empirical manifestation of the intelligible, moral world spoken of in the first *Critique*. But it is not clear how far Kant thinks it is realisable without divine aid. In the *Religion* it is deemed to be the manifestation on earth of the Kingdom of God and we are told that to found a moral people of God is the work of God himself (6:100).

We have in place already the points that enable us to understand the basis for Kant's assertion that happiness is not realisable outside of a moral community but can be expected as the outcome of living within one. In a society of wholly virtuous individuals all conduct would be in accordance with the laws of impartial right, so no one would pursue their interests at the expense of others' pursuit of theirs. Conditions for the maximal realisation of freedom on the part of all would thereby be created. Moreover, these individuals would not merely regulate their behaviour by strict duties preventing them from interfering with the plans of others. They would also act upon the duties of virtue Kant describes and endorses in the *Metaphysics of Morals* (6:382–3). Under this heading comes benevolence – an active concern for promoting the welfare of others. Each individual would be fostered in the pursuit of his or her own life-plan by others having as their end that others should flourish and enjoy well-being. Happiness for all is thus very much on the cards.

But there is plenty of material in Kant telling against the assertions in A809/B837. Recall the passage from the *Critique of Judgement* in which Kant portrays the frightening prospect that awaits the would-be virtuous individual who denies the (possible) existence of a providential God (5:452). Some of the ills that surround human beings in the world it describes will not be present in the ideal moral community. Deceit, violence and envy will not be rife. Some of the human causes of deprivation, diseases, and untimely death now present will be absent. But nature will still be capable of throwing much at individuals, and the community as a whole, that will bring about illness and death. Drought, contagions and all manner of naturally produced violence are no respecters of virtuous individuals or communities. So even in such a community happiness cannot be guaranteed. Human beings will still be finite creatures of nature and doing their moral best *in the hope* that external circumstances will crown virtue with happiness.

We have registered an obvious objection to the notion that being virtuous in a moral community is a sufficient condition for happiness. We can draw on the deeper thoughts about human happiness that Kant himself has to enforce this objection. We have noted that there is a shallow side to Kant on this topic: happiness as contentment with one's lot as a finite being of needs just is the satisfaction of all one's desires. The deeper side to Kant realises that there is a work of prudential reason required to make happiness attainable – in the form of making a system, a ranking of one's desires and in learning from experience what desires, when met, actually produce contentment. There is no reason to think this prudential, experientially based wisdom about the happy life comes just with being morally virtuous. Indeed, being morally virtuous for Kant is the state of a finite, rational individual who has gained the necessary strength in commitment to the moral law that enables him or her to keep the fight going against those inclinations of a self-regarding kind that tempt against obeying the moral law. Virtue as a condition of moral strength (see, for example, *Morals* 6:405) brings home the point that the state of a moral but finite individual is a conflicted one. Such individuals must always struggle not to subordinate respect for the moral law to inclinations in maxim making. The end of this conflicted state could only be reached if what we attained was not virtue but holiness (see the next section). If virtuous persons are in this conflicted state, how can they be happy?

Kant has other places where he declares that happiness is simply not realisable for creatures like us. His deepest level of thinking on this topic shows that he regards *the essential conditions of living as a human creature* to prevent the realisation of happiness. We have another reason for thinking that the attainment of happiness is impossible even with divine aid. What needs to happen is an escape from the human condition (more on this below). Here is one of Kant's statements of this point:

But what of *contentment* [*Zufriedenheit*] (*acquiescentia*) during life? – It is unattainable for man: either from the moral point of view (being content with his good conduct) or from the pragmatic (being content with the well-being, which he tries to create by skill and prudence). Nature has put pain in man as a spur to activity, which he cannot escape, so that he may constantly progress toward something better; and even in the final moment of life, our contentment with the last portion of it can be called contentment only comparatively (partly through comparing ourselves with the fate of others, partly with ourselves); but is never pure and complete satisfaction. – To be (absolutely) content in life would amount to idle rest and the stilling of all incentives, or the deadening of all sensations and connected activity. But such a thing is as little compatible with man's intellectual life, as is the stopping of the heart in an animal's body, where death follows inevitably, unless a new stimulus comes (through pain). (*Anthropology* 7:234–5)

There are three central points here: (1) being free of pain or having no more desires that demand satisfaction will mean the end of an active, human life; (2) *Zufriedenheit* involves comparison of one's present state with past states and with possible future ones, so the present satisfaction of desires does not necessarily bring contentment; (3) *Zufriedenheit* involves comparison with others' state of being. This last point is made much of by Allen Wood in his treatment of Kant on happiness. He brings out Kant's belief that human beings are by nature prone to be happy only if they feel themselves to be better off than their fellows. Our social condition is such that we compare ourselves with others and our subject to vices such as envy. As Kant puts it in the *Religion*: 'Envy, the longing for power, avarice, and the hostile inclinations connected with these, forthwith assault his [man's] nature, easily satisfied in itself, when he is among human beings' (6:93–4). The sense of our own self-worth is dependent on our feeling that we are superior to others (see Wood 2001:271–2). Presumably, some of this sense that happiness only comes with a sense of superiority over others would be lessened in those human beings who are wholly virtuous, albeit that they might still have to struggle against it.

The message that human beings are inherently incapable of happiness is repeated in a number of other central Critical texts. In the *Groundwork* at 4:417–18 Kant stresses the fact that we cannot aim at happiness successfully because only experience will tell us what we really need to will when we try to will happiness. Only experience will tell us what plans bring happiness, and we are forever learning. In the third *Critique* at 5:430 a central point of the *Anthropology* passage is reaffirmed: our 'nature is not of the sort, to stop somewhere in possession and enjoyment and to be satisfied'. The point about the unattainability of happiness is rammed home in *The End of All Things*. Here it is linked to the most fundamental of facts about us: that we are beings in time and therefore are subject to change. This means that even if we enjoyed a life that lasted forever, we would not attain happiness, and with it the highest good, so long as it was a mutable life in time:

When we assume the moral-physical state of man to be at its best, namely as a constant progression and approach to the highest good (marked out for him as goal): he still (even with an awareness of the immutability of his disposition) cannot combine *satisfaction* with the prospect of an eternally enduring alteration of his state (the moral as well as the physical). For the state in which he now is will always remain an evil in comparison with a better one, into which he always stands ready to enter; and the representation of an endless progression toward the final end is nonetheless at the same time a prospect of an endless series of evil which, even though they may be outweighed by a greater good, do not bring satisfaction, for he can think that only through the final end being *attained* at last sometime. (8:335)

This remarkable passage seems to envisage the divine grant of everlasting life, yet still holds no confidence in our achievement of happiness. The final end hinted at in *The End of All Things* is an escape from time altogether.

What Kant's deepest reflections on happiness show is that the very fact of being finite agent – and thus one with inclinations and needs – means that happiness is always in prospect and never attained. It is an asymptotic, but not an achievable, goal. This entails that the highest good, insofar as it includes happiness as one of its components, is also an asymptotic, but not an achievable goal. It also entails that the highest good does not become achievable even with divine aid and action – while it includes happiness as an essential part.

Is there an alternative to the inclusion of happiness as a component of the highest good? There is: the highest good consists not of a perfected moral state (be it virtue or holiness) united with happiness but of that state united with blessedness – *Seligkeit*. *The End of All Things* speaks of an eternal *Seligkeit* which some or all human beings might hope for (8:328–9). A state of *Seligkeit* is attainable only when its subject enjoys 'complete independence from inclinations and needs' (*Critique*$_2$ 5:118). At one point in the *Reflexionen* Kant speaks of it as being therefore a state that belongs to God only – since it would be a state marked by complete independence of physical causes. It would thus be a form of happiness springing solely from the self and independent of anything external (18:460). In the second *Critique* Kant commends the Christian portrayal of blessedness as something that can come to human beings in eternity (by which Kant must mean a state transcending time, if he is to be consistent with the message in the *End of All Things*):

> But the moral law itself *promises* no happiness; for this is not necessarily connected with observance of the law according to concepts of a natural order. The Christian doctrine of morals now supplies this absence (of the second indispensable component of the highest good) through the representation the of the world, in which rational beings devote themselves with their whole soul to the moral law, as a *kingdom of God*, in which nature and morals come into a harmony, foreign to each of them of itself, through a holy author who makes possible the derived highest good. *Holiness* of morals is prescribed to them as a law even in this life, while the well-being proportionate to this, which is *blessedness* [*die Seligkeit*], is represented as attainable only in an eternity ... (5:128–9)

The above reflections are taking us down the following path: the highest good consists not in the union of virtue and happiness, as is described at the start of Chapter 2 of the Dialectic of the *Critique of Practical Reason*, but rather in the union of *Heiligkeit* and *Seligkeit*. There are two issues that then emerge. First the highest good, contrary to Kant's official account, does not present itself as a synthesis of two heterogeneous elements (as Mariña points out, 2000:333). It does not do so because blessedness is just the other side of the coin that is holiness, understood as including 'complete independence from inclinations and needs'. The second issue is that the highest good can no longer be a state on earth, but only something that could be realised in some transcendent realm. This would at least have to be a realm free of time. These issues will arise again when we turn to the topic of virtue and holiness.

In this section we have been addressing the third set of fundamental questions to be asked about Kant's moral argument:

(3) What is happiness? Why is it a necessary object of our wills? Is it attainable even if there is a God?

Pursuing these questions has revealed major problems in the moral argument. Kant has a variety of views on the nature of happiness. He has no convincing argument for the conclusion that all finite rational agents must pursue happiness as an end of action. The deeper and more pessimistic strands in his account of happiness suggest that not even God could bring about happiness, where that is understood as the satisfied life of the finite rational creature who has a non-moral as well as a moral nature. God might be the agent of our transformation into timeless, inclination-free beings, but then we would not have happiness in the standard sense of 'physical happiness' (Kant's phrase from *Religion* 6:67). We would instead have the blessed life of those who lack any physically based inclinations at all.

Virtue and holiness

Perhaps this section is better titled 'virtue or holiness'. It is a striking fact about Kant's presentation of the moral argument in the second *Critique* that the highest good is *introduced* as involving the union of virtue and happiness but is *developed* as involving the union of holiness and happiness. It is with this fact in mind that we framed our fourth set of questions about Kant's moral argument: What is virtue? Does Kant mean virtue or holiness to be the moral part of the highest good? Is either attainable even with God's help?

The definition of the highest good at the opening of Chapter 2 of the Dialectic of the *Critique of Practical Reason* could not be clearer. The concept of a person possessing the highest good is the concept of notions of happiness and virtue being allotted to that person: *Tugend und Glückseligkeit zusammen den Besitz des höchsten Guts in einer Person ... ausgetheilt* (5:110). In many of Kant's writings on moral philosophy a clear distinction is drawn between virtue/*Tugend* and holiness/*Heiligkeit*. Virtue is the condition of moral perfection that a finite, rational creature can aim at. Holiness is possible only for God (see, for example, *Lectures Theology* 28:1075). Virtue is the condition of complete moral strength that the good human being seeks. Its full possession would bring complete conformity of a human being's actions with the demands of the moral law, because its possessor would have the moral strength to resist all motivating factors (like the inclinations) that tempt human beings to act contrary to that law. This understanding pervades the discussion of virtue in the *Metaphysics of Morals*. In a typical passage in that work, Kant writes:

> *Virtue* is the strength of a human being's maxims in fulfilling his duty. – All strength can be recognised only by the obstacles which it can overcome; in the case of virtue, however,

these are natural inclinations, which can come into conflict with the moral purpose, and since it is the human being himself who puts these obstacles in the way of his maxims, virtue is not merely self-constraint (for then one natural inclination could seek to defeat another), but also a constraint in accordance with a principle of inner freedom, therefore through the mere representation of one's duty in accordance with its formal law. (6:394)

Similar accounts of virtue can be found elsewhere (see *Anthropology* 7:147). Virtue, as moral strength in resisting the pull of motivational factors that would take us away from acting on moral maxims, can only be the morally perfect state of a physical being. God or an angelic being would not face a choice between formulating maxims in accordance with the demands of morality or in accordance with inclination. Kant goes so far as to indicate sympathy for the view that virtue as an ideal eclipses holiness 'which is never tempted to break the law'. He quotes the poet Haller: 'Man with his faults / Is better than a host of angels without will' (*Morals* 6:397$_n$). This thought makes obvious sense. There can be no moral merit in having a will that is morally pure where there is no possibility of it being impure. Virtue is an achievement for human beings. Holiness is not an achievement for God or an angel.

Things could not be clearer then: the highest good for human beings, the highest good on earth, is the union of virtue and happiness. It is not the union of holiness and happiness, because holiness is the inclination-free, and thereby morally pure, state of a God or angelic being. So when Kant defines our moral end in the first *Critique* by stating that 'It is necessary that our whole course of life be subordinated to moral maxims' (A812/B840), he must have virtue in mind.

Kant's various statements about virtue as a human end sometimes give support to the thought aired in Chapter 5 that the highest good is merely something that we have an obligation to *strive toward* rather than *attain*. This much is clearly stated in the first *Critique* at A315/B371–2. Virtue is there held up as an Idea: necessary as a standard for judging ourselves and others, but impossible of attainment. The same thought is in the *Metaphysics of Morals*: 'Virtue is always in *progress* and yet always starts again *from the beginning*. – The first point holds because, considered *objectively*, it is an ideal and unattainable, even though it is a duty to approximate constantly to it' (6:409). Such sentiments are linked to Kant's claim that the duty to become morally perfect, that is to become a person who always acts out of pure motives of duty, is a wide, imperfect one (see *Morals* 6:393). Thus the moral law in this instance merely prescribes the duty 'of seeking with all one's means: that in every action conforming to duty the thought of duty for its own sake is the sufficient incentive' (6:393). If such statements are taken at their face value then they seriously undermine the moral argument. For they leave the door open for the riposte that our duty is not to attain the highest good but merely to make progress toward it. As noted in Chapter 5, the argument is decidedly weakened if we allow the highest good to be merely an asymptotic goal.

The goal of virtue as moral strength also raises the thorny question of how, on his own premises, Kant can maintain that the notion of God helps us to imagine the highest good to be attainable. He seems wedded to the principle that any thing that counts toward a human being's moral merit or advance must be the responsibility of that person. Moral merit (unlike wealth or similar external goods) can only come from within. Moral strength can only come from within. *Religion* 6:44 records this point with crystal clarity:

> What the human being is or shall become in a moral sense, good or evil, he must make or have made himself. Both [that is: good and evil] must be an effect of his free choice, for otherwise they could not be imputed to him, consequently, he could be neither *morally* good nor evil.

This thought creates tensions in Kant's account of God as the purveyor of grace and it will be explored at greater length in Chapter 7. It is enough to note now that he holds to it and that it has an obvious plausibility. It appears to flow tautologically from the very meaning of the notion of the moral that moral merit and strength must be self-created.

In the light of the foregoing, readers of Kant should be surprised at the presentation of the argument for the postulate of the immortality of the soul (Section 4, Chapter 2 of the Dialectic of the *Critique of Practical Reason*). It begins with affirming our necessary pursuit of the highest good in the world, states that '*complete conformity* of dispositions with the moral law is the supreme condition of the highest good', but then identifies that morally perfect human condition with holiness/*Heiligkeit* and not virtue/*Tugend* (5:122). The three paragraphs of this section then run out the following argument for the postulate of immortality (5:122–4):

1. Holiness is a mode of perfection that no rational being in the sensible world can ever attain at a given point of time.
2. It is nonetheless rationally required.
3. It can only be envisaged via an endless progress toward moral perfection.
4. Such an endless progress requires the thought of immortal life.
5. This still does not enable us to conceive that holiness will ever be attained in our endless duration.
6. So we must suppose that God takes an eternal, timeless perspective on this uninterrupted progress toward moral perfection and counts it as the actual attainment of holiness.
7. He then is able to distribute an appropriate share in the highest good in accordance with his perception of a trajectory toward moral perfection.

This is one of the most puzzling arguments in the Critical corpus. The relation between steps (5) and (6) in my summary appears shrouded in mystery. Just how does the divine perspective on progress *toward* holiness enable us to conceive how God can treat that progress as *achieved* holiness? This is one of the key questions arising from Kant's account of God as a source of grace and so we will leave it to the next chapter. For now we need to concentrate on the issue of why Kant equates moral perfection with holiness and not with virtue. He has the point from the first *Critique*, A315/B371–2, that virtue is an ever-receding goal of human striving, and so one might think that he can launch his case for the postulate of immortality without transposing the argument into one concerning holiness. The introduction of the concept of holiness seems to bring further problems. Holiness is not a state that human beings can attain, while they are human beings. But it looks as though they cannot even strive for it, since they cannot strive for a condition where they are no longer physical, and thus no longer human, beings. Moreover, holiness would seem to be a state linked not to immortality as an endlessly enduring life in which moral progress continues but to immortality as a state beyond time in which change is no more. Kant in the argument for this postulate opts for a picture of eternal life as duration without end that he rejects in *The End of All Things*. We have recorded already Kant's insightful claim in the *End* that an endlessly enduring life is a vision of an enduring series of ills in which contentment would be impossible (8:335).

In addition to the above, the following problem strikes us. If holiness is a God-like or angelic state free of inclinations, transcending physical nature, and is the supreme condition of the highest good, then there is no need for the talk of God's perspective on our endless progress toward it. God could (give or take some rather major worries about personal identity!) endow us with this state. He could take us out of time and into eternity. He could annul our physical, temporal existence in favour of a timeless one. We would then be free of inclinations and thus of those things which compete for our allegiance to the moral law.

There is, in the light of all these points, reason to think that Kant means something else by *Heiligkeit* in these passages than the God-like, angelic state of non-physical being. Alan Wood has argued that there is a distinction to be made between divine holiness in Kant and a human mode of holiness. It is the latter which is the supreme good for human beings and the necessary condition of the highest good for finite rational creatures such as us. Wood writes:

> The supreme good, the highest moral good, will consist in the goal of perfect virtue, 'the complete fitness of intentions to the moral law'. Such is the final goal of all moral progress, and constitutes what Kant calls 'holiness of will'. This 'holiness', however, must not be confused with the holiness of the *divine* will, which consists in an absolute and necessary determination of the will by the objectively practical. Kant describes the holiness which is the unconditioned moral perfection of the finite rational being also as the ideal of the 'Son of God' or the 'ideal of humanity well-pleasing to God'. (Wood 1970:92).

As indicated at the close of this quotation, Wood thinks that this form of non-God-like holiness is embodied for Kant in the crucial example of Christ. Wood cites *Religion* 6:64 – a passage in which Kant describes the Holy One as afflicted by just the same needs, the same sufferings, the same natural inclinations and hence also the same temptations to transgression as we are. Thus the Christ-figure is not like God. God has no natural inclinations and is not morally pure by virtue of the fact that he has made a decision to give priority to the claims of duty over those of inclination. For God, as Kant repeatedly claims, moral rules and principles do not impose obligations, do not wear the mask of imperatives, and do not appear as commands (see, for example, *Critique*$_2$ 5:82).

Let it be admitted that there is a conception in Kant of a form of finite holiness: moral perfection realised (or realisable) in a being with needs and inclinations. The question that needs to be explored is how this form of holiness relates to virtue *qua* moral strength, as this is defined in the *Metaphysics of Morals*. It is notable that in the *Religion* (at 6:47) Kant distinguishes two forms of virtue. The background to this distinction lies in Kant's assertion of humanity's radical evil, whereby we are ready to subordinate maxims based on duty to maxims based on inclination. An 'innate' corruption of the power of choice pervades humanity and prevents human beings attaining unconditioned moral perfection. Discussion of radical evil in humanity will be found in the following chapter. Kant introduces the first type of virtue by defining it as the firm resolve to comply with one's duty which has become habitual. This form of virtue is acquired over time: 'Therefore virtue in this sense is acquired little by little and means for some a long practice (in the observance of the law), through which the human being passes from a tendency to vice through gradual reformation of conduct and consolidation of his maxims to an opposite tendency'. What is notable about this form of virtue is that it does not constitute moral perfection. It does not do so because it is compatible with – and, indeed, is likely to involve – mixed motives in obeying the moral law. Kant continues:

> But not the slightest change of heart is necessary for this; only a change of [external] morals. A human being regards himself as virtuous whenever he feels himself constant in his maxims of observance to duty: though not from the supreme ground of all maxims, namely duty; but, for example, an immoderate human being turns to moderation for the sake of health, a liar to honesty for the sake of reputation, an unjust human being to civic righteousness for the sake of peace of peace or profit, etc.; all in conformity with the precious principle of happiness.

This account of virtue could be read as stating that the strength required to maintain a constant conformity to the demands of morality may call upon a wide range of non-moral motivation. Virtue here involves constancy in acting in accordance with duty, but not constancy in acting solely out of respect for duty. This account of virtue seems to me to be contrary to the account of virtue-as-moral-strength in the Metaphysics of Morals. There 'the strength of a human being's maxims in fulfilling his duty' is said to be 'a constraint in accordance with a principle of inner freedom, therefore through the mere representation of one's duty in accordance with its formal law' (6:394). Such a passage clearly suggests that in acquiring virtue as moral strength the subject attains an ability to be moved by respect for the moral law without reliance on other motives. The strength acquired is that which enables mere representation of something as a command of duty to trump any inclinations that tempt one to act immorally.

The account of the two forms of virtue at 6:47 continues by contrasting becoming legally good with becoming morally good. Legal goodness is manifested in the first form of virtue where 'not the slightest change of heart' has taken place. Moral goodness displayed in action is motivated by respect for the law. It introduces a second, noumenal notion of virtue:

> that someone should become not merely a legally good, but a morally good (pleasing to God) human being, i.e. virtuous according to his intelligible character (*virtus noumenon*), who, when he recognises something as his duty, needs no other incentive than the representation of duty itself: that cannot be done through gradual reform, so long as the foundations of the maxims of the human being remains impure: but rather must be effected through a revolution in the disposition of a human being (a transition to the maxim of holiness in the same).

The above passage evidently draws upon the *Religion* account of radical evil. Intelligible virtue arises out of a change of heart whereby we are in revolt against our fundamental, evil disposition – away from that disposition where we are ready to subordinate maxims based on duty to maxims based on inclination. (More on this revolt in the next chapter.) We can move closer to outer conformity with duty's requirements, understood in the fashion of the *Religion* passage, through gradual improvement. But we cannot acquire intelligible virtue in the same fashion. We need a revolution instead. This is another kind of moral strength: the strength that comes with a reorientation in one's fundamental disposition away from evil. The phenomenal/noumenal contrast kicks in at this point. It is a key theme in Kant's ethics that nothing in what others or I can empirically discern about my actions can prove that they are the outcome of a pure moral disposition. A typical affirmation of this point is found in the following from the *Metaphysics of Morals*:

> For it is impossible for a human being to see into the depths of his own heart so as to be completely certain of the purity of his moral intention and the integrity of his disposition in even a *single* action, even when there is no doubt about the legality of his action. Many times a man mistakes his own weakness, which counsels him against the venture of a misdeed, for virtue (which is the concept of strength); and how many have lived long and guiltless, who are *fortunate* in having escaped so many temptations; how much pure moral content lies in any action's disposition, which remains hidden from the agent himself. (6:392–3)

Ordinary self-awareness does not give us insight into our fundamental disposition. At most we can infer that we are motivated by respect for the law in its purity by inference from the moral constancy of our actions. But here we confront our old friend the curve-fitting problem. Our conformity with the moral law may have become constant in our finite lives up to the point of death, but 'even those empirical proofs of the genuineness of the disposition are entirely lacking, given that there is no further life-conduct upon which to base the verdict on our moral worth' (*Religion* 6:71). Perhaps we have become constant in our conformity to the law, but, as Kant says, we have been merely lucky. If temptation had come our way, the conformity would have vanished. Of course, the curve-fitting problem would go away if we had an infinity of conforming acts about which to hypothesise. Any finite number of outwardly good acts is compatible both with the hypothesis that we have real virtue and the hypothesis that we merely have the lesser kind Kant defines. But an infinite number of outwardly good acts would change the story – hence Kant's linking of a postulate of immortality to the moral argument. But even in this case we need the second half of his story. Suppose we go on endlessly doing good acts. At any one point in the sequence we have only a finite number (we evince a potential, and never an actual, infinity of actions). So true virtue is not demonstrated at any point in the infinite after-life. We need the divine perspective, that of omniscience, to get us from the perceived sequence, which is always finite, to the certain perception that virtue/holiness has been attained.

To this point we have seen that Kant's account of virtue is complex, to say the least. In the *Metaphysics of Morals* virtue appears to be an acquired moral strength that brings with it an ability to act out of respect for the moral law. In the *Religion* and the second *Critique* there appears to be a two-fold notion of virtue: empirical virtue and intelligible virtue. The former we can progress toward, acquiring gradually. The latter is something that we cannot acquire gradually, because it involves a radical transformation, a revolution in the human heart. The second, 'higher', notion of virtue appears to be correlated with a form of holiness that could be manifested by a finite being with needs and inclinations. The Christ-figure exemplifies it. Problems still remain. If it is not clear how the postulate of God makes the original simple notion of virtue appear attainable, it is just as unclear how that postulate makes the higher notion of virtue attainable. For we still have Kant's fundamental principle that morally meritorious states can only come about through the moral agent's own efforts. To quote *Religion* 6:44 once more 'What the human being is or shall become in a moral sense, good or evil, he must make or have made himself'.

A further problem emerges once it is seen that this allegedly finite form of holiness is still infinitely beyond the reach of human beings. Thus Kant asks in the *Religion* how we can realise in us 'the idea of a humanity well-pleasing to God', how we can obey the Biblical injunction 'Be ye holy'. The answer is not comforting: 'The distance, however, between the good, which should produce in ourselves, and the evil, from where we start, is infinite, and, so far as the deed is concerned, i.e. the conformity of life-conduct to the holiness of the law, it is not exhaustible in any time' (6:66).

In the *Critique of Practical Reason* Kant draws the moral that holiness cannot be attained by the human being. Holiness of the will is a practical Idea, that is, the notion of something that can never be given. It is a model. Finite rational beings can only eternally approximate to it. All that finite practical reason is entitled to is the assurance of constancy in continued and unending progress of its maxims toward this model. (5:32–3). This constancy in continual progress toward holiness is then called virtue. This may be yet another sense of 'virtue'! Even the acquisition of this virtue 'as a naturally acquired ability can never be perfected' (5:33). Here Kant no doubt has in mind the point noted above: assurance that one will continue to act in accordance with the law may just reflect the fact that one is lucky enough not to have faced circumstances in which one's moral strength is deeply tested.

Thus we have seen that Kant has a variety of ways of describing the state of moral perfection that human beings are supposed to strive for: virtue, noumenal virtue, holiness, etc. But at each point at which the description of moral perfection is spelled out we have the same message: moral perfection is not attainable by us while we are finite creatures. This creates major problems for the cogency of the moral argument. We might think this difficulty – that one side of the highest good cannot actually be attained – creates more work for the postulate of God to do. The postulate is needed not only to explain how both sides of the highest good can be achieved in unison, but also to explain how one side of it is possible at all. We have, however, noted the major point of Kantian principle preventing any clear view of how God's activity could enable human beings to attain virtue/holiness: moral progress has to be down to us.

In the context of the presentation of the argument for immortality in the second *Critique*, the role of God is thoroughly obscure. We are told that we can hope for endless progress in virtue after death and trust that the timeless perspective of God on that progress will enable him to see if/that we have the necessary purity of moral will that is holiness. But: if God's timeless, omniscient gaze can overcome our ignorance of whether we are really acting out of respect for the law and not merely in conformity with the law, why does it need an endless series of actions to make this out? Why cannot it just discern the 'intelligible' character of our acts and motives after a finite length of time? And if God were to give us the happiness or blessedness that is the due reward of virtue/holiness, would he not have to give it to us at some point in our pre- or post-mortem lives? But at any such point the endless progress would, *a fortiori*, not be completed. He would be giving us happiness/blessedness after a finite span of existence. The argument for the postulate of immortality ends with the baffling, apparent admission that even the apparatus deployed in this part of the proof will not enable us to conceive how the human being becomes virtuous/holy at some given point in an endless life:

> thus he cannot hope, indeed never in this, or in any foreseeable future moment of his existence, to be fully adequate to the will of God (without indulgence or remission, which do not harmonise with justice), but only to be so in the endlessness of his duration (which God alone can survey). (5:123–4)

'In the endlessness of his duration' looks as if it means 'never'. What does not take place at any moment or moments does not ever take place.

From the standpoint of alternative ethical theories (such as an Aristotelian one) Kant's account of virtue and a praiseworthy moral disposition will no doubt be subject to stringent criticism. But we have been drawing out the internal difficulties within this part of the Kantian system. One such difficulty is that stemming from Kant's insistence that for virtue to be virtue it must be the result of our own efforts – thus making the role of divine aid mysterious. Another internal problem stems from Kant's characterisation of even the finite, non-divine, brand of holiness as intelligible/noumenal. As such it cannot be inferred from phenomenal acts. He is then faced with the problem of how holiness can be attained in the temporal life of a human being. Our critique has been directed at casting doubt on whether making that life endless can overcome the gulf between the sensible and the intelligible, the phenomenal and the noumenal.

The highest good as an immanent or transcendent end

We now reach the fifth and final set of questions to be asked about the moral argument: Is the highest good an immanent or transcendent end? Is it attainable in the world of appearance or some temporal continuation thereof? Or can it only be a state reached after temporal existence has been left behind?

There are numerous places in which Kant writes of the highest good as something that is to be expected in the world. The *Critique of Practical Reason* speaks of the highest good as something realisable in this world at 5:125, 5:126 and 5:134. *Theory and Practice* has a similar idea at 8:279 and the *Religion* at 6:5, 6:7$_n$ and 6:136. The notion that the highest good consists in the union of virtue and happiness ties in with this insistence that it is something to be found in the world. *Tugend* and *Glückseligkeit* are states of finite rational beings like us. They are states of a being with a physical nature: *Tugend* is that state of moral perfection a being who has physical inclinations can attain; while *Glückseligkeit* is the satisfied life of a physical being.

To be set against the affirmation of the immanent character of the highest good are those passages we have come across in which Kant affirms that happiness is impossible for finite rational creatures and moral perfection cannot be attained in a finite life span. Not surprisingly, then, we find Kant stating or implying that the highest good can only be imagined as realised in a future life or an intelligible realm, that is a state of existence in which our physical natures are left behind. Passages suggesting this include: A811/B839, A814/B842 (first *Critique*); 5:115, 5:118, 5:119 (second *Critique*); and 6:161 (*Religion*).

The question of whether the highest good is realisable on earth is not made any clearer by its link to notion of a perfect ethical community on earth. This is said in the *Religion* to constitute 'the visible representation (the schema) of the invisible Kingdom of God on earth' (6:131). Kant speaks about Christ's preaching of the coming of this Kingdom of God on earth. But it noticeable that he draws back from concluding that it can be fully realised in human history. He does so by endorsing Christ's message that 'so far as happiness is concerned, which constitutes the other part of the human being's unavoidable wish, he told them from the beginning: that they could not count on it in their earthly life' (6:134–5). The ethical community may be the *representation* of the Kingdom of God, and thus the representation of the highest good, but it is not evident that it is the highest good in its fullest sense.

If the moral argument turned around our obligation to bring about the highest good on earth, it would face a crushing objection. Let us read it as imposing that obligation upon us and then as applying the 'ought implies can' principle to evoke divine aid as the only means we can see of realising the obligatory end. This is the crushing objection: God is evidently not bringing about the highest good for human beings on earth. It is just a plain fact that human beings live and die without achieving the highest good in this life. God is not acting to give these human beings the highest good in this world (see Mariña 2000:341). Read in this way – as concerning a good to be realised in this world – the moral argument hits a paradox that is sufficient to blow it out of the water. It has a key premise that the highest good cannot be conceived by us to come about if natural causality alone governs the world. It then evokes the possibility of another kind of causality, a moral one, to overcome the gap between how the world appears to us and what we aspire to become. But the postulate of moral causality does not change the fact that our existence in this three score years and ten is governed by natural causality. Postulating the existence of God cannot alter this obvious fact. If a moral causality is postulated it must then be a hidden one. If it is hidden, it is hard to see how it can be judged to be operating or not operating by reference to what happens in this life. The outcome of the postulated mechanism can only be in the remote future – so far off that the present a-moral state of things is not evidence against its coming to be. And, let us note, this future cannot simply be some future human society in which morality rules. Leaving aside Kant's point that even in a wholly moral community physical human beings may well never attain happiness, such a future human community provides no answer to the question of how all those who lived before its inception can attain the highest good. These folk don't attain the highest good because they don't live in this community. They might fertilise the soil that allows it to grow, but that is hardly achieving the highest good for themselves.

The future that the hidden mechanism is bringing about and which will contain the highest good must be a future for all of us. So it must involve a postulate of immortality for each and every one. If the highest good is literally a Kingdom of God on Earth, then it must be one in which all the dead arrive reborn. (The earth would be a mite crowded in that eventuality.) But we have already documented Kant's teaching in *The End of All Things* that happiness for the finite being in time is an impossibility in any event. If we honour that message, then the highest good cannot literally be life in any kind of human community. Kant's deeper reflections in happiness all point, as we have noted in this chapter, to the conclusion that it is only the *Seligkeit* of a life in which our finite, physical and temporal natures have left behind which can provide true *Zufriedenheit*. And this means that the happiness side of the highest good can only be realised in a transcendent state.

We have already seen the strong temptation in Kant to identify the moral element in the highest good not with happiness but with holiness. Holiness is pre-eminently the state of a God-like or angelic being who has no physical nature and thus no inclinations whose pull could affect maxim making. Even if we recognise a finite form of holiness as manifested in the Christ-figure, it still seems to be Kant's teaching that a finite, physical creature cannot attain holiness in the temporal process. At best, such a creature only advances continually toward it. To add to the material in support of this point in the previous section, we can cite a lengthy passage from the second *Critique* (5:83–4) in which Kant affirms that the moral disposition in its complete perfection, since it is an ideal of holiness, is not attainable by any creature. The ideal of holiness would be reached, Kant states, when the agent is in a state of thoroughly liking to fulfil all moral laws, but precisely this state would involve leaving behind his creaturely nature. For

> this would mean that he would not find in himself even the possibility of a desire that would tempt him to deviate from them; for overcoming such a desire always costs the subject some sacrifice and therefore requires self-compulsion, that is, inner necessitation to what one does not completely like to do. *This stage of moral disposition, however, can never be reached by any creature.* For, as a creature, he is thereby dependent with respect to what he requires for complete satisfaction with his condition, he can never be altogether free from desires and inclinations which, because they rest on physical causes, do not of themselves agree with the moral law, which has quite a different source, and with that it is always necessary, with respect to those desires, to base the disposition of his maxims on moral necessitation, not on ready conformity, but on respect which *demands* compliance with the law, even though this happens reluctantly, not on love, which is not concerned about any inner refusal of the will contrary to the law, even though it is necessary for him to make this latter, namely, bare love for the law (which would then cease to be a *command*, and morality, having passed subjectively into holiness, would cease to be *virtue*), the constant albeit unattainable goal of his striving. (first emphasis mine)

The message of these many words is clear: moral perfection consists in unmediated love for the law and this is not attainable for the finite, rational creature. Moral perfection cannot be had in this life.

Thus Kant's deeper reflections on happiness and moral perfection lead him to the view that the highest good is not of this world. It is manifested only in a state of being in which our finite, physical and temporal existence is left behind. In that state holiness would be possible and we would enjoy the *Seligkeit* that comes with escaping the ways in which our first-order physical desires and our second-order desire for superiority over others make us forever unhappy. But this means that the highest good cannot be a union of two heterogeneous things as so many of Kant's expositions of the moral argument suggest (see Mariña 2000:333, and also Wike 1994:156–63). It is not a union of virtue and happiness. It is the escaping of our nature as finite rational beings. That nature leaves us divided. As finite we seek happiness but cannot attain it. In part we cannot because we are rational. As rational we make comparisons between our own state and that of others and between our present state and past and future states. As rational we are also moral. As moral agents we struggle against the claims of inclination and our resentful, competitive feelings toward others. This state of struggle permanently adds to our unhappiness. As moral agents we nonetheless seek a purity of will that we cannot attain. The highest good as a transcendent state is a mode of being in which these divisions in the human being have been overcome. But they are only overcome when our human nature has been left behind.

The cogency of the moral argument

In taking stock of Kant's moral argument we ought to remind ourselves of its essential elements:

1. It is rationally and morally necessary to attain the highest good (happiness arising out of complete virtue).
2. What we are obliged to attain, it must be possible for us to attain.
3. Attaining the perfect good is only possible if natural order and causality are part of an overarching moral order and causality.
4. Moral order and causality are only possible if we postulate a God as their source.

I venture this conclusion: in the light of our discussion of this argument over two chapters we can see that it has very little cogency. Problems abound with it at every turn and many of these problems arise out of its author's own reflections on the key elements in it.

Amongst the problems we have discovered are the following. Kant has no convincing argument for the claim that we are under a rational necessity to pursue happiness, and thus none for the conclusion that someone who has ceased to strive for happiness is irrational. He himself tells us that happiness is unattainable, not due to the lack of apparent moral order in the world, but due to essential conditions of our natures as finite creatures. His deeper reflections on happiness also clearly entail that not even God could make us happy while we were human creatures, for our state of happiness is in large measure the function of whether we have desires for the right things in the right sort of way. His 'ought implies can' principle is bedevilled by ambiguity over whether it is our duty to attain the highest good or merely seek after it. He has a doctrine of asymptotic goals that feeds on this ambiguity and according to which it is not irrational for reason to direct itself by reference to goals that it knows it can never attain. He also teaches us that the duty to seek moral perfection is a wide and imperfect one. It is not clear, and he is not clear, whether the highest good has to be thought of as really attainable or merely possible of attainment. It is not clear, and he is not clear, whether the postulate of God required to make the highest good realisable (or possible of realisation) involves thinking that there is a God or merely that there might be a God. Thus whether the moral argument rules out unbelief or merely a virulent, dogmatic form of it is left open. The account of the highest good on which the argument is based in the second *Critique* and elsewhere unravels on Kant's own, deeper reflections in its constituent elements of happiness and moral perfection. He is caught between a synthetic and monistic interpretation of it. He is also caught between an immanent and transcendent reading of it. He also makes plain that he thinks the argument is based on our subjective limitations and needs. It rests on *our* difficulties in envisioning how nature could bring about a union of the two elements that make up the highest good (in the standard account of it – which later unravels). It rests on the imaginative advantage *we* find in conceiving the mechanism that will unite the two elements in terms of a God with human-like attributes. Finally, Kant himself throws doubt on whether God can assist us in gaining the key element in the highest good – moral perfection.

The above catalogue of problems highlights the importance of the objection to the argument from the 'very subtle and clear headed' Wizenmann (5:143$_n$). To Wizenmann the argument looked like wishful thinking dressed up as a proof. It is obviously fallacious, he pointed out, to reason from a need we have to the objective reality of God. We have seen that Kant's response to Wizenmann asserts that the moral argument is based on a need of *reason*. The claim that the need that leads us to orient our lives via the postulate of God is reason's need (*Orientation*: 8:137) is also important for the path Kant sets out in *Orientation*. *Glaube* in God is pure, rational faith. This insistence accounts for why, in rejecting the metaphysical path to God of Mendelssohn, Kant does not need to embrace the faith-philosophy of Jacobi. But in the light of the problems found in the moral argument it is not at all evident that reason demands the postulate of God.

In the *Critique of Pure Reason* the moral argument is introduced by reference to three great questions which human beings must ask of themselves: What can I know? What should I do? What may I hope? (A805/B833) The critique of reason that Kant undertakes delineates the limits of knowledge. What we should do as individuals is plain: 'Do that through which you will become worthy of happiness' (A808–9/B836–7). The hope that we then entertain is that the highest good of moral worthiness crowned by happiness is realisable. But it is obviously one thing to claim that this is a characteristic human hope and another to say that reason itself forces that hope upon us, and yet another to say that reason 'inexorably leads' (A814/B842) us to postulate a divine, original good as the sole possible source of the highest human good.

I have argued elsewhere (Byrne 1998:90ff.) that Kant has uncovered the essence of religion in the notion that religion provides us with symbolic representations of some mechanism or other whereby the threat of evil to human meaning can be overcome. Religion is rooted in the human response to evil. By 'evil' here we mean those factors in human nature and human circumstances that militate against attaining a full, assured form of the human good. Religion responds to evil by offering a metaphysical, ontological commitment made through the means of imaginative symbols. It contains some version of the thought that the given world, with its structures of agency and causation, is not all that there is but masks deeper levels of reality, agency and causation that are friendly to the attainment of human good. There seems to be reason for saying that without this thought nothing could count as a religious view of reality. Kant remains faithful to this thought, essential to a religious outlook.

A way of summing up this idea about the essence of religion is this: it is the purpose of human religious systems to provide human beings with a theodicy, where a theodicy is a way of maintaining hope for the human good in the light of evil. This is a much broader understanding of theodicy than is customary. A theodicy is normally understood as a defence of the goodness and justice of God in the light of suffering and evil in his creation. In his own *Theodicy* Kant defines the enterprise thus: 'the defence of the highest wisdom of the creator against the charge, which reason brings against it for whatever is contrary to purposiveness in the world' (8:255). But Kant's own definition, and subsequent discussion, indicates that theodicy deals more broadly with reason's perception that the world appears not to be purposively ordered in the light of demands of morality. It contains moral evil. It contains physical evil (pain). And it contains a consistent mismatch between the two, namely a 'disproportion between crimes and punishments in the world' (8:257). Kant, immediately after noting this pervasive disproportion, focuses on the objection it offers to the thought that God is holy, good and just. But we can see that these facts are more generally a blow to the thought that the world is morally ordered, that there is some coincidence between the sensible world and the intelligible, moral world that we hope lies behind it. Kant unites the two kinds of teleology treated across the second and third *Critiques* in his reflections on theodicy. We discern/expect teleology in the world and assume therefore that the world is the product of wisdom and then confront dysteleology. Dysteology presents us with a profound mystery:

> For we have the concept of *artistic wisdom* from the organisation of this world, a concept which, in order to attain to a physico-theology, is not wanting in objective reality for our speculative faculty of reason. Similarly we also have a concept of a *moral wisdom*, which could have been implanted in a world in general by a most perfect creator, in the moral idea of our own practical reason. But of the *unity in the harmony* of that artistic wisdom with moral wisdom in a sensible world we have no concept and we cannot hope to attain one. (8:263)

We must suppose that, despite appearances, our willing of moral deeds is at the same time co-ordinated with the will of the author of nature and in line with the teleology that truly governs the world. But we cannot attain cognition of the intelligible world and see the way in which the intelligible world grounds the sensible world. We have no insight that solves the problem raised by evil (8:263–4). Kant's *Theodicy* is in truth a rejection of customary attempts to justify God's ways to humanity that proceed by speculating on what God's ends and means may be in ordering the world as he does. The world is a closed book for us (8:264) and we can only continue in obedience to the moral law and assume there is some kind of moral wisdom governing the world. Kant's hero is Job, precisely because Job ends by acknowledging his ignorance and the mystery of the divine purposes.

Kant's treatment of evil, both in the moral argument and in his *Theodicy*, shows that he is fully aware of its paradoxical place in the discussion of religion. Evil is an objection to core ideas of religion. It counts against the insistence that there is a teleology in reality enabling the human good to be attained. Yet awareness of evil is a moving force in postulating a divine mechanism which will ensure that there is such a teleology.

The postulate of God is linked to the hope that the highest good is attainable. Our lengthy discussion highlights the question of whether we are being irrational if we abandon this hope. We have seen that Kant thinks that abandonment of this hope leads to moral despair of the deepest kind. The morally upright person who is also a dogmatic atheist will in the end realise that the moral life is impossible. It is time to revisit once more the passage in the *Critique of Judgement* (at 5:452) in which Kant makes this point most forcefully. Recall that Kant waxes there on the extent to which the moral agent intent on becoming virtuous will be surrounded by deceit, violence, and envy. Righteous agents will be subject through natural forces to all manner of evils (deprivation, diseases and untimely death) irrespective of their worthiness to be happy – 'like all the other animals on earth'. There will be no escape from this mismatch between virtue and happiness 'until one wide grave engulfs them all (whether honest or dishonest, it counts the same here) and hurls them, who had the ability to believe themselves to be the final end of creation, back into the abyss of the purposeless chaos of matter from which they were taken'.

In the light of our discussion to this point, we can ask what Kant's thought about moral teleology offers to ward off this fearsome vision. He cannot offer those who would recoil from it the assurance that, with the postulate of God, happiness is attainable. If by happiness we mean the satisfied life for a finite rational creature, then happiness is not on Kant's menu. And even if it were, God could not serve it up. At most, postulation of God and immortality could offer endless life (or a succession of lives) beyond the grave in which we continued to pursue satisfaction in life through the attempt to fulfil our ends. There are serious problems in supposing that this offer meets the case in a coherent fashion. If an after-life provides me with further opportunities to attain the happiness I was seeking, then it must be one in which I can continue with the projects and plans I had pre-mortem. Likewise, if I am to continue whatever progress in virtue I have made pre-mortem, then, post-mortem I will have to live a life in which the person I am, with my character traits, can acquire, strengthen and exercise the virtues. So both the pursuit of happiness and that of virtue imply that, post-mortem, the substance of my life proceeds as before. I can pick up again with the relationships, roles and the like I had pre-mortem. A little reflection will show that such an idea makes little sense.

Kant might be aware of these difficulties. Such awareness would provide one reason for his toying with the transcendent, non-synthetic account of the highest good. But that account copes with the vision of nature flinging those 'who were capable of having being believed themselves to the final end of creation, back into the abyss of the purposeless chaos of matter from which they were drawn' by lifting these human beings out of a finite, human existence at all. They would cease to be physical beings. Every one of their ends as finite creatures would be annulled. They would no longer be a person with a certain career, family or friends. Mariña says of the nightmare vision of the moral life on earth just leading to death-as-annihilation that it means engaging 'in a battle towards the acquisition of virtue, the inevitable outcome of which is known beforehand; as such, it is to display the courage of a fool' (2000:345). But there is no virtue for us in the here and now and minus God, there is also no virtue for the being who no longer has a physical nature. The highest good as transcendent and non-synthetic involves regarding virtue *qua* moral strength as something to be abandoned in favour of acquiring a will that knows no temptation and thus that cannot but choose the good. But since beings with a holy will would not face temptation, struggle and the like, their opportunities for choosing the good will be limited. Here we stumble across a thought common to many versions of speculative theodicy: God placed human beings in an imperfect world in which they are subject to all the ills confronting finite, contingent creatures because only in that world would they face significant choices. Only in such a world would it be possible for them to display virtue. Kant is aware that being a finite, contingent creature is necessary for virtue and, as noted above, sympathetic to the idea that this virtue is more valuable than the holiness of a non-finite, non-physical creature (*Morals* 6:396). So a riposte to Mariña opens up: being contingent and facing death is the only background against which courage and other virtues are possible at all. The courage of fools may be all that is available. Note also that battles towards goals, the inevitable outcome of which is known beforehand, do not make the fighters of them fools. Kant knows this. He has a developed account of asymptotic ends that fully recognises that it is worthwhile setting ourselves goals we know beforehand we will never achieve (see *Critique$_1$* A663/B691).

Kant does have a teleological conception of reality in which human beings are to think of themselves as the final ends of creation. This is part and parcel of his moral argument. That teleological vision leads inevitably to a theodicy (in my general sense) and a theology. Many writers past and present have agreed with his underlying thought: 'no teleology, then no morality'. We must be grateful for the pertinacity displayed in his attempts to articulate this thought, the depth of his treatment of the issues, and his honesty in bringing to light the numerous complexities and difficulties lurking beneath its surface attractiveness.

Chapter 7

Kant's Moral Theology Explored

God and the foundations of morality

Kant's moral argument for God's existence shows plainly enough that he wished to associate the idea of God with the foundations of morality. In so doing, he offers us a moral theology that serves to fill out the picture of God provided by natural theology. He links the notion of God with three roles a highest being might play in the foundations of morality: holy lawgiver, beneficent governor and just judge (*Critique*$_2$ 5:131$_n$). We have documented already the key letter to Lavater in which Kant summarises the essence of his account of true faith in these terms: 'the sum of all religion consists in righteousness and that we ought to seek it with all our power in the faith, that is, unconditional trust, that God will then supply the good that is not in our power [to bring about]' (10:180). The references to God's role in morality in these sources is linked to Kant's oft-stated definition of religion in his Critical writings: 'the recognition of all duties as divine commands' (*Critique*$_2$ 5:129).

The problem for the interpreter of Kant's philosophy of religion is how to understand the essential connection between God and the foundations of morality that Kant posits. In particular, the issue arises of whether Kant's moral theology requires the positing of an actually existing deity who issues real commands, who provides real supplements to human efforts to achieve righteousness and who really speaks as the voice of conscience in human beings. This option is but vaguely outlined in these words. The alternative, again vague, is that Kant's moral theology requires merely the *idea* of a holy lawgiver, beneficent governor and just judge: in other words, some subjective posit.

The broad interpretative issue just broached is connected with two others that need mention now. One is the status of the *Opus Postumum* in the interpretation of Kant's moral theology and the other is the significance of his distinction between moral theology and theological morality. In order to treat both we will need to dip back into Kant's account of religious language.

Many of the notes Kant left on his desk for his would-be final book, and later published as the *Opus Postumum*, contain the clear message that the God of moral theology exists merely as a subjective posit. God is not intended to be a real existent outside of the human mind and conscience. The discussion at 22:116 illustrates. Here Kant introduces God as a being who is 'entitled to command and capable of commanding all rational beings according to laws of duty (the categorical imperative) of moral-practical reason'. But this is no real existent:

> However, the existence of such a being can only be *postulated* in a practical respect, namely, the necessity so to act as if I stood under this fearful [*als ob ich unter dieser*

furchtbaren ...] but yet, at the same time, beneficial guidance ... ; the *existence* of such a being is not thereby postulated in this formula [of regarding all my duties as divine commands].

There are a number of places where we are told that the assumption of God required in connection with the moral law is merely hypothetical (22:125–6; cf. 21:53). More radical still are places where God is said not be a substance outside me (21:21), denied to exist as a real, independent substance (22:27), or identified with an ideal rather than a substance (22:54).

Many commentators agree that the *Opus Postumum* remarks on God and morality portray God as a subjective posit required to make sense of the moral law, rather than a real being somehow behind it. They divide over whether this stance involves a radical change of view over that predominating in the works of the 1780s and early 1790s or an organic development from them. There is a tradition of reading the *Opus Postumum* that holds it to embody a fundamental shift in Kant's position on the relation of religion to morality (see Ward 1972:160). Guyer, on the other hand roundly declares that the work 'clearly manifests Kant's loss of organisational powers but it is not a lapse into senility or second childhood and a surrender of his lifelong beliefs' (Guyer 2000:405). In my opinion, the view of God in the *Opus Postumum* as a mere subjective or problematic posit can be made to cohere in general terms with that in the earlier texts, albeit it develops it somewhat. The *Opus Postumum* reading of God as an 'as if' posit fits the gloss provided on the moral argument in the previous two chapters. Kant thinks we are committed to at least the real possibility of a source of teleology in the world sufficient to make the highest good in turn possible. But the picture of this source as at once the *ens realissimum* of transcendental theology and the personal God of natural and moral theology is down to us and our psychological needs. The *full picture* of God produced by natural and moral theology is a subjective posit. It does not, in its positive content, depict a reality. It serves to meet our needs. It is an orienting and not a referential thought.

Key to any discussion of the continuity between the *Opus Postumum* and the *Critiques* – and indeed to the whole matter of how to interpret the notion of God as moral lawgiver, ruler and judge – is an understanding of Kant's account of religious language. Thus, John Hare, who wants Kant to be committed to a real divine commander, has to assert that the Critical boundaries around knowledge and thought about God merely reflect a very strict definition of knowledge and need not trouble us: 'Kant is not an agnostic, except that he does not "know" [that God exists] in his own very restricted sense of "knowing", according to which we can only know what we could possibly experience with the senses or what is apodeictically certain' (Hare 2000b:466). To this we can add Hare's opinion that Kant never moves from these modest restrictions on knowledge of the supersensible to restrictions on their meaning: 'Kant does not ... extend the prohibition on claims about knowledge to claims about meaningfulness; he does not, that is, deny the possibility of meaningful language about God's work on our behalf' (1996:274; if stress were placed on 'work' in the last clause, it might have some truth to it). Hare thinks 'as if' readings of Kant rest on a so-called 'cushion hermeneutics'. This arises when the deeply religious concerns of a past author are interpreted in the light of contemporary secularist trends, thereby discounting that author's genuine religious commitments (Hare 2000a:273).

If my case in the previous chapters is sound, then it is Hare who has been reading his own religious commitments into Kant: the cushion is on the other foot. For a start, we know that Kant does not deny knowledge of God because he has a very strict threshold for genuine knowledge. He has a consistent teaching across a number of Critical works to the effect that *Glaube* in God is not even on the scale that runs from opinion to knowledge. It lacks *any* objective certainty. We also know that, when he moves from natural teleology and moral teleology to the postulation of God, Kant makes explicit that it is down to us and our ways of thinking that the God-concept is used to underpin belief in teleology. The use of the concept reflects what will animate the specifically human intellect's belief in natural and moral order (see *Critique*$_3$ 5:397–8 and *Critique*$_2$ 5:145). These strong moves toward a subjective reading of the God-postulate fit in with the account of religious language documented in Chapter 4. According to that, beyond the mere assertion of a transcendent ground of order, talk about God is symbolic and does not identify what God's nature might be like in itself. From that account it follows that there must be a strong element of 'as if' in the definition of religion as the recognition of all duties as divine commands. This conclusion holds because the account of religious language entails that our concept of God contains no assured reference to, or portrayal of, a personal deity who might issue commands. This also follows for a personal deity who might rule the cosmos or judge human actions. We shall see below that there are places prior to the *Opus Postumum* where this conclusion about the God of moral theology is made clear.

Those who think that there is a substantive, and not merely pictorial, role for God as commander, ruler and judge in Kant's moral theology will accept that they face at least a prima facie problem in Kant's rejection of theological morality in favour of moral theology. The distinction is drawn in the first *Critique* at A632$_n$/B660$_n$. After the mention of moral theology in the text of A632/B660, the note defines theological morals as that morality contains moral laws that *presuppose* the existence of a supreme ruler of the world. Moral theology, on the other hand, is defined as the conviction of the existence of a highest being that is grounded on moral laws. The distinction is also drawn in *Lectures Theology* at 28:1002, where theological morality as defined as a morality in which 'the concept of obligation presupposes the existence of God'. Moral theology determines the content of the concept of God after the moral law's form and content is determined and not before. One thing that is wrong with theological morality is that it attempts to make human knowledge of duties dependent on human knowledge of God and his commands. Given Kant's radical agnosticism about God, this must be a mistake. Another thing that is wrong with theological morality is that it is bound to introduce heteronomy into the ethical life. Both the *Groundwork* and the second *Critique* are famous for their message that the authority of the moral law is immediate and unconditional. Acts are without moral worth unless they are motivated solely by respect for the demands of impartial, universal legislation. If they are motivated by consideration of interests or motives outside of mere respect for the law, then the categorical imperatives of morality are reduced to hypothetical imperatives of self-love. Nothing outside my self and its recognition of the demands of the law can be necessary for my obedience to the claims of obligation. In this key respect, the rational, moral agent is self-legislative. We get heteronomy every time we place the determining ground of the human moral will in something external to its self-legislative powers, its respect for impartial and universal law *per se*. What binds is the form of the moral law and no material principle independent of it. Placing the determining ground of morality in the will of God is no exception to this rule (see *Critique*$_2$ 5:64). Appeal to God's will or perfection is just another way of introducing a material principle into ethics (*Critique*$_2$ 5:41) and all such principles take away the immediate, unconditional character of the moral law. When the law is subject to a material principle it will bind only insofar as obedience to it is the means of gaining some end beyond or outside it.

One of the targets Kant has in view in rejecting theological morality is the thought that God is the author of the moral law. In a simple divine command theory of ethics, the moral law exists because God has authored it by way of issuing prescriptions and proscriptions to human beings. One reason why this view is mistaken for Kant is that it ignores the fact that the moral law binds the rational will as such. The law holds for all rational beings whatsoever and not merely those who live under the contingent conditions defining human existence (*Groundwork* 4:408). God *qua* rational being therefore stands under the law – though by dint of God's holy will he does not experience moral laws as commands (*Groundwork* 4:414). Hence his commands cannot make or unmake the law. If he is bound by the law, the law must be logically prior to his will. Any willing by God will be in accord with the moral law. Kant is moreover adamant that the moral law has no author and, specifically that God is not its author. The moral law is unlike a positive law that can be created through some agent's will – which is just what it would be if a crude version of divine command theory were true (see *Morals* 6:227, *Lectures Ethics* 27:283 and *Moral Mongrovius II* 29:633–4).

In denying that the moral law has an author, Kant is in effect making a distinction between positive laws and laws of reason. In the *Moral Mongrovius II* at 29:634 he states that 'It [the moral law] inheres in the essence of things. By the same token, God is not the author through his will of the proportions of mathematical figures'. We might see in the comparison with 'the proportions of mathematical figures' this point: the moral law consists of a set of a necessary truths; necessary truths cannot be created by will or command.

Kant does, in the above passages, distinguish there being an author of a law from there being a legislator (*Gesetzgeber*) of that same law. The moral law can have a legislator. But what Kant might have had in mind by that is best considered when we examine such positive meaning as can be found in the claim that in religion duties must be regarded as divine commands.

Morality, commands and legislation

The definition of religion in terms of the recognition of all duties as divine commands is found widely in the Critical corpus – in the *Conflict of the Faculties*, the second and third *Critiques*, the *Metaphysics of Morals*, the *Religion* and the *Proclamation*. In all cases, the definition fits in with the portrayal of a moral theology, in which what is primary is our awareness of duty. The definition is not meant to rest on the thought that there is a knowledge of God and of his commands from which duties can be derived. Here is the extended definition from the second *Critique* at 5:129:

> In such a fashion the moral law leads through the concept of the highest good, as the object and final goal of pure practical reason *to religion, i.e. to the recognition of all duties as divine commands, not as sanctions, freely chosen and in themselves arbitrary ordinances of a foreign will*, but as essential laws of every free will in itself, which must nevertheless be regarded as commands of the supreme being because only from a will that is morally perfect (holy and beneficent), at the same time omnipotent, and so through agreement with his will, can we hope to achieve the highest good, the striving for which the moral law makes our duty.

The passage continues by insisting that we are not to heed our duties for the sake of the happiness that comprises part of the highest good, something which 'would destroy the whole moral worth of actions'. Rather the moral law commands me to make the highest good the end of my conduct and 'I cannot hope to effect this except by the agreement of my will with that of a holy and beneficent author of the world'.

In the above quotation Kant's writes of the *Erkenntniß aller Pflichten als göttlicher Gebote*. In other places he uses: *Beobachtung* (observation), *Beurtheilung* (judgement/assessment), *Inbegriffs* (embodiment) of all our duties a divine commands. These terms are indicative of the fact that in religion we do something: we associate the performance of duties with the notion of a divine commander. Outside of the *Opus Postumum*, I find no instances where Kant describes the recognition of duties in terms of 'as if/*als ob*' they were divine commands. However, in two places in the *Metaphysics of Morals* he adds the Latin *instar* after the *als*, indicative perhaps of the sense 'after the fashion of' (see 6:443 and 6:487).

The second *Critique* passage is surely important for the way in which *aller Pflichten als göttlicher Gebote* is linked to the teaching of the moral argument. One clear implication of the definition of religion is this: in religion we associate moral laws with teleology. In religion we see obedience to these laws as something that will generate the highest good. We associate the fulfilment of our duties with the notion of a cosmic order. Moral theology thus changes our view of moral laws. They are no longer merely laws for the human will but ordinances associated with a postulated cosmic teleology. Through obeying the moral law, we act in harmony with this postulated teleology and thus can hope to attain the highest good. This gives moral laws a link to an essentially metaphysical conception, while not seeking to derive those laws from the commands or nature of a metaphysical entity. While the connection of the definition of religion with the thought behind the moral argument gives the moral law an objective dimension, that same connection provides support for reading *aller Pflichten als göttlicher Gebote* as in effect portraying all duties *as if* they were the commands of a God. In other words, it associates the moral law with a subjectively generated picture. This is made plain in the two crucial paragraphs commenting on the objective force of the moral argument at 5:145–6 that we have already had occasion to highlight. Recall that, in characterising the impossibility of linking the moral law to cosmic teleology without thinking of God as the moral author of nature, Kant tells us that the impossibility is '*merely subjective*, i.e. our reason finds it *impossible for it* to conceive' of such a connection coming about through a merely natural mechanism (*Critique*$_2$ 5:145). He amplifies this point:

> But as for the manner in which we are to represent this possibility to ourselves, whether in accordance with universal laws of nature without a wise author presiding over nature or only with this presupposition, reason cannot decide this objectively. Here a *subjective* condition of reason enters in: the one way in which it is theoretically possible for it to conceive of the exact agreement of the realm of nature with the realm of morals as the condition of the possibility of the highest good, which at the same time is the only way that is conducive to morality (which stands under an *objective* law of reason). (5:145)

Thus what *aller Pflichten als göttlicher Gebote* does is tell us that religion associates the moral law with cosmic teleology as a matter of an objective need of reason – reason's objective necessity to pursue the highest good as an end. But there is a further association with a subjectively generated need to see this law as specifically issuing from a divine commander, whose will transforms moral laws from things which we merely bind rational beings into laws that the cosmos also respects. It is merely as if the moral law issues from a divine commander, but it has to be seen as connected to a cosmic teleology. The interest of pure practical reason that decides for the assumption of a wise author of the world is described as 'free' (5:145–6), though practical reason must opt for some belief in a cosmic teleology.

That this is the right reading of Kant's definition of religion is suggested by some further passages in the corpus. The *Metaphysics of Morals* in particular contains passages placing a strongly subjective reading on *aller Pflichten als göttlicher Gebote*. Thus we are told that this definition expresses:

> only the relation of reason to the *idea* of God, which reason makes for itself, and a duty of religion is not thus made into a duty *to* ... God as a being existing outside our idea, since we hereby abstract from the latter's existence. – That all human duties are to be thought in conformity with this *formal* aspect [of religion] (their relation to a divine will given a priori) has only a subjectively-logical ground. Namely, we cannot very well make obligation (moral constraint) vivid for ourselves, without thereby thinking of *another* and his will (of which reason in giving universal laws is only the spokesman), namely God's – But this duty *with regard to God* (actually to the idea, we ourselves make of such a being) is a duty of a human being to himself, i.e. not objective, an obligation to render certain services to another, but only subjective, to the strengthening of the moral incentive in our own lawgiving reason. (6:487)

There is a lot going on in these remarks. A new respect in which the moral law is seen under the aspect of divine commands is introduced. The picture thus associated with the moral law is a way of expressing its sovereignty over the human will. To see the moral law as a set of divine commands is, in this regard, a way of seeing it as holy and sacred, as unlike a positive law which we may make or unmake, regard or disregard. The picture is thus connected with the 'hymn' to the majesty of 'the moral law within me' at the close of the *Critique of Practical Reason* (5:161–2). The moral law is to be seen under the image of divine command because it is holy, sacred. We personify the moral law through the association with God (see also *Lectures Theology* 28:1076, *Morals* 6:488–9, *Lectures Ethics* 27:713). The passage tells us that the association between morality and divine commands is merely subjective. We make the unconditional, non-positive, absolute status of the moral law *anschaulich* – vivid, clear, concrete, intuitive – by dint of seeing it as if it were the result of divine commands. The subjective character of the association between the moral law and divine commands is cemented by the assertion that we can have no duties to God. This notion – there are no obligations, duties, or indeed moral relations to God – is asserted at a number of other places (*Lectures Ethics* 27:713, *Morals* 6:491). Thus moral laws cannot gain their authority because they arise from God's commands and because we have an obligation to obey him. In these passages Kant is adamant that we can only talk with sense about the obligations and moral relations of one human being to another. We cannot have any obligations to God.

The subjective, pictorial nature of the link between moral laws and divine commands is cemented in Kant's account of God's association with the voice of conscience in the *Metaphysics of Morals*. This touches on God's role as 'just judge'. Kant's discussion begins with the assertion of inevitability of the phenomenon of conscience as the judgement on the rightfulness of our acts before the tribunal of reason. The phenomenon of conscience is like 'that of adjudicating a case (*causa*) before a court' (6:438). It is, however, absurd for one and the same person to be both the accused and the accuser before a court, so in order to represent the trial of our actions before the court of conscience/reason, we have to think of someone other than ourselves as the judge in this case. 'This other may be an actual person or a merely ideal person that reason creates for itself' (6:438). Kant then pursues the option that the judge in the court of conscience is an ideal person. The ideal person must be seen as a scrutiniser of hearts – that is, not primarily of our external actions. He must be thought of as imposing all obligations, as that 'to whom all duties whatsoever are to be regarded as also his commands'. He must also be thought to have the property of omnipotence so as to give effect to those laws (6:439). So, from the phenomenon of conscience, we are led to accept that the concept of an omnipotent moral being called 'God' 'is always contained (even if only in an obscure way) in the moral self-awareness of conscience' (6:439). The subjective, essentially pictorial character of the association between morality and a divine lawgiver is then spelled out:

> This does not amount to saying: the human being is justified, through the idea to which his conscience unavoidably leads him, to *assume as actual* such a supreme being outside of himself – still less that he is *obliged* by his conscience to do so; for the idea is not given to him *objectively*, through theoretical reason, but only *subjectively*, through practical reason obligating itself to act in keeping with it [the idea]; and through using practical reason, the human being, *by means of the analogy* with a lawgiver for all creaturely, rational beings, is merely guided in regarding conscientiousness (which is also called *religio*) as responsibility before a holy being (morally lawgiving reason) distinct from us yet present in our inmost being, and of submitting to this being whose will is the rule of justice. The concept of religion is here for us only 'a principle of judging all our duties as divine commands'. (6:439–40)

This passage clearly indicates the subjective, orienting character of the thought of God as the moral *Gesetzgeber*: we are to act 'in keeping with this idea'.

Thus far we have distilled a minimally objective but mostly subjective function for the thought that God in a moral theology is the holy lawgiver of morality. Now we must turn to the suggestion that there is, for Kant, an objective role for the divine legislator to play. He is not the author of the moral law but is the author of the obligation associated with that law. Various strands in Kant move some commentators to attribute this conclusion to Kant.

In one of his general accounts of the nature of law, Kant distinguishes the office of legislator from that of the author of law thus: 'One who commands ... through a law is the lawgiver (legislator). He is the author ... of the obligation in accordance with the law, but not always the author of the law' (*Morals* 6:227). A lawgiver/legislator will only be the author of the law in that case where the law is merely a positive one. In legislating or giving a non-positive law, what might the *Gesetzgeber* do by way of authoring 'the obligation in accordance with the law'? A possible answer is indicated in the *Reflexionen* at 19:300: a legislator is one who connects the law to compulsion. In other words, the legislator attaches sanctions to breaking the law. In the passage from *Moral Mongrovius II* cited early on in this chapter, this thought in relation to God and the moral law seems to be taken seriously. After telling us that God is not the author of the law, Kant adds (or strictly: his students' notes add) that God attaches a new obligation to it. A legislator is one who has in his power the happiness that accrues to obedience to the law (29:633). God's will provides for the bindingness of the moral law 'only when he has the blessedness of his creatures in his power and uses it as a condition; thus he obliges everyone who wishes to be blessed to obey him'. The implication (the passage is not clear) is that, minus divinely provided rewards and sanctions, the atheist cannot see moral laws as binding. On this score the notes tell us that:

> An atheist is also able to recognise moral duties insofar as they issue from freedom and reason themselves. On the one hand, we are worthy of happiness through the moral law; on the other hand, we want and need this [happiness]. The moral law gives us obligations but not incentives [*Triebfedern*]. These are given to morality by religion. (29:634)

Here then is a way in which God might be the *Gesetzgeber* of morality: he is the author of the obligation in accordance with the moral law and by attaching sanctions to obedience to it (specifically, through associating obedience with happiness and disobedience with its loss), he gives us a motive to obey it.

Students of Kant's moral philosophy who have been brought up on the *Groundwork* and the *Critique of Practical Reason* will rush for the smelling salts at this thought that God might be needed as the legislator of the moral law. Why should these obscure notes by Kant's students be allowed to overthrow the clear message to be found in those canonical texts that the moral law obligates immediately and unconditionally? What has happened to the distinction between theological morals and moral theology? Don't panic: we have been here before. The teaching seemingly present in *Moral Mongrovius II* merely adds the terminology of God as legislator to matter we encountered in Chapter 5 in citing the first *Critique*'s presentation of the moral argument. That told us that everyone regards the moral laws as *commands*, which however they could not be, if they did not connect a priori suitable consequences with their rule, and thus carry with them *promises* and *threats*. But this they could not do, if they did not rest in a necessary being as the highest good, which such a purposive unity can alone make possible. (A811–12/ B839–40)

The connected thought 'Without a God and a world now not visible to us hoped for, the glorious ideas of morality are, indeed, objects of approval and admiration but not incentives for resolution and practice' (A813/B841) can also be found in other lecture notes from the Critical period (see, for example, *Lectures Ethics* 27:278 and *Lectures Theology* 28:1003).

We can either ditch this aspect of the God-as-legislator theme or take it seriously. A method of ditching it is to say that it is a throwback to the pre-Critical ethics that only emerged fully-fledged with the *Groundwork* of 1785. Commentators on Kant record that his pre-Critical ethics included at one phase the view that while the moral law could be discovered by reason, something affective, something to do with feeling, was required to make that law engage with the human will (see Allison 1990:68). The first edition of the *Critique of Pure Reason* can then be seen as simply retaining this pre-Critical distinction between apprehension of the law and the motive to obey it. Consequently, it has a pre-Critical way of linking God and morality via the concept of the highest good. Dutiful actions then need to be motivated by the incentive of future happiness, rather than in the later account by respect for the moral law alone. (So contends Allison, 1990:67; he says the first *Critique* embodies a 'semi-Critical' ethics.) Such a way of ditching what lies behind this version of the God as legislator raises, as we have noted before, the question of why Kant should let it survive in the 1787 second edition of the *Critique*. Moreover, the notes from *Moral Mongrovius II* date from lectures given in 1785.

If we don't ditch this role for God as legislator, two options remain: inconsistency in Kant's mature views on ethics or a hidden harmony amongst them.

The case for seeing Kant as inconsistent will specifically charge that he fails to make up his mind on the implications of moral impurity for human obedience to the moral law. We noted in Chapter 5 that one way of interpreting the first *Critique*'s attempts to link morality and incentives is in the light of comments in the *Religion* on the manner in which the motive of respect for law 'needs still other incentives besides it in order to determine the power of choice for what duty requires' (6:30). We found a possible connection between the first *Critique* statements and acknowledgement of a lower form of virtue in human beings, one that embodied a habitual obedience to the claims of the moral law, but which was compatible with – and, indeed, is likely to involve – mixed motives in obeying the moral law (see *Religion* 6:47). If we use these thoughts about moral impurity and a lower form of virtue from the *Religion*, we *may* have space to see the first *Critique* comments as more than lazy leftovers from a pre-Critical ethical stance and as fitting in with the points gleaned from notes from Kant's lectures. But now comes the allegation of major inconsistency: this line of thinking not only goes against the clear teaching that the moral law is to be obeyed immediately and unconditionally if actions are to have any moral worth, but also against Kant's plain warnings against mixing a principle appealing to non-moral incentives with one resting on respect for the moral law *per se*. There is no way a principle appealing to a material goal, such as hope for a divinely given reward of happiness, could mix with the formal principle of respect for the categorical demands of the moral law in a coherent moral life. Even while telling us that our necessary end, the highest good, involves the thought of harmony with the will of a morally perfect and all-powerful being, Kant insists: 'Here again, then, everything remains disinterested and grounded merely on duty; without being required to base it on fear and hope as incentives, which, if they became principles, would destroy the entire moral worth of actions' (5:129). This is but to remind us of the clear teaching concerning the essence of morality found in the *Groundwork* and the second *Critique*, as stated in such passages as:

> the *formal practical principle* of pure reason, which in accordance with the mere form of a possible of a universal law-giving through our maxims must constitute the supreme and immediate determining ground of the will, is the *only possible* principle that is suitable for categorical imperatives, i.e. practical laws (which make actions duties), and in general for the principle of morality, whether in assessment [of action] or in application to the human will in determining it. (5:41)

In line with this message, we would have to conclude that, if it were the task of the putative legislator of the moral law to attach incentives to its observance, then this activity would only destroy the ability of the moral law to 'make actions duties'.

The apparent gross inconsistency in Kant on the relation between morality, divine legislation and incentives is surely linked to another apparent inconsistency: that contained in his account of the problems that beset the would-be virtuous atheist. On this score we have noted (in Chapter 5) that Kant appears to say contradictory things. On the one hand, the atheist cannot escape the force of the moral law through denying the existence of God; on the other hand, moral despair awaits those who deny the real possibility of the highest good. It is tempting to argue that Kant must have a consistent thought animating both of these assertions, for he enters both claims within a few pages of each other. Thus, in the *Critique of Judgement* he tells us at 5:450–51 that one not convinced of the existence of God cannot judge himself to be free of the obligations imposed by the moral law. We then get an orthodox statement of the immediate and unconditional character of the bindingness of the moral law: 'Every rational being would still have to recognise himself as always firmly bound to the precept of morals; for its laws are formal and command unconditionally, without regard to ends (as the matter of the will)' (5:451). But within the next two pages he says of the righteous atheist who has given up on the possibility of the highest good that:

> if he is to remain faithful to the call of his moral inner vocation and not weaken the respect, by which the moral law immediately influences him to obedience, through the nullity of the one final ideal end that matches its high demand (which cannot occur without doing injury to the moral disposition), then he must assume ... the existence of a *moral* author of the world, i.e. of God ... (5:452–3)

A possible way to find a hidden harmony in Kant on this matter and reconcile apparently conflicting statements from the same texts is as indicated in Chapter 5. *Individual* moral acts are possible for this atheist, but *in the long-term* only disabling moral despair awaits, and such despair will end up by weakening the ability to do specific acts for the law's sake. So Kant could be saying that 'the moral disposition' is, and can only be, the disposition to act on particular moral demands immediately and unconditionally. He might also be asserting that to have this moral disposition in a rational manner requires an accompanying pursuit of the end of morality: the highest good. (Note that the disposition encouraged by theological morality would, in contrast, be that of doing individual right acts because they were commanded by God.) Belief in the real possibility of the highest good is not an immediate precondition of doing individual right acts, but it is of the disposition to do them. This is why abandonment of belief in the real possibility of the highest good leads in the long-enough term to the loss, or weakening of, the ability to do right acts as right acts should be done. From this line of thinking comes the famous statement in the second *Critique* that, minus belief in the possibility of the highest good, the moral law becomes fantastic and inherently false (5:114).

Whether this distinction between the incentive to adopt the moral disposition and the incentive to do individual moral acts saves Kant's bacon I leave readers to judge.

Let us return to the role of God as the legislator of the moral law. Patrick Kain summarises the essence of legislating for Kant as 'the giving or "declaration" of a principle or law with which someone shall or is obliged to comply, a declaration that the principle expresses the legislator's will, a declaration typically backed up by sanctions and/or rewards' (Kain 2004:280). Thus Kant's God does not author the moral law but declares (presumably through the human reason itself) that this law is his law and backs up the moral law by sanctions and/or rewards. The happiness that is in his power to attach the law, the sanctions that he can attach to the law (see *Moral Mongrovius II* 29:633–4), should then not be seen as reward and punishment attaching to particular acts. Rather, they may consist in nothing other than the connection between obedience to the law and the bringing about of the highest good. They support the moral disposition, rather than give direct incentives for the doing of individual acts. One thing a legislator can do is take a law that s/he has not authored and make it the law of a given territory, that is make it operative over a group of people. One might see the divine legislator as doing that with the moral law. He makes the moral law operative in the cosmos and over all human beings by attaching a non-natural causality to moral acts, thereby making them productive of the highest good.

We have treated of the suggestion in the *Moral Mongrovius II* that God is the legislator of the moral law insofar as he is the author of the obligation arising out of the law. Our lengthy discussion of that suggestion has brought us – surprise, surprise – back to where we were at the start of this section. As legislator of the moral law, God's role is to transform moral laws from things that rational beings alone must obey into laws that the cosmos also respects. This transformation makes the highest good possible. To the extent that the connection between the moral law and the highest good makes the bindingness of the moral law possible, then to that extent

God is the author of the obligation attaching to the moral law. Out of this analysis we will be able to separate the merely pictorial functions of the thought of a divine legislator from its objective functions (as indicated in the above). To this notion of God as moral legislator we can attach the thought that the moral law is divine legislation because it is to be seen as holy, sacred.

The matter of whether Kant's account of God as moral legislator can be seen as consistent really boils down to two questions. First: is his doctrine of the highest good compatible with the formalism of his Critical moral philosophy? Second: is it compatible with the repeated assertion in such texts as the *Groundwork* that each and every rational agent is self-legislative in the moral sphere? To the first question we must reply: it is if we accept Kant's distinction between the highest good as the necessary end of the moral life versus the highest good as providing the motive to perform morally lawful actions. To pursue the second question further, we need a résumé of how the individual, human moral agent is self-legislative in morality.

There are a number of respects in which the human agent self-legislates the moral law. These do not involve the human agent authoring the law – we know that the moral law has no author for Kant. They do, however, involve the concept of legislation described above: a declaration or resolve that the principles of the moral law expresses the human being's will, a declaration typically backed up by sanctions and/or rewards. First the human agent who acts out of respect for the moral law acts on maxims which s/he wills to be universal laws fit for all rational agents. This is specified in the first formulation of the Categorical Imperative in the *Groundwork*, which bids is to act only in accordance with maxims we can at the same time will to be universal laws (4:421). So the maxims of such an agent are at once rules for his/her will and at the same time rules for the will of every rational agent. Thus his/her maxims are laws for others and the agent has legislated for all in formulating and acting upon his/her own maxims. Furthermore, the moral agent incorporates universal, impartial rational legislation into his/her will when acting out of respect for duty by acting upon its principles solely because of their lawful character. The moral law then becomes the law for his/her will, and thereby it ceases to be an alien law, compliance with which depends on external sanctions. The human agent can through these processes also be seen to be creating rewards and punishments attaching to obedience to the maxims that thereby become self-legislated laws. The very structure of the moral agent's attitudes will entail the reward of self-contentment when dutiful maxims are followed through and the punishment before the court of conscience if they are not followed through that consists of the opposite to self-contentment: a sense of guilt and self-loathing. These are sanctions internal to the law and its self-legislation by the agent.

The notion of the moral agent as a legislator of the moral law is only compatible with God's putative role as moral legislator if we avoid making hope of divine reward and fear of divine punishment necessary incentives for individual moral acts. For we see that the notion of self-legislation by the moral subject is just an aspect of the key claim that the moral law binds immediately and unconditionally in acts that are done from duty, as opposed to being merely in accordance with duty. These key ideas point to the intrinsic authority possessed by the moral law, and are thus hard to fit in with any account of God as moral legislator that sees God as necessary for providing moral laws with their authority.

Is there anything further we might associate with the notion of God as moral legislator? It may be argued that there is an essential role for God *qua* legislator within Kant's idea of a Kingdom of Ends. In Kant's ethics the ideas of the Categorical Imperative and the self-legislation it makes possible lead to the notion of a Kingdom of Ends. Each rational being is an end in itself, and never to be treated merely as a means by any other. Moral action should be seen as the means whereby a Kingdom of Ends is brought about: 'a systematic union of rational beings through common objective laws' (*Groundwork* 4:433). In the *Religion*, this Kingdom, or at least a representation of it, is presented as something that might come about on earth in the form of a moral community. That would be one in which the moral law alone sufficed to guide the actions of all its members and merely statutory laws would have withered away. A section of Part III of the *Religion* tells us that 'The Concept of an Ethical Commonwealth is the Concept of a People of God under Ethical Laws' (6:98). This section links the idea of a moral community, which approximates to the Kingdom of Ends, to a divine legislator. Its opening move is this: 'If an ethical commonwealth is to come into existence, all individuals must be subjected to a public legislation, and all the laws binding them must be capable of being regarded as commands of a common lawgiver' (6:98). In an ethical commonwealth the people cannot see themselves as the lawgiver, for humanly legislated law can bind only external actions. In an ethical commonwealth, laws will be directed toward the morality and not the legality of actions and that means the laws must legislate for the 'inside' of human actions. The legislator of these laws must be aware of the inner quality of actions and, at the same time, be someone whose will would not make merely statutory duties but would be identical with the principles commanding true duties. Only God will suit this two-fold requirement:

> Therefore only such a one can be thought of as the supreme lawgiver of an ethical commonwealth, with regard to whom all true duties, and thereby also the ethical, must be represented at the same time as his commands; on account of which he must also be one who is acquainted with the heart, in order to penetrate to the inmost parts of the dispositions of each, and as must be in every commonwealth, see that each gets what accords to the worth of his actions. This is however the concept of God as a moral world ruler. Hence an ethical commonwealth is conceivable only as a people under divine commands, i.e. as a people of God, and indeed according to the laws of virtue. (6:99)

Kant states at the start of the next section that 'To found a moral people of God is, therefore, a work whose execution cannot be expected from human beings but only from God himself' (6:100). But before we rush to the conclusion that the *Religion* contains an account of a further, substantive role for God as moral legislator, we need to note some limitations attaching to this story.

We should first register the fact that Kant does not describe any actions God undertakes in his role as facilitator of the ethical community – nothing concrete attaches to the idea of God's penetration to the heart of each individual, or of his giving to each according to the worth of his actions. Indeed, given the fundamental structure of the Critical philosophy, one cannot see how God could do anything concrete in this regard (as: intervene in human society and start doling out rewards and punishments). At 6:100–01 Kant appears to acknowledge this by urging us not to go after our private moral concerns on the assumption that God will look after those of the race as whole. 'He must rather proceed as if everything depended on him.' With this commitment to do what we can comes the hope that 'a higher wisdom' will provide the fulfilment of our efforts (6:101). This last comment is in the spirit of the latter to Lavater and consistent with the general, unspecific moral hope that the highest good can be realised somehow. Furthermore, we can record the clear similarities between this *Religion* invocation of God as judge and ruler and the passage on God as judge in the court of conscience in the *Metaphysics of Morals* at 6:438–40 we have already discussed. The *Metaphysics of Morals* passage is one where the idea of God figures as just that: as an idea. It guides us in 'regarding conscientiousness (which is also called *religio*) as responsibility before a holy being (morally lawgiving reason) distinct from us yet present in our inmost being, and of submitting to this being whose will is the rule of justice' (6:440). The passage is also concerned with the idea of God as an inner judge, through which we could represent the workings of conscience. But it does not require a God doing any real work independently of our representations. The *Religion* passage likewise speaks of what we must 'think of' and how duties 'must be represented' by us.

John Hare is one who has maintained that there is some real work for Kant's God to do in relation to the realm of ends and its embodiment in an ethical community on earth. In relation to the realm of ends and its embodiment on earth, there is what Hare describes as 'a co-ordination problem':

> We have to believe that a system is in place and is being maintained in which the ends of the other members of the kingdom are consistent with each other's and ours. ... The world might be the kind of place in which I can only be happy if other people I affect are not. (2000b:470)

My non-moral inclinations might be such as to clash badly with those of others. That will make it very difficult to share in membership of a Kingdom of Ends with those others, for in such a kingdom I will have to share in and promote those ends, while at the same time having hope that my happiness is realisable as well. God, according to Hare's reading of Kant, does the co-ordinating. But – my first objection – how does he do this co-ordinating? What actual work is there for God to do in this connection? Kant describes none. It is difficult to see how, consistent with human freedom and Kant's banishment of divine action from the world known through the senses (or, at the very least, banishment of any way of our discerning such action), God could do anything by way of altering the starting reality that the non-moral desires of potential members of the Kingdom of Ends conflict. Moreover, it seems that for Kant this co-ordination problem is amongst those that morality itself is designed to solve.

In a community governed by moral laws there would be no conflict between the outward actions performed on the basis of its members' non-moral inclinations. They would act in accordance with such perfect duties of right as 'do not steal' and 'do not make false promises'. Such duties create conditions in which all may freely pursue their non-moral goals with maximum freedom. They restrict freedom of action on one's inclinations to the extent that such action will limit the freedom of others to pursue their inclinations. They thus eliminate conflicts in inclination-pursuit and enhance the total amount of freedom available in the community. (See Kant's account of 'The Universal Principle of Right', *Morals* 6:230–31.) So, our obeying the duties of right would solve this aspect of the 'co-ordination problem'. Furthermore, a society of individuals wholly committed to observance of the claims of morality will also obey the imperfect duties of virtue. They will thus set themselves the ends of virtue. These include, as we have noted already, the end of realising one's own perfection and the end of realising the happiness of others (see *Morals* 6:382–8). The cultivation of these ends will surely involve fighting against those non-moral drives that work to create conflict between human beings. Insofar as I cultivate in my life the end of realising the happiness of others, then I will move away from that competitive unsociability that bids me see my happiness as possible only through gaining superiority or advantage over others. The unjust desire to acquire superiority for oneself over others will be directly tackled by cultivation of the ends of virtue. Thus morality itself creates a system in which the ends of the other members of the kingdom are consistent with each other's.

Thus, for a variety of reasons, I do not see how there is work for God to do in co-ordinating human inclinations and ends. There may be work for God to do in seeing to it that my happiness is possible in the moral community. Though we have noted in Chapter 6 that Kant toys with the notion that membership of the moral community would be self-rewarding, guaranteeing happiness for all who partook of that membership, further reflection shows that this is not so. Membership of the moral community does not free individuals from contingency, or guarantee that all their most heart-felt goals are jointly realisable, or ensure that fulfilment of those goals will actually bring them overall contentment. But this area of concern raises no new considerations over and above those already dealt with in discussing the moral argument in Chapters 5 and 6. There may also be work for God to do in perfecting us as moral agents so that there are people ready and willing to create the moral community on earth. But that problem (of whether divine agency is necessary for making human beings good) amounts to the separate issue of the role of God's grace in Kant's system. It is to that issue that we must now turn.

Kant on radical evil and divine grace

When Kant writes to Lavater of the religious faith that God will supply the good that is not in the power of human moral agents to bring about on their own, he undoubtedly has in mind not just the good of happiness but also virtue, moral goodness. He has in view the gap between our commitment to eschew evil in thought and conduct and the reality that we remain throughout our lives mired in evil. This is the gap over which the doctrine of grace in traditional Christianity has provided the bridge. God makes moral demands upon us. We cannot fulfil them through our own unaided efforts. God's grace provides the assistance to meet those demands. Kant wishes to ally himself with this doctrine in some way or other. He starts out from the same recognition that there is this gap.

The general idea of a gap between, on the one hand, the moral demands placed on human beings and, on the other, their want of moral perfection, needs to be replaced by a more detailed picture. With that picture will come distinctions among kinds of divine help in the overcoming of human failings. Any account of Kant's linking of the notion of God to that of divine grace must keep in view three sorts of divine grace. I will distinguish them as distributive grace, transforming grace and justifying grace. By 'distributive grace' I mean the divine willingness to award human beings happiness or blessedness despite the fact that they never attain moral perfection. The need for distributive grace in Kant's system is established by his teachings that moral perfection cannot be attained but that nonetheless the highest good must be attainable. By 'transforming grace' I refer to the alleged divine ability and willingness materially to assist in transforming the evil human being into the good human being (sometimes referred to in Christian theology as 'sanctifying grace'). Transforming grace, if it were coherent and actual, would get us across one part of the moral gap we are focusing on. But supposing we could get across that gap and become wholly good *qua* moral agents, another gap would remain. Byrne moves from moral imperfection to imperfection, with or without divine aid. The perfect Byrne is still left with guilt from the bad acts he performed while an imperfect being. For Byrne to enjoy a perfected relation with God, he needs to expunge that guilt. God's justifying grace is whatever divine mechanism is required to do the expunging (sometimes referred to as 'atoning grace'). In Christian thought, of course, the mechanism has been understood to involve some necessary role for Christ as the atoning saviour of humankind. Grace of this kind is effected or made possible through Christ's atoning for human sins. Here is another gap to overcome: between the guilty human being (even if now perfectly good) and the righteous God who cannot admit that human being into full fellowship with him while the stain of guilt remains.

It is evident that only the first two types of grace are of any interest to the non-theist. Those who do not look to the end of life in perfected relationship with God have no need whatsoever of justifying grace. But will not the atheist still be worried about the fact that s/he must die guilty of past wrong-doings even if moral perfection is achieved? I don't see why. It is surely just a fact about the human condition for the atheist that all do some wrong at some time and that, at the best, there is always the stain of some past wrong on anyone's character. That is simply one of the marks of human imperfection. The atheist may be, should be, concerned to gain forgiveness for significant wrongs done to fellow human beings from those human beings. But s/he will see no reason to seek a 'your guilt has altogether gone' verdict from the Universe at death. There is no reason, for example, why *that* sense of guilt should disable thought and action or rationally lead to self-loathing. Why loathe yourself merely because there are always some wrong thoughts and actions in one's 'record'? It is precisely the cultivation of loathing such as this that atheists will see as one of the psychological sicknesses encouraged by religion.

Kant's own moral theology does not allow of a four-square instance of Christian justifying grace. For his philosophy is notably shy of descriptions of the final human end as perfected relationship with God in a life to come. Rather the final end of human life, indeed the final end of Nature, is achievement by human beings of the highest good, which we know is the union of moral perfection and happiness. This

Kantian end for humanity allows of something *analogous* to justifying grace, namely distributive grace. This would arise if God is faced with the possibility of annexing happiness to something that is not quite achieved moral perfection, the possibility of God taking something less than moral perfection as deserving the 'reward' of happiness. What this peculiarly Kantian context for divine grace does is allow for a slide between the various forms of grace to be possible in his work.

When Kant treats of the argument for the postulate of immortality in the *Critique of Practical Reason* (5:122–4), he seems to have that moral gap in mind which calls for the first type of grace: distributive grace. Recall the argument:

1. Holiness is a mode of perfection that no rational being in the sensible world can ever attain at a given point of time.
2. It is nonetheless rationally required.
3. It can only be envisaged via an endless progress toward moral perfection.
4. Such an endless progress requires the thought of immortal life.
5. This still does not enable us to conceive that holiness will ever be attained in our endless duration.
6. So we must suppose that God takes an eternal, timeless perspective on this uninterrupted progress toward moral perfection and counts it as the actual attainment of holiness.
7. He then is able to distribute an appropriate share in the highest good in accordance with his perception of a trajectory toward moral perfection.

God's atemporal vision of our unending progress toward moral perfection seems to have nothing to do with transforming grace – with what will make us morally perfect. God's view of us does not effect a change in us from worse to better. The argument supposes that we are indeed on a never-ending journey toward moral perfection. We never reach the goal of moral perfection, but God is going to distribute happiness nonetheless. He will give it to those who are indeed irrevocably committed to this never-ending journey. He will take their commitment to be equivalent to their actually being morally perfect. This is a gracious act on his part, because the human beings who have this commitment do not actually deserve happiness, since they have not reached the necessary end of a morally perfect life.

It must be admitted that there is no mention of the notion of grace in connection with the argument for the postulate of immortality in the *Critique of Practical Reason*. Indeed the vast majority of occurrences of *Gnade/Gnaden* in the Critical corpus are found in the *Religion* (with a few in the *Conflict* and one in the first *Critique*). But there is every reason to see the divine distribution of happiness on the back of a mere progress toward moral perfection as a form of grace – distributive grace. It fits Kant's definition of grace in the *Religion*: 'the decree of a superior to award a good for which the subordinate possesses no more than (moral) receptivity is called grace' ($6:75_n$; 'receptivity' in the note is contrasted with 'legal claim' in the text of 6:75). Moreover, when Kant comes to describe the function of grace in crucial parts of the *Religion* (as in the General Remark on grace at the end of Part I), he seems to be envisaging the mechanism described in the immortality argument.

It can be seen that the Kantian system throws up a problem to which both distributive and transforming grace might be the solution: moral perfection is unattainable by finite rational creatures, even if they live endlessly. The problem leads to another: how then can the highest good be possible after all? Distributive grace can solve this problem through a divine mechanism bypassing the need for moral perfection to be the condition for the attainment of the highest good. Transforming grace can solve it by allowing moral perfection to be achieved by a non-human mechanism of moral regeneration. At first glance, the appeal to one form of grace in this pair excludes the appeal to the other. If distributive grace is operative in bringing about the highest good for human beings, transformative grace is not needed, and *vice versa*. A closer examination of the *Religion* on evil and grace will enable a clearer picture to emerge of the work both distributive and transformative grace might do and why Kant suggests some role for justifying grace.

The *Religion* enforces the sense of a gap between the demand for moral perfection and our actual performance through its teaching (set out in the first of its four parts) that human beings suffer from radical evil. Since this teaching has been described and analysed by numerous commentators (see, for example, Allison 1990, Frierson 2003, Wood 1970), I will only give a brief account of it here.

At the core of the doctrine of radical evil is the claim that experience of human failings and evil deeds indicates that each and every human will is fundamentally corrupt. Human nature is characterised by the possession of three core dispositions: animality, humanity and personality (*Religion* 6:26ff.). Our disposition to animality is a form of self-love shown in our three drives for self-preservation, for propagation of the species and for communication with human beings. We have these three drives mechanically and not through the instruction of reason. Our humanity is a form of self-love displayed in our unsocial sociability. It is a form of self-love dependent on comparisons with others, giving rise to vices such as envy. These are vices of culture. By contrast 'The propensity to *personality* is the receptivity to respect for the moral law, as of itself a sufficient incentive to choice' (*Religion* 6:27). The disposition to obey the moral law can never be wholly lost to the human being. Even at our worst, we cannot repudiate the moral law: 'The law imposes itself on him irresistibly through his moral predisposition; and if no other incentive works against it, he would also adopt it into his supreme maxim as sufficiently determining his choice, i.e. he would be morally good' (*Religion* 6:36). All our experience shows that human beings are not morally good (that is, not morally perfect). Other things than perception of the demands of moral reason move us to act. So being moral is a struggle for us.

The thought about the highest good as a less than overwhelming incentive fits in with the portrait of the evil in human nature that Kant diagnoses as radical in the *Religion*. This evil manifests itself in the frailty, impurity and depravity of human nature. Our frailty is indicated in the way in which the good – the law – is objectively or ideally an irresistible incentive, but in reality weaker in us than non-moral motives, such as are provided by our inclinations (6:29). Our impurity manifests itself in the way in which the motive of respect for law needs still other incentives besides it in order to determine our choice for what duty requires, incentives such as desire for honour, good-hearted instincts, sympathy and above all self-love (6:30). Our depravity shows in our corrupt propensity to subordinate the claims of the moral law to non-moral ones (6:30). The claim that we are radically evil is not the claim that we are all utterly morally depraved. It is obvious that many of us, much of the time, act in accordance with the claims of the moral law and, at least apparently, against those of self-love. Radical evil is to do with our fundamental moral disposition. In particular, do we fully and wholeheartedly give priority to the moral law in formulating and acting upon maxims in conduct – as our predisposition to personality demands? The answer, from experience, is that we do not. Rather, we know that 'Every man has his price' (Kant quoting Walpole, 6:39). Our 'price' is our moral breaking point, the point at which non-moral incentives are sufficient to make us abandon moral ones and go along with the claims of self-love. All of us are evil in virtue of our fundamental propensity (*Hang*) to subordinate moral incentives to non-moral ones at some point or other, when the price is right.

The reader might object that the doctrine of radical evil looks to be no more than the assertion that we are not morally perfect. It might appear to the sceptical to be compatible with there being many degrees of evil and goodness in human personalities, and to be no more than the decision to call those who do not reach the ideal limit of goodness 'evil'. Whatever the merits of this scepticism (and they are considerable in my opinion), Kant thinks that he is entitled to a positive, substantive assertion that all suffer from evil. Given that the disposition to personality can never be extirpated from us (if it were we would become diabolical, not human, creatures), we must make a substantive decision to allow occasions when morality does not hold sway in our lives. An incentive opposed to the moral law must have influence over our wills. It could not have this influence if we did not incorporate it into our maxims. Thus we must have made some kind of choice for evil (see 6:24). This thought allows Kant to speak in rigoristic terms of there being either one or other of two fundamental propensities in our lives. A human being cannot be morally good in some parts and at the same time evil in other parts (6:24).

Our universal display of a moral breaking point in choice shows an evil in us. For that evil to be imputed to us, it must be the result of some kind of choice we have made. We can find no temporal origin for the choice, since from the earliest times at which we could make responsible choices our propensity to evil is displayed. If we thus turn from a temporal to a rational origin for our evil, we must acknowledge that it is as if we each make a timeless choice of a supreme, overarching maxim to govern our conduct. This overarching maxim is to the effect that the moral law shall not be the supreme condition of valid maxim making. We then get radical evil 'since it corrupts the ground of all maxims' (6:37), and is thus a corruption in the human will as such. It is not to be thought that the intelligible, non-historical choice of a supreme maxim *determines* the incorporation of specific maxims associated with individual actions. Every action we perform has to be regarded as free and original (6:41). But the character of specific maxims and acts is such as to be explicable, from a rational point of view, only on the assumption that we have all chosen the overarching maxim that makes us evil.

The radical character of the evil we are mired in shows in the fact that it does indeed affect our very power of maxim making. Since it corrupts the very ground of all maxims, it must be inextirpable by the human will: 'for this could only happen through good maxims, which, if the subjective supreme ground of all maxims is assumed to be corrupted, is something that cannot happen' (6:37). The inextirpable character of our propensity to evil creates one form of moral gap. We have freely chosen this propensity, which is a bad one. Therefore we are responsible for it and we ought to get rid of it. But it is inextirpable, so we cannot. Into this gap we might imagine that God's transforming grace steps in.

Before locating the entry of grace into whatever remedy there may be for radical evil, let us note that the doctrine is not original to the *Religion*. A version of it is to be found in the *Groundwork* 4:405. Here Kant notes that human beings face a powerful counterweight to the moral law in their lives. This is the satisfaction of their needs and inclinations under the umbrella of happiness. From the conflict between the unremitting claims of reason and those of happiness:

> From this there flows a *natural dialectic*, that is, a propensity [*Hang*] to confuse those strict laws of duty and to cast doubt upon their legality, or at least upon their purity and strictness and where possible to make them more suited to our wishes and inclinations, i.e. to corrupt them at their ground and to destroy all their worth, which not even common practical reason can in the end call good.

The doctrine of radical evil also seems to cohere with the teaching of the *Metaphysics of Morals* to the effect that the duty to become morally perfect (that is, to always act out of respect for the moral law, out of the purest of motives) is a wide and imperfect duty, and not a narrow, perfect duty. This entails that our duty is merely to strive with all our might to achieve the end of purity in maxim making (*Morals* 6:393). Inextirpable, radical evil is not here cited as the reason why we can never actually attain perfection, but it would explain it. Yet this seems to confront us with a new problem: if we are radically evil, how we can we adopt the end of moral perfection and do something that counts as striving to attain it?

The question thus raised provides another reason for delving into the miasma that is the General Remark on grace at the end of Part I of the *Religion* (6:44–53). The second paragraph of the Remark rehearses the problem just stated: how can an evil human being make him or herself good? How can an evil tree bring forth good fruit? We still face the moral demand to become good and by 'ought implies can' it must be possible for us to become good human beings (6:45). This is the gap that reference to transforming divine grace should be able to bridge. But the first paragraph of the Remark begins with a statement of principle apparently forbidding any such use of transforming grace: 'What the human being is or shall become in a moral sense, good or evil, he must make or have made himself' (6:44). As noted previously, it seems all but tautological to say that what redounds to my moral merit should be produced by my own will. Kant, however, envisages a compromise on this strict principle toward the end of the paragraph. He writes of supernatural co-operation coming to those in pursuit of moral goodness after they have made themselves 'antecedently worthy of receiving it'. Intending good persons must make the break from evil themselves, be worthy of the divine aid that might take them further along the path. Moreover, any such aid will only be of use to them if they incorporate 'this positive increase of force' into their maxims. In this way transforming grace may contribute to the coming to be of a goodness which is nonetheless still attributable to the agent who has achieved that goodness.

Goodness of the kind required cannot come to be through a gradual process, affirms Kant (6:47). It requires a transformation in inner principles of action. The war against radical evil in human nature must begin with a revolution that amounts to a change of heart. The revolution/change of heart involves what Kant describes as 'a revolution in the mode of thought, but a gradual reform in the mode of sense' (6:47). That is to say, there must be a radical change at the level of the intelligible, free ground of our actions, which change will show itself in the gradual, increasing conformity of our outward actions to the demands of the moral law. Kant explains this change of heart in greater detail:

> if by a single unalterable decision a human being reverses the supreme ground of his maxims, through which he was an evil man (and thereby puts on a new man): he is so far as his principle and attitude of mind goes, a subject receptive to the good; but only in incessant labouring and growth is he a good human being: i.e. he can hope, that through the purity of the principle, which he has adopted as the supreme maxim of his choice, and through its stability, to find himself upon the good (though narrow) path of a constant progress from bad to better. (6:47–8)

The immediate continuation of this quotation deals with God's role in relation to the change of heart. But before we tackle the question of God's action in helping to overcome radical evil, we need to ask exactly what the change of heart consists in and how, if at all, it eliminates radical evil.

One natural way of understanding the change of heart is this: it involves replacing the choice of the supreme maxim allowing us to subordinate respect for the moral law to non-moral incentives with a new supreme maxim. Post the change of heart our propensity to evil has gone because we have a new supreme maxim 'Always make respect for the moral law trump consideration of non-moral incentives'. Kant's description of the change of heart – 'if by a single unalterable decision a human being reverses the supreme ground of his maxims, through which he was an evil man (and thereby puts on a new man)' – implies this reading. Some have interpreted the change of heart in this way. To do so, however, creates problems.

The first problem is that Kant's account then seems to fall into patent contradictions. We would have a contradiction between the affirmation of the possibility of the change of heart and the claim that the propensity to evil cannot be extirpated by human powers. There is, in addition, the general tension in supposing that a propensity not acquired at any time, which is therefore timeless in a manner of speaking, could be got rid of at a 'later' time. What is timelessly true of any entity cannot cease to be true of that entity at some time. If the moral revolution is understood as ridding oneself of the *Hang* toward evil, then (as Quinn has argued, 1984:198–9) Kant is committed to an inconsistent triad. The triad is formed of the thesis of radical evil, the thesis of rigorism and the thesis of the possibility of the change of heart. Rigorism tells us that human beings can only have one supreme maxim: either a good or an evil one. That rules out the co-existence of the original evil supreme maxim alongside a new, good supreme maxim post the change of heart. The thesis of radical evil rules out the possibility of our once having an evil supreme maxim and later a good supreme maxim, for that thesis makes the choice of the original evil maxim both inextirpable and independent of all temporal conditions. Hence, 'there is no possible world in which (1) the thesis of rigorism is true, (2) every human being adopts a morally evil supreme maxim and (3) some human adopts a morally good supreme maxim' (Quinn 1984:199).

The second main problem with conceiving of the change of heart as an annulment of the original *Hang* toward evil is that Kant manifestly conceives of the change of heart as compatible with continued moral lapses. There is a revolution of the will at the intelligible level, but only a continued, gradual progress toward good in our outward actions. We are not morally perfect in our outward acts. If the revolution got rid of the original, radical evil, how could this be? If human beings were no longer radically evil, then they would no longer have a moral 'breaking point' and would never be in the position of acting other than out of respect for the moral law. It might be argued that even if the evil supreme maxim is got rid of and replaced by a good supreme maxim, evil-doing is still possible. Might not weakness of will remain? Might not imperfections in self-knowledge persist, such that we mistake a demand from self-love for one from morality and act wrongly in consequence? (For a view like this see Sullivan 1989:128 and 130.) The problem with this attempt to save the reading of the change of heart under discussion is that such impediments to right action are described by Kant as aspects of our radical evil, and thus could not remain if that evil were extirpated. At 6:37 these impediments are mentioned under the headings of frailty and dishonesty and are linked to 'a radical perversity in the human heart'.

In the light of the foregoing, let us assume that the change of heart leaves the original propensity to evil seated in the human will. What then might it consist in? In brief, it might amount to this: a new commitment by the human agent to the imperfect duty to strive after moral perfection, that is to the goal of acting, not merely in accordance with the law, but out of respect for the law.

Acknowledging their radical evil, virtuous human beings have undertaken a change of heart by committing themselves, once and for all, to cultivating the duty to be virtuous. They have adopted a resolute disposition to strive after holiness and fight the evil within them. This resolution to strive after holiness shows itself in a gradual improvement in their outward conduct. Less and less do they allow themselves to set aside the strict claims of morality. Their moral breaking point gets further and further off. Their 'price' increases. Their fundamental dispositions are now more complex. They still have the original propensity to evil – which is inextirpable by human powers – but that is mixed with an underlying disposition that marks their revolt against that propensity. In this sense, there is a new 'man' post the change of heart, albeit the *Hang* to evil remains. (For accounts along these lines see Frierson 2003:122ff. and Wood 1970:230ff.)

Advantages flow from this reading of the change of heart. The Quinn-style charge that Kant's account is mired in contradiction is rebutted. Rigorism is not violated, if we heed the levels at which human beings have good and bad dispositions. Human beings post the change remain evil (not morally perfect) in their most fundamental disposition. But *good* human beings are in revolt against this evil; that, together with their improved record in outward conduct, is the mark of their goodness. The fact that they continue to be capable of immoral acts is explained. A reason is supplied why moral perfection (perfect virtue/holiness) is a never-to-be-achieved goal. The explanation is that even the good person committed to moral perfection is always in revolt against a radical evil in his/her nature and therefore struggling against a fundamental impediment. The good person might then be said to have a kind of imperfect virtue: not moral perfection but an unchanging commitment to strive after it, a commitment constituted by a will in revolution against our radical evil. This account will even give some sense to the notion of divine transforming grace. Back to the opening of the General Remark on grace at 6:44: we must make ourselves worthy of this kind of grace by undertaking the change of heart, by commencing our revolt against radical evil, by resolving to obey the imperfect duty to become perfectly virtuous/holy. But having made ourselves thus worthy, we might hope that 'some supernatural co-operation' (6:44) is forthcoming to aid us in the fight. Transforming grace thus does not produce the change of heart, but might assist in the war against radical evil that the change of heart occasions (cf. Mariña 1997:388). God might, for example, grant good persons greater self-knowledge or strength of will, thus aiding them in the struggle they are embarked upon. In general terms, we can note that Kant sees no opposition between, on the one hand, the change of heart and its transformative effects being the responsibility of agents and, on the other, there being external sources of aid for moral regeneration which the individual may draw upon. It is the teaching of Parts III and IV of the religion that the remedy for radical evil is in part social. That is to say, when people of good will join together in public associations to bring about the ethical community, they are increasing the resources available in the struggle against evil (see, for example, 6:94). So from this point of view there is no objection to there being aids to moral regeneration stemming from a communion of an individual human being with other agents.

This brings us to the role of grace as described at the end of Part I of the *Religion*. The General Remark closes by classifying grace as one of the *parega* that reason helps itself to in the religious sphere. It is an idea which is not itself produced or certified by reason, but which reason makes use of in picturing the answers to certain problems. A *parergon* is thus the object of a reflective, not a dogmatic, faith (6:52). Kant displays his view of the severe limitations upon the use of the notion of grace in the following:

> For it is impossible to make them [the effects of grace] theoretically cognisable (that they are effects of grace, not immanent nature), because our use of the concept of cause and effect of objects of experience cannot be extended beyond nature; the assumption of a practical use of this idea is completely self-contradictory. For the employment would presuppose a rule, concerning the good (for a particular end) which we ourselves must do to accomplish something; to expect an effect of grace means the very opposite, namely that the good (the morally good) is not ours, but the act of another being, that we can only earn it by doing nothing, which contradicts itself. (6:53)

Therefore the idea of an effect of grace is, he concludes, incomprehensible. Since it is theoretically and practically of no use, I conclude that it serves merely an imaginative and pictorial purpose, such that it fosters or enlivens hope in the struggle against evil. The fact that there is a contradiction in making practical use of the concept of grace is linked to Kant's repeated rejection of the thought that there might be means of grace of a 'mechanical', non-moral kind in this or that religion. Transformative grace could certainly not come about through attendance at rites or ceremonies. In this Remark Kant distinguishes between religions of rogation and moral religion. The former are those that think that divine grace can come about through means other than making oneself a better human being. The latter place the onus on individuals to make themselves worthy by their own efforts of whatever divine aid is forthcoming (6:51–2).

Transforming grace being theoretically incomprehensible and practically self-contradictory when thought of as coming from a supernatural agency, Kant tries his hand in the *Conflict* at a more anthropological understanding of it. The principle that effects moral transformation is presented as belonging to human nature, albeit a 'supersensible' aspect of it. He writes:

> If by nature we mean what in man is the ruling principle of his demand for *happiness*, and by grace the incomprehensible moral disposition that lies in us, i.e. the principle of *pure morality*, then nature and grace not only differ from each other, but are often found opposed to each other in conflict. But if by nature (in the practical sense) we mean our ability to achieve certain ends by our own powers in general, then grace is none other than the nature of the human being, insofar as he is determined to actions by his own inner, though supersensible, principle (the representation of his duty), which, if we wanted to explain, although we know no further ground for it, we represent as an impulse to good produced in us by the Godhead, the predisposition to which we did not establish in ourselves, and so as grace. (7:43)

In the terminology of the *Religion* 'the principle of pure morality' is our disposition to personality. This is an original possession of human nature. It is thus prior to any particular choices we make. It is supersensible by virtue of being an expression of our natures as free, intelligible beings. For these reasons, the stimulus to good it provides for us can be aptly represented as coming from without, as external to individual choices made in time by the will in time. On this account, talk of grace is merely a pictorial way presenting a renewed influence of 'the principle of pure morality' in those who have undertaken the change of heart.

I have indicated how there might be a role for transforming grace in relation to the problem of radical evil, even though it is a role of which we have no theoretical comprehension and cannot use practically. However, we find that when Kant sets out the role of grace in relation to radical evil most fully, he is not talking about transforming grace at all. Kant gives an account of what divine grace does in relation to the problem of radical evil in the continuation of the passage from *Religion* 6:48 quoted above wherein the change of heart is described. Kant has told us that the one who has accomplished the change of heart finds him or herself on 'the good (though narrow) path of a constant progress from bad to better'. Thus far there has been no role for God, but then we have this:

> For him who penetrates to the intelligible ground of the heart (the ground of all maxims of choice), to whom this endless progress is a unity, i.e. for God, this amounts to actually being a good human being (pleasing to him); and thus far the change can be regarded as

a revolution; for the judgement of human beings, however, who can appraise themselves and the strength of their maxims only by the ascendancy they gain over sensuous nature in time, the change is to be regarded only as an ever-continuing striving for the better, thus as a gradual reform of the propensity to evil, of the perverted cast of mind. (6:48)

This passage envisages a role for God that is remarkably similar to that outlined in the argument for the postulate of immortality in the *Critique of Practical Reason* (5:122–3). To be aware that a human being is really in revolt against the propensity to evil entails knowledge of the inner ground of that person's maxims, of the character of the intelligible self. All that is available to a sense-bound awareness is a record of more and more outward acts being in conformity to the moral law. Such a record, however, is perfectly compatible with one's having made a move merely to the lesser form of virtue that Kant describes at 6:47. This amounts to 'only a change of [external] morality', as evinced, for example, when an immoderate human being converts to moderation for the sake of health – not out of respect for the demands of the law. As noted in the previous chapter, no finitely long record of behaviour in accordance with the moral law could prove that the higher form virtue and not the lesser form had been taken up in someone's life. It needs a God's-eye view to discern this. Moreover, even one who has undergone a genuine change of heart and has taken up the higher form of virtue is still not morally perfect, but only on the road toward it, for this person's will is in revolt against radical evil and that entails that he or she still suffers from it to some degree. That is why this person is on 'the good (though narrow) path of constant progress from bad to better'. God has to both discern the genuine change of heart from the false and take the change of heart to be equivalent to achieved moral perfection.

None of this amounts to God exercising a transforming power of grace. Though the immediate context to the discussion of grace in the General Remark to Part I of the *Religion* does not evince this, Kant must be contributing to an account of God's distributive grace. The grace outlined at 6:48 brings about no change to a human character. The 6:48 account seems to offer, for example, no help in understanding how the *Religion*'s favoured social version of the goal – the moral commonwealth – is brought any closer. Rather, grace supplies knowledge of the human will's true status and a way of counting a decisive inner step toward a goal, followed by continued outer progress, as if it were attainment of that goal. Presumably, if Kant's God was exercising an effective transforming grace, then the good human being would not be good as merely labouring against evil and becoming better, but would be established as holy and thus free from any potential for future evil. The Preface to the first edition of the *Religion* provides a context for the whole discussion. It sets out the goal of the highest good, its two elements and the need for a higher, moral, most holy, and omnipotent being who alone can unite the two elements of this good (6:5). Grace in the passage under discussion fits in with that context, insofar as it explains how God might bring the highest good when we never get the first element (moral perfection) in its complete form. But this is what I call distributive grace.

In summary, while the General Remark to Part I of the *Religion* toys with the idea of God's transforming grace, it does not in the end do anything with it. It is declared to be theoretically incomprehensible and practically incoherent. The real work in overcoming the gap between human imperfection and moral demands is given to distributive grace. Let us now see what Kant can make of justifying grace.

The first 10 or so pages of the second part of the *Religion* rehearses the problem that gives rise to the need for the form of grace described at 6:48. We have the difficulty that our deeds are always imperfect even after a decisive revolt against the active and cause of evil in us opposing the seed of goodness we possess (6:57). And the solution involves the God's-eye view that takes the unending progression of the good in us toward conformity to the law in the light of insight into the inward disposition behind it and counts it as a perfected whole. Therefore 'the [good] human being ignoring his standing deficiency can still expect to be generally well-pleasing to God, at whatever time his existence may be ended' (6:67). These early pages bring in an explicit link to Christian symbolism by connecting the humanity-as-morally-perfect element of the highest good with the idea of a humanity well-pleasing to God and to an instantiation of that idea in a perfectly good human being, who is the embodiment of the good principle on earth. This person would execute in his person all human duties, spread goodness far and wide through teaching and example, and willingly take on suffering for the sake of others (see 6:61). The link to the Christian symbol of the Christ, the Son of God, paves the way for introduction of a role for justifying grace. At 6:72 we get this problem for the human being mired in evil, but fighting it post the change of heart: 'Whatever he may have achieved in the adoption of a good disposition, and, indeed, however steadfastly he may have persevered in such a disposition in a life conduct conformable to it, he nevertheless started from evil, and this indebtedness is never possible for him to wipe out' (6:72). So, even the human being who is good, in the sense of being in genuine revolt against radical evil, is still guilty of performing evil deeds (be it before, during or after the change of heart). As being guilty, the good human being cannot expect to be well-pleasing to God, but rather to deserve punishment from God's hands, and there is nothing he or she can do to remove this guilt. We are clearly now moving to that form of the moral gap which might occasion the need for justifying grace.

Kant's solution to this problem is typically opaque. It involves at least the following elements: God taking the trial and suffering involved in the conversion that is the change of heart as satisfaction for guilt incurred in life conduct; God viewing the person post conversion as morally a 'new' human being, not liable for the faults of the 'old'; linking such elements to the Christian symbolism of a personified good principle who suffers and dies for the old humanity (see 6:74–5). At 6:75 God is described as taking the resultant mix as enabling him to remit the punishment due to our guilt. This is classed as a function of his grace. Once again, appeal to a concept of grace is deemed fitting by Kant because a God's-eye view of our state is needed. From an empirical point of view we are merely in progress toward becoming a person who is good:

> It is always therefore a verdict of grace alone, although (because based on a satisfaction that for us lies only in the idea of an improved disposition which, however, only God cognises) it is fully in accord with eternal justice, when by means of this good in which we believe, we are relieved of all liability [for the acts of the 'old man']. (6:76)

Justifying grace works here, allegedly, because God takes the new disposition, and the transition to it, in the one who has undertaken a change of heart as capable of deflecting the rigorous justice which would otherwise be that person's due. And it requires God's eye view to see that disposition as real.

The Kantian account of justifying grace has puzzled many commentators and given rise to accusations of incoherence. (For discussion of it see Quinn 1986 and Mariña 1997.) I do not wish to go into its merits here, but rather to point out that it seems to have little to do with the root problem behind the letter to Lavater, namely the gap between the strict demands of the moral law and the apparent inability of human beings to meet them. As noted at the start of this section, we have here an extra problem. It is one that arises when we add to the elements of moral demand and human performance the further thought that there is a God who is seeking sinless human beings to enjoy an eternal relationship with him. This God then has a problem with the fact that even human beings who have become perfect, either via grace or their own efforts, have a legacy of guilt. This problem of God's seems to be wholly alien to the nest of problems described in the Critical corpus surrounding how the two elements of the highest good can be achieved. The concern with human guilt brings in something new. That is to say, it is only by the most external imposition that the Critical problem of how humanity can achieve moral perfection can be transformed into one requiring justifying grace as its solution. We must in that case confront not just the difficulty of how humanity can achieve a disposition that is in perfect conformity to the moral law, but the difficulty of how humanity can become free of any guilt arising from wrongdoing. The goal of history and creation for the Critical Philosophy includes the moral perfection of humanity. It is not at all clear that it includes, save by way of external attachment, the guiltlessness of humanity.

In summing up the function of Kant's God as a purveyor of grace, we can see that he cannot give any real substance to the idea of God as the source of transforming grace. God as a transformer of the human heart is not ruled out absolutely, but Kant has no concrete role for God under this guise and he tells us that such grace is theoretically uncognisable and practically useless. He does have a role for God's distributive grace, and one that is connected with a pessimistic strand in a number of his works about the actual achievability of moral perfection by human beings. We will see in the next chapter that something like distributive grace was also ascribed to God by deistic thinkers writing before Kant. Kant does indeed claim to have a role for God's justifying grace. This is something that would take him beyond deism into distinctively Christian territory, but we have noted a serious question about the need for this role in his system.

How far Kant's thinking about God is distinctively Christian and how far it is deistic are matters we turn to in the final chapter.

Chapter 8

Kant, Christianity and Deism

Kant and Christian truth

There is a debate over whether the Critical Philosophy's account of religion is or is not compatible with Christianity. This debate often focuses on the question of whether Kant's religious outlook is a deistic or a Christian one. The debate encompasses a number of more detailed questions: Does Kant allow for the real possibility of revelation? Does he allow of divine action in the world, specifically for miracles? Does Kant reduce true religion to natural religion? Does he reduce religion to morality? Does he allow any real role for a redeemer and saviour in history, specifically in the person of Jesus Christ? Does he allow rational assent to key Christian doctrines?

This chapter will address these detailed questions about Kant's general religious stance. As noted in Chapter 1, some contemporary thinkers want to claim that Kant is a Christian thinker (see Palmquist 1989). Without going over the question discussed in Chapter 1 as to Kant's own religious adherence, I shall argue that Kant's Critical interpretation of religion is antithetic to Christianity, at least as Christianity is normally understood. Kant does in at least one major respect reduce religion to morality. While departing in some respects from the positions of central deistic thinkers such as Blount and Tindal, he is much closer to eighteenth-century deism than he is to orthodox Christianity.

The question of whether Kant's religious philosophy is or is not compatible with Christianity interacts with the questions of what the general intent of the *Religion* is and of the nature of the overall religious stance it is meant to endorse. Kant offered his own gloss on the general intent of the *Religion* in a letter of 4 May 1793. In it he states that his aim is to show how the possible unity of the Christian religion with the purest practical reason is to be understood (11:429). Thus *Religion* is meant to show how the aims and truths of practical reason, purified as far as possible of the contingent and empirical, can be united with the Christian faith. Examination will show that Kant prosecutes this goal but only by dint of a striking re-interpretative strategy with respect to Christianity. In the light of that re-interpretative strategy, it turns out to be no surprise that he can outline a possible union of Christianity and purest practical reason.

We can link Kant's own gloss on the *Religion* with the account within it of the range of religious positions a philosophical account of religion can choose between (*Religion* 6:153–7). Starting off with his standard definition of religion as the recognition of all of our duties as divine commands, Kant distinguishes revealed religion from natural. The former is a religion in which knowledge of duty is derived from knowledge of God. The latter is a religion in which I must know something is my duty before I can acknowledge it as a divine command. He thus uses the natural/revealed religion contrast as the equivalent of his theological morality versus moral theology distinction. This is not a particularly authentic or helpful way of defining 'revealed religion' and 'natural religion'. In relation both to eighteenth-century usage and Kant's own argument, it would be better to define them thus: natural religion is that religion all of whose truths are knowable by the use of unaided reason alone (a definition Kant adopts a few paragraphs later at 6:155); revealed religion consists of, or contains, religious truths which we could only know by virtue of a divine supplement to human reason, viz. divine revelation in history.

After distinguishing natural and revealed religion, Kant then sets out the options:

> He, who declares mere natural religion morally necessary, i.e. for duty, can also be called rationalist (in matters of faith). If he denies the reality of any supernatural divine revelation, he is called naturalist; should he allow this [revelation], but assert that to recognise it and accept it as actual is not necessarily demanded for religion, then he can be called pure rationalist; but, if he holds that faith in it [revelation] is necessary to universal religion, then he would be called pure supernaturalist in matters of faith. (6:154–5)

The way this passage is drafted suggests that Kant has introduced rationalism and then defined three positions which rationalists can adopt: they can be naturalists, pure rationalists or supernaturalists. The drafting is then odd, for supernaturalism is not a version of rationalism but its negation. A number of key assertions in the *Religion* (and elsewhere) indicate that Kant cannot countenance supernaturalism.

The drafting of the above passage appears even more puzzling in the light of the first sentence of the next paragraph, which affirms that a consistent rationalist cannot be a naturalist:

> The rationalist must by virtue of his title hold himself within the limits of human insight. Hence he will never in the manner of a naturalist dispute or deny either the inner possibility of revelation in general or the necessity of a revelation as divine means for the introduction of true religion; for regarding this no human being can settle anything through reason. (6:155)

So, having apparently introduced supernaturalism and naturalism as versions of rationalism, they are swiftly said to be incompatible with it. This leaves pure rationalism in possession of the field.

At first blush, Kant's apparent rejection of naturalism seems consistent with a great theme of his Critical treatment of the divine: the affirmation of the limits of human knowledge of God with the aim of undercutting both religious dogmatism and naturalistic dogmatism.

Kant continues by setting out in some detail the option that a religion might be objectively natural while subjectively revealed. This option seems to comport well with pure rationalism. It will provide one way in which Kant can affirm his own moral theology while officially allowing room for a genuine revelation in

Christianity's scriptures. An objectively natural religion will consists of truths, all of which could have, and perhaps ought to have, been discoverable by the unaided human reason. Thus it might consist wholly of the truths of Kantian moral theology. It can be subjectively revealed if God's disclosure of those truths 'at a certain time and a certain place might be wise and very profitable to the human race' (6:155). To use deistic terminology, an alleged revelation in history might be admissible if it were a republication of the religion of nature.

More understanding of Kant's treatment of religion and revelation will be provided by considering in greater detail why he cannot admit of supernaturalism, the explicit role he allows for revelation and the consistency, or otherwise, of his rejection of naturalism.

Supernaturalists hold 'that faith in divine revelation is necessary to universal religion'. Many things are wrong with supernaturalism according to Kant. Chief among its errors is this: it ignores the fact that nothing in religion can be true unless it is universally true. Kant's rationalism is shown in his commitment to the notion that all truths of religion are truths of reason, that is: universal truths which are not about specific people or events in history and which can, in principle, be known by anyone, no matter when and where they live. This point is made more than once in the *Religion*. At 6:109 it comes out in the identification of 'the most important distinguishing mark of truth' in religion with 'the legitimate claim to universality'. He tells us that 'The distinguishing mark of the true church is its universality' (6:115). Supernaturalists occupy a stance displaying a fundamental incoherence. They claim certain truths are parts of the faith that is universally binding on all human beings, the faith that is saving faith, but at the same time they hold that these truths are revealed in history or are about what happened in history. Thus supernaturalism bases itself upon a faith in revelation. But a faith based on a historical record and/or about what happened at certain times in history is, in virtue of the fact that is a historical faith, incapable of being transmitted in such a way that it commands universal conviction (6:109). Kant explains the point a little more fully:

> Now historical faith (which is based upon revelation as experience) has only particular validity, namely for those in contact with the history on which the faith rests, and contains like all experiential cognition not the consciousness that the object believed in must be so and not otherwise, but only, that it is so; thereby it contains at the same time the consciousness of its own contingency. (6:115)

One reason why religious 'truth' based on revelation cannot be universal is that, necessarily, it cannot be known by those who live prior to the people to whom it is revealed. If those born before this favoured part of history could know of this saving truth in advance, then its revelation in history would not be necessary. Moreover, it will be a highly contingent matter whether all members of the human race who live after the revelation have sufficient evidence of the relevant historical happenings to be able to be sure of its truth. If any specific historical candidate for true revelation is selected by supernaturalists, they will have to admit that in practice there are many generations of people who have lived and died subsequent to it and who have had no effective knowledge of it. Moreover, historical goings on are matters about which we have beliefs that are more or less probable. If the relevant historical goings on were located 1,800 or more years ago, beliefs about them will not have an overwhelming probability. There is an undercurrent of Kant's thinking on these matters that insists that something as important as religious truth must be knowable with certainty (more on this in what follows).

The positive outcome of this rejection of the key claim of the supernaturalist is this: statements that are part of true religion must be necessary truths of reason. Thus our quotation from 6:115 continues: 'Therefore this faith [historical faith] can suffice as an ecclesiastical faith (of which there can be several), but only the pure faith of religion, which is grounded entirely on reason, can be recognised as necessary and thus as the sole one marking out the true church'. This quotation does not unambiguously proclaim the message that true religion consists only of necessary truths of reason, but this one does: 'The true, unique religion contains nothing but laws, i.e. such practical principles, of whose unconditional necessity we can become conscious, which we therefore recognise as revealed through pure reason (not empirically)' (*Religion* 6:167–8). True religion thus consists of nothing but universal, necessary, moral laws that are discoverable by reason. Supernaturalism is out because there are no religious, saving truths that depend on historical revelation to be known. Religious truths are the wrong kind of truth to depend on history in this way. Given that the laws of pure rational religion can be known a priori (see *Conflict* 7:61) – as befits universal and necessary truths – they cannot be known through history. Historical evidence and historical goings-on are irrelevant to them.

It has been argued that Kant's point that 'true religion is universal, revealed religion cannot be' is weak. Perhaps there are some, indeed many people, who because of contingent circumstances cannot rise to the knowledge of the relevant truths of reason (cf. Wood 1991:13). But this ignores Kant's main point about universality. I may through ignorance be unaware of the relevant universal and necessary laws of reason that make up true religion. These limitations can, however, be overcome in principle. A fact such as that I was born before some supernaturalist's favoured revelation in history cannot. Moreover, Kant evidently has in mind that even if an historical truth (such as 'Jesus rose from the dead') was believed by all *compos mentis*, adult human beings, it would not be a genuinely universal truth. Its being believed universally would be accidental. Only necessary truths in Kant have true universality, for only such truths rest on grounds that make them universally knowable (see Savage 1991: 59 and *Critique$_1$* A:1). Genuinely universal truths have universal grounds. They are true a priori. They are universally knowable because they deal in what *must* be so, not merely what *is* so.

As the above quotation from 6:167–8 indicates, Kant thinks that religious truths are universal and necessary because they are identical with the general principles of morality. As we know full well, religion is the recognition of duties as divine commands. The matter of religion thus comes from morality:

> Religion is not distinguished in its matter, i.e. object, at any point from morality, for it is concerned with duties as such, but rather its distinction from morality is merely formal, i.e. its legislation of reason uses the Idea of God, which is derived from morality itself, to

give morality influence on the human will to fulfil all its duties. This is why there is only one religion. (*Conflict* 7:36)

This is why, Kant affirms, there are no distinct religions – although there are different forms of faith in divine revelation.

If the substantive truths of religion are thus moral truths, then there is, after all, a sense in which Kant does reduce religion to morality (for a contrary view see Palmquist 1992). It also follows that the question of how universal religion is, when understood as the question of how far it has spread through humanity, is just the question of the universality of conscience. Kant's view on this facet of human awareness of religion is given by his repeated reference to moral/religious truths being engraved on our hearts by God (as at 6:84, 6:85 and 6:104). Thus, to uncover the revelation of reason, we merely have 'to consult a document indelibly kept open in every soul and which needs no miracles' (6:85). We do not have to rely on information others might hold about what happened a long time ago in some far off land, for 'everyone can recognise by himself, through his own reason, the will of God which lies at the basis of his religion' (6:104).

Kant's teaching on the content and matter of true religion should surely settle the question of whether or not his Critical system allows him to endorse Christianity. The account of true religion as containing nothing other than universal, necessary, practical laws entails that what is distinctive in Christianity is not part of true religion. This conclusion follows if we assume that Christianity is the faith that it is because it consists of more than a set of universal, practical laws. Christianity is indeed commonly taken to include more than universal, practical laws, for amongst its essential credal commitments we find propositions about the actions of God in history. For Christianity to be true the statements in such summaries as the Apostles' Creed must be true, and to be a Christian one must affirm them as true:

> I believe in God, the Father almighty, creator of heaven and earth. I believe in Jesus Christ, his only Son, our Lord, who was conceived by the Holy Spirit and born of the Virgin Mary. He suffered under Pontius Pilate, was crucified, died, and was buried; he descended to hell. The third day he rose again from the dead. He ascended to heaven and is seated at the right hand of God the Father almighty. From there he will come to judge the living and the dead. I believe in the Holy Spirit, the holy catholic church, the communion of saints, the forgiveness of sins, the resurrection of the body, and the life everlasting.

To accept such a creed as this is manifestly to be committed to a set of historical (and metaphysical) truths that go beyond universal, practical laws. Kant says over and again that being religious entails no commitment to any historical claims. Thus in the *Conflict of the Faculties* we are told that religious faith 'which is directed solely to the morality of life-conduct, of action, holding historical, even biblical teachings for true has in itself no moral worth or unworth and belongs under the heading of the indifferent' (7:47). Crucially for Kant, whatever truths there are in Christianity, they do not introduce a sacramental system human beings must lay hold of in order to become well-pleasing to God. Religious faith is directed solely to the morality of conduct. As often as he tells us that belief in historical claims is not necessary for true faith, Kant rams home the message that the only way of becoming well-pleasing to God is through morally upright conduct. Kant states that he accepts that the following is true without need of proof: 'Everything, save for good life-conduct, which the human being can do to become well-pleasing to God, is mere religious delusion and counterfeit service of God' (*Religion* 6:170). Moral improvement alone is the sole condition for attaining eternal life (*Conflict* 7:37). Recall that Kant's stated aim for the *Religion* is to present how the possible unity of the Christian religion with the purest practical reason is to be understood. This is an easy goal to accomplish *if* the principle for interpreting Christian scriptures adopted is that of seeking for their moral meaning alone. And this is Kant's hermeneutic. The supreme norm for interpreting Scripture is the religion of reason (*Religion* 6:114) and thus the moral philosopher must take priority over the scriptural scholar in determining the authentic meaning of Biblical texts. Generalising about all holy books, Kant writes: 'For the reading of these holy books, or the investigation of their content, has as its final purpose the making of better human beings; their historical element, however, which contributes nothing to this, is something in itself quite indifferent, which one can regard as one wishes' (6:111).

Given the above, it cannot be that, for Kant, the alleged actions of God in Jesus have to be known about in order for us to have a true and saving faith. Nor can it be the case that, while explicit faith in what God has done in Jesus is not required, God must have been at work at the ontological level in the Redeemer to make salvation possible. Nor can it be the case that the actions of God in Jesus brings something about which we can later tap into via a sacramental system preserved in a religion *about Jesus*. When Kant gives his own interpretation of the sacraments of the Christian faith in the General Remark to Part IV of the *Religion*, he gives them a moral function. We know already that Kant holds all genuine religious truths to be universal, necessary, a priori. Thus they will simply not describe anything that was or was not happening in first-century Palestine. This means that while there may be truth in the ideas of the Incarnation, Passion and Resurrection of Christ, the truth is of a universal sort and does not depend on what happened in and through the individual man Jesus of Nazareth. What we have in Part II, Section 1 of the *Religion* is the presentation of Jesus, the God-man, as the personified 'ideal of a humanity well-pleasing to God' (6:61), that is as the representation in a text of something that is universal in import. Hence Kant is able to state that 'the good principle did not descend among humans from heaven at one particular time but from the first origins of the human race in some invisible way ... and has by rights its first dwelling place in it [humanity] (6:82). What Christian narratives portray is an 'intelligible moral relation' (*Religion* 6:78) in the form of stories, whose historical truth is a matter of indifference for true faith. The a priori content of true religion does not depend on putative acts of God in history, but stories about those acts can serve as ways of enabling us to gain a better grasp of them. All-in-all, it does not appear as if Kant can allow any substantive truth to the claim that 'Jesus saves'. Hence, his system is antithetic to Christianity.

It must be conceded that Kant does allow that the appearance of the good principle in an actual human being, specifically in Jesus, could result in some gain for us all. He goes so far as to say that 'by being an example of this [the good principle] (in the moral idea) he [i.e. Jesus] opened the doors of freedom to everyone who, like him, chooses to die to everything that holds them fettered to earthly life to the detriment of morality' (6:82). I take this to mean something like the following. Belief in an actual personification of the good principle, as in Jesus, assures those who undertake the change of heart, and who seek to acquire a will in revolt against evil, that such a revolution is possible. Thus it can give them greater confidence in undertaking the change of heart. This is one of the ways in which Kant attempts to rebuild bridges between the a priori truths of true religion and the contingent and historical features of ecclesiastical faith. Kant's further efforts in this direction will be explored in greater detail below when considering his precise relation to deism.

Kant can give one unproblematic role to Jesus, namely that of being 'the first to expound a religion, pure, striking comprehensible to the whole world (a natural one) and whose teachings, as preserved for us, we can therefore test for ourselves' (*Religion* 6:158). This is a common way of praising Jesus in Enlightenment thought. Jesus is the first, or the clearest, or, in some other way, best preacher of natural religion. As long ago as 1695 Locke had criticised those who 'made Jesus Christ nothing but the restorer and preacher of pure natural religion', so this portrayal of Jesus must have had some antiquity before Kant took it up. Locke states that such a portrayal does 'violence to the whole tenor of the New Testament' (Locke 1999:5). He does so because he believes the New Testament, particularly by way of Paul's Epistle to the Romans, makes faith in Jesus and his resurrection mandatory for true belief and for the possibility of salvation. If Jesus Christ is nothing 'but the restorer and preacher of pure natural religion', it might be helpful to know about him, but hardly necessary. And while the human race may have gained through this mission on earth, it cannot have been essential to their salvation.

Kant as pure rationalist

We have noted how in the *Religion* at 6:155 Kant appears to box himself into a corner and force on himself the option of pure rationalist. Pure rationalism rejects the dogmatic dismissal of the possibility of revelation contained in naturalism. We have seen why and how Kant rejects supernaturalism. He affirms that there is nothing that is necessary and true in religion save what is found in natural religion. Religious truth is universal truth and thus cannot be essentially bound to some historical revelation. But there are parts of the *Religion* and the *Conflict of the Faculties* that appear to show Kant accepting the option outlined at 6:155–6 to the effect that rational religion might be objectively natural but subjectively revealed. We have noted that this means that, while true religion consists wholly of the truths of Kantian moral theology, it has also been disclosed by God 'at a certain time and a certain place' (6:155). Such a disclosure will not have been strictly necessary for human beings' grasp of pure religion, but may have been advantageous to them. This stance allows rationalism to be accommodated with belief in a miraculous revelation from God to the human race in the fashion Kant appears to endorse in a letter to Fichte of 2 February 1792:

> a religion may contain no other articles of faith, than those that also exist for pure reason. This proposition is to my mind entirely innocent and denies neither the subjective necessity of a revelation nor of miracles (since one can assume that, if it is possible at all, the actual

occurrence of such a thing could be rationally understood as well, without revelation, even though reason would not have introduced these articles by itself. Even if miracles were necessary at the beginning, they are no longer so; this religion is now so grounded, that its articles of belief can henceforth be maintained of themselves). (*Correspondence* 11:321)

While he is not strictly outlining his own position in the above, rather trying to render the sense of Fichte's, the view presented fits in perfectly with the form/content distinction applied to religion and revelation in the *Conflict*. The matter of religion is morality and because of that there is only one religion (7:36). But the matter of that one religion is, we have seen, distinct from its form. There are 'different forms of belief in divine revelation ... i.e. different forms of sensible representation of the divine will, in order to give it influence on our minds, amongst which [forms] Christianity, as far as we know, is the most suitable' (7:36).

The end of the above quotation shows that the distinctions between subjective and objective revelation and between the form and content of religion allow Kant to at least state that Christianity is superior over other faiths. It is not that Christianity contains truths that no other religion does not or could not possess, but it was clear from the moment of its founding that it proclaimed nothing other than pure moral religion as the way to become well-pleasing to God. In this regard, it marked a radical departure from Judaism. The universal history of the Church begins with the origin of Christianity, which was founded on an entirely new principle (as compared with the Judaism out of which it grew) and effected a total revolution in doctrines of faith (*Religion* 6:127). In Christianity the marriage between the matter of religion, universal practical laws and the form of a given, historical faith is at its most perfect. This is the faith in which the moral philosopher has least work to do in bringing out the moral matter that lies at the heart of any ecclesiastical, historical faith worthy of our attention. In an extended discussion in the *Religion* from 6:159 to 163, Kant takes the Jesus of the Gospel according to Matthew and seeks to show that Jesus had it in mind from the beginning to preach a faith in which a moral service to God was paramount and a cult of mere mechanical means of grace was superstitious. Thus Christ is honoured as 'the founder of the first true church' (6:159).

In order to fill out and defend the picture offered by pure rationalism, Kant needs to defend both the need for God to publish natural religion in history and the real possibility of revelation and miracle. Why 'and miracle'? There is one main reason why, if miracles are not afforded the status in the Kantian system of being really possible, revelation is not really possible in it. This is that miracle, along with the fulfilment of prophecy, is the fundamental apologetic ground for accepting that something is revealed. Granted that a candidate for revelation must comport with what reason shows to be true, what might show that a truth allegedly revealed was not simply discovered by the rational powers of the human transmitter of it, such as Jesus? The answer has traditionally been: genuine revelation is attested by miracles, which because of their nature can serve to vouch that there is a supernatural source behind the prophet's words. The connection between miracle and the authority of those claiming to utter revelation was well established in the eighteenth-century debate. Locke, for one, declared in 1695 that: 'The evidence of our savour's mission from heaven is so great, in the multitude of miracles he did before all sorts of people'

(Locke 1999:142–3). Kant acknowledges the link himself in the *Religion*: miracles associated with Jesus have some kind of logic as a way of marking out the break with Judaism Jesus was making and as helping his ideas to gain entry into the minds of his contemporaries (see, for example, 6:127–28 and 6:163). We might also wonder how some truth could be marked out as supernaturally revealed, rather than rationally discovered, unless its occurrence in the mind was not miraculous, that is unless it was the product of direct divine causation and not wholly naturally explicable. Kant endorses this point in the *Religion*: a supernatural revelation is a miracle (see 6:85). The real possibility of miracles would include their epistemic possibility. Miracles cannot serve to vouch revelation if we have no means of rationally deciding whether they have taken place or not.

The need for revelation apparently allowed by Kant relates to his progressive view of human history, as outlined in such works as *What is Enlightenment?*, *Conjectures on the Beginning of Human History* and *Idea for a Universal History with a Cosmopolitan Purpose*. These give us the collective message that, though all human beings have it in them to be free and enlightened creatures, a process of slow development through conflict is required in human history for this capacity to produce a fully free and enlightened community. We have seen that Kant has an example (albeit it is very much fuelled by prejudice) in ancient Judaism of a faith in which the truths of natural religion, of pure moral religion, have been overlain by mere statutory rules and a belief in mechanical forms of grace. The need to demonstrate a break from a past, merely statutory faith, it appears, can give revelation a legitimate purpose. It can serve as a means of propagating natural religion: 'the doctrine of revelation, upon which a church is founded and which stands in need of scholars as interpreters and preservers, must be cherished and cultivated as a mere means, though a most precious one, for giving meaning, diffusion, and continuity to natural religion even among the ignorant' (*Religion* 6:165). While not exactly a ringing endorsement of the need for revelation, this passage does at least concede that there are folk who are ignorant, and presumably they are ignorant of the truths of natural religion. Despite the fact that moral faith rests solely on reason and 'lies as close to every human being, even the simplest, as though it had been literally inscribed in his heart' (*Religion* 6:181), there are still the ignorant, to whom the preaching of natural religion via the vehicle of a revealed faith is seemingly necessary.

One reason why 'the ignorant' might require a revealed faith, albeit temporarily, is given in the way Kant appeals to the need to link the preaching of the truths of pure moral religion with something that will enliven the human imagination. In the following, having just told us that universal religion cannot be essentially bound to a local historical faith, Kant nonetheless affirms

> yet, because of the natural need of all human beings, to demand for even the highest concepts and grounds of reason something sensible=tangible, some experiential confirmation or the like (a need which must also be actually taken into account when the purpose is to introduce a faith universally), some historical ecclesiastical faith or other, usually found already, must be used. (*Religion* 6:109)

In this way ecclesiastical faith can serve as the vehicle for the pure faith of rational religion. Kant has labelled his temporising position on reason and revelation 'pure rationalism' because it is not tainted by naturalism, but, from another perspective, it is impure rationalism. The senses, the imagination, have a role in religion alongside that of reason. Kant can thus envisage a role in the history of the race for the different confessions. They serve as 'vehicles for religion' (*Peace* 8:367$_n$), helping to spread the message of religion through their sensibly tenable stories and institutions, until, in a fully free and enlightened world community, they die. These faiths can play their part in propagating the truths of moral religion and in uniting people of good will into moral communities – thus hastening the coming of a perfected, worldwide moral community. But in the end

> It is thus a necessary consequence of the physical and, at the same time, the moral predisposition in us, which is the foundation and at the same time the interpreter of all religion, that in the end religion will gradually be freed of all empirical determining grounds, of all statutes which rest on history, and unite human beings provisionally for the furthering of the good through the means of ecclesiastical faith, and so at last pure rational religion will rule over all, 'so that God may be all in all'. (*Religion* 6:121)

There is one place, 6:135$_n$ where Kant muses that ecclesiastical faith might always be useful as a vehicle.

To this account of an apparent need for revelation, Kant adds statements not ruling it out as a possibility. The principal passage in which he states that it would in effect be dogmatic to rule out the possibility of revelation ('for regarding this no human being can settle anything through reason', 6:155) has already been quoted in the above. In a similar fashion, Kant takes pains at places not to reject miracles dogmatically. The General Remark at the close of Part II of the *Religion* is devoted to miracle. It is made plain that belief in miracles is 'in general dispensable' (6:84) given that, one day, a moral religion is established, for claims of moral religion rest on reason alone and require no testimony from miracles for their authority. The Remark then underscores the argument that it would have been 'entirely conformable to the ordinary human way of thinking' if the break from a religion of mere cult (Judaism is in his mind) to a new moral religion was 'adorned by miracles'. 'Adorning' the new religion (Kant surely should have written *Glaube* not *Religion* because there is only one religion and it is timeless) with miracles fits in with the mode of understanding attaching to the old faith (6:84). He concedes that the life and passion of the teacher of this new faith might be miraculous and that we can leave the merit of these miracles undisturbed. The one thing we must not do is to make it 'a tenet of religion that knowing, believing, and professing them [the miracle stories] are themselves something whereby we make ourselves well-pleasing to God' (6:85). Kant continues by stating that there are rational human beings who have no practical belief in miracles. They do not rule miracles out, but – expanding on Kant's text – since they embrace natural religion directly, they do not need a subjective revelation, unlike 'the ignorant'. Kant then tells us that we have only a general concept of the miraculous, insofar as we can think of God as the creator and ruler of the world who from time to time (Kant's words: 'in special cases') 'promotes' deviations from natural laws (6:86). But this general concept tells us nothing about particular alleged miracles: 'Here reason is as paralysed'. This tolerant, agnostic, non-dismissive stance to miracles was conveyed by Kant in some of his lectures (see *Lectures Metaphysics* 28:217–21, 28:869–75, 29:871 and *Lectures Theology* 28:1111–12).

Kant as naturalist

It is not possible to write a chapter on Kant's philosophy of religion without confronting the question of whether he is consistent in what he says. The question must be faced as to whether his avowed setting aside of an 'impure' rationalism, that is one tinged with a naturalist rejection of revelation, is wholly sincere. Now we have noted in Chapter 1 the great store Kant set by honesty in academic publishing, asserting that he will never say that which he does not believe, although he may lack the courage to affirm all that he believes (*Correspondence* 10:69). We will, however, find numerous points in Kant's writings where he appears to reject the real possibility of both revelation and miracle. And we do know that Kant was concerned about whether the text of the *Religion* would pass the Prussian censors. After an initial success in evading the censors' condemnation, Kant was in receipt of a royal reproof in 1794 forbidding further publication of such ideas in the future (see Kuehn 2001:361ff.). Given the points in favour of naturalism from Kant's own writings laid out below, we must conclude that his defence of the real possibility of revelation is either artful or confused.

When Kant states that the rationalist will never deny the intrinsic possibility of revelation (*die innere Möglichkeit der Offenbarung*) his conclusion is bolder in appearance than in reality. We know that he thinks intrinsic possibilities are endless, being constrained only by the principle of self-contradiction. Candidates for acceptance from within the opinion-knowledge scale must be at least real possibilities. Real possibility depends on a relation between a concept and something outside it: the form and possibilities of experience. As we shall see below, Kant cannot represent revelatory communications as falling within possible experience. Moreover, the idea of revelation presupposes other notions that Kant has told us cannot be known to represent real possibilities. Notably, it depends on the notion of a personal deity willing and able to communicate with his creatures. It is clear from our discussion in Chapter 4 that Kant reckons we have no assurance that such a notion corresponds to a real possibility. Our assurance extends only to the real possibility of there being some ground of teleological order in reality. Universal needs of reason force us to assume that such a ground exists. This point also affects belief in miracle. Kant understands these in a traditional fashion: suspensions of the laws of nature by a God (see *Lectures Metaphysics* 28:217). But if the notion of a deity able and willing to cause events in nature from without represents no real possibility to us, then the notion of a miracle cannot represent a real possibility either. It was shown in Chapter 4 that the *Religion* does not dissent from the general doctrine of sense and the specific teachings about religious language that produces these Critical boundaries on substantive speculation about God. Far from it: the four places in the *Religion* where Kant discusses matters relating to religious language:

6:65$_n$, 6:139, 6:142, 6:182–3 fully cohere with his highly agnostic account of what it can mean to talk about a personal God.

Moving on from these general considerations, we have to face the fact that Kant contends in more then one place that revelation is impossible. 'Revelation is impossible' is my gloss on these passages. The justice of the gloss will be seen in the light of the fact that 'revelation' refers to a relational activity: an agent reveals some message to some subject. Thus if we rule out subjects being able to know that revelation has taken place or being able to comprehend it, then we rule out revelation. Ruling out revelation as a real possibility can be done from both ends, as it were. We might claim to have sufficient knowledge of God's nature to rule it out. This move is one that is undercut by the Critical Philosophy, which tells us that we cannot know either way what is really possible for God to do and not do once contradictions have been eliminated. But we can also rule out the real possibility of revelation from the other end. We might know enough about the operation of human cognition to know that creatures like us could never recognise a revelation. That knowledge may be amply sufficient to rule out the real possibility of a God revealing things to creatures like us. This is just the conclusion that Kant appears to come to in a number of places.

The ruling out of divine revelation to beings like us is a significant theme in the first and main essay in *Conflict of the Faculties*, which essay, we should note, was composed in 1794 and thus close to the publication of the four parts of the *Religion*. We know that Critical restrictions on knowledge eliminate the possibility of direct experience of God. Since original revelation from God to human beings would involve some form of direct encounter with God, this restriction must rule out revelation. Kant makes the connection in the *Conflict* thus 'A direct revelation from God ... would be a supersensible experience, which is impossible' (7:47). More generally, the *Conflict* tells us that 'if God should really speak to a human being, the latter could still never *know* that it was God, who was speaking to him. It is absolutely impossible that a human being should apprehend the infinite by his senses, distinguish it from sensible beings, and *recognise* it from that' (7:63). Some might argue that all that this passage tells us that is that we cannot *know* a revelation is genuine, leaving open the possibility that we might have a reasonable belief that revelation has taken place (see O'Brien 2000:537). After all, in traditional Christian apologetics, from Aquinas to Locke and beyond, acceptance of revelation is founded upon evidence of an indirect kind (such as miracles) that falls short of demonstration. But note that the above passage tells us that it is 'absolutely impossible' for a human being to apprehend the infinite and distinguish it from the sensible. Further, there is no account in Kant of how short of proof we might have reasonable belief in revelation. It is important in this connection to note that the passages on miracle quoted above allow in theory that miracles occur but leave open the possibility of dissent from miracle stories. Yet some of these stories would have to be substantively probable for them to serve their traditional apologetic purpose. Kant evinces no concern whatsoever to join the side of those traditional eighteenth-century apologists who followed Locke in viewing some miracle stories about Jesus and the Apostles as so probable that they lent moral certainty to the claim that Christianity contained a genuine revelation from God. In this regard, a studied agnosticism about the truth of particular miracle stories is as good as out-and-out scepticism as a means for ditching their traditional apologetic role in support of revelation. Some of the stories have to be convincing.

There are places where Kant points to the positive possibility that we may recognise the teachings of a book like the Bible as divine. This will be when its teachings are seen to be in accord with the 'concepts of *our* reason, insofar as they are pure-moral and thus infallible' (*Conflict* 7:48; see also 7:46). But the fact that Jesus is recorded as teaching the truths of rational, moral religion is precisely not sufficient to show that he is the purveyor of revelation, where that means a message coming from a supernatural deity. The very fact that a religious figure preaches the truths of natural religion shows that he or she could have grasped those truths by use of the human reason alone and thus serves to undermine, rather than support, any claim that we have revelation in front of us. This portrayal of Jesus as teaching rational, moral truths is precisely the one used by the deists in contending that he had no new revelation for us. For the concept of revelation to get a foothold we need the notion of a message that contains would-be truths above reason and is surrounded by signs of coming to the messenger from the deity.

There is a similar ruling out of revelation in the *Reflexionen*. Kant states that 'Above all the judgement that something is an appearance of God (a theophany) amounts to enthusiasm; given that one cannot at all have such an intuition, we cannot apprehend revelation' (*wir können die Offenbahrung nicht in uns aufnehmen*; 19:644). These statements fully cohere with the way in which the *Religion* rules out any attempt to distinguish the effects of nature and grace in our experience of ourselves. Nowhere in experience, Kant tells us, can we recognise a supersensible object; indeed 'To want to perceive heavenly influences is a kind of madness ... which nonetheless always remains a self-deception detrimental to religion' (6:174). Kant simply rules out any intelligent, rationally guided, human participation in messages and influences coming from the divine to particular persons.

The *Conflict* does allow revelation from God to human beings in the sense known to apologetics as 'general revelation'. This is the thought that, since the human faculties are created and designed by God, then the discoveries of reason can be regarded as God speaking to us (see 7:67). Reason is even referred to as 'the God within us' (7:48). But of course this will not help the pure rationalist who wants to leave room for a supernatural revelation in history. Perhaps it is in this connection that we should understand Kant's remark that the mark of something's being a divine revelation is the harmony of the message with 'what reason pronounces worthy of God' (7:46). Note well that for someone such as Locke, genuine revelation would cohere with reason while at the same time dealing in truths that were above reason. Truths above reason are those we can accept on the basis of trusting the messenger who delivered them, even while we cannot judge them to be truths by reference to what reason can directly discover. But Kant rules out there being any religious truths that are thus 'above reason' in Locke's sense (see Locke 1975:IV, 17, 23). We have documented earlier in this chapter his contention that all religious truths belong to a universally available moral, rational religion. In the case of Locke's truths above reason, our ground for assenting to revealed claims is the fact that they are revealed. There is absolutely no sense in Kant that he can admit revelation as an objective ground of assent. In particular, he cannot accept that claims that are opaque to human reason can be accepted on the strength of the alleged fact that they are revealed. We cannot accept 'mysteries' such as the Trinity on this basis, for concerning them 'God has revealed nothing to us, and can reveal nothing, for we could not understand it' (*Religion* 6:144). This is why in the pages prior to this quotation he attempts to give a moral interpretation of the Trinitarian formulae (see 6:141–2).

These Kantian strictures on revelation must have implications for how any human subject is to tell whether any particular event is a miracle or not. Granted that some events may be naturally inexplicable so far as we know, Kant has no doctrine to explain how human beings could rationally discern divine action in history. As noted above, pleading for a theoretical agnosticism about whether miracles really occur it is not enough to ground the established apologetic use of miracles. They cannot then serve as part of the 'external evidences' for Christian faith. There is one place in the *Nachlass* where Kant clearly and explicitly states that miracles are in principle impossible. This is in a short essay *Über Wunder*. This brief two-page note is dated 1788–90 by the editors of the Academy Edition (the note is found at 18:320–22). It is related in content to passages from the *Metaphysical Foundations of Natural Science* (1786) in which Kant declares his allegiance to the Newtonian principle that action and reaction must always be equal to one another. The principle is linked to the claim that all action in the world is interaction (4:544). This will be seen to be the affirmation of some kind of conservation principle for goings on in the spatio-temporal world. There is a system of bodies. Motion is exchanged between items in that system, but there cannot be actions that come from without, that are not interactions between items in the system. *Wunder* tells us that neither through a miracle nor the operation of a spiritual (that is, non-material) being in the world can a motion be induced in the world without creating an equal motion in the opposite direction. Failing this law, motion could be produced in the world from within empty space (18:320). Kant is after 'all action is interaction', specifically interaction between entities in a common system of space and time. Kant distinguishes outer and inner miracles. The former concern events in space. The latter events that are in time – presumably inner miracles would encompass the miraculous, because supernaturally caused, occurrence of ideas in the human mind and thus bear on the topic of revelation. All actions in space must have determining factors in space; ditto for actions in time. Miracles would involve action in the world as from empty space/time and this is impossible: 'motion in empty space is however a contradiction, that would involve a relation of a thing to a nothing, for empty space is a mere nothing' (18:321).

The upshot of this rehearsal of Kant's doubts and strictures concerning revelation and miracle is that it is hard to see how he can after all agree with the stance of the pure rationalist. Recall this individual will never 'dispute or deny either the inner possibility of revelation in general or the necessity of a revelation as divine means for the introduction of true religion; for regarding this no human being can settle anything through reason' (6:155). It turns out that Kant does dispute the real possibility of miracle and revelation. He finds that human beings can determine things through reason regarding our lack of a capacity to discern and take up revelation. Without that capacity there is no revelation to us. To put this point more generally: there is much in the Critical Philosophy and its implications that seem to rule out any intelligent, reason-guided participation by human beings in a divine–human interchange through supernatural revelation and miracle. These doubts have clear implications for the real possibility of Jesus Christ giving us, via a supernatural revelation, a republication of the truths of natural religion at the start of the Common Era in order to awaken our hidden awareness of the one, true moral religion. We cannot now see how he could have done so: no one would have the means of discerning that he was preaching the truths of moral religion *because they had been revealed to him*. The thought that there was supernatural causality at work in this man's life and preaching turns out to be deeply problematic. Of course, it could be true that this life and preaching, and its subsequent preservation in the New Testament, was instrumental in awaking lots of people from ignorance of the moral religion they should have known about. It could be true that, because of the evolutionary and progressive character of reason in human history, the race has had to rely on ecclesiastical, historical faiths like Christianity to spread the message and work of the one true, moral religion. But these truths could obtain regardless of whether Jesus and the Christian Church had a genuine revelation. It might just be a general truth about reason in history that it has relied on, and needed to rely on, individuals and organisations who spelled out the truths of natural religion in forms that could be taken up by the senses. The stories told in the *Religion* about the role of Jesus and about the character of ecclesiastical, historical faiths as vehicles could all be true in the absence of any revealing other than the occurrence of general revelation through reason. And this is what the rationalist who is a naturalist will maintain. The suggestion that it is fitting that these re-publications of natural religion be accompanied with miracle stories may only be an anthropological comment. People find this association between a new faith and miracles appropriate. This is why reforming efforts like those of Jesus are wrapped up in miracle stories. It may also explain why the Critical philosopher should not seek to cast doubt on these stories in public or dispute the claim that Jesus was divinely inspired.

Kant and deism

Scholars debate whether Kant is a deist, whether his philosophy of religion goes beyond deism or not (cf. Wood 1991 *passim* with Hare 1996:41–5). In large measure this debate is over whether Kant allows for the real possibility of revelation and gives it a substantive role in human history. Enough has been said in the previous section to indicate that and why I disagree with the assertions to the effect that Kant sees special revelation as a vehicle in God's dealings with human beings. So I have taken sides on this issue already. But it must be said that the question of Kant's relation to deism is beset by vagueness, a vagueness founded on the fact that 'deism' and 'deist' were without precise sense in the eighteenth century. What can be done is to plot the many similarities between Kant's philosophical theology and that of those thinkers who were paradigmatic deists in the decades before 1781, while at the same time indicating the distinct emphases and themes in Kant that set him apart from at least many deists.

The word 'deism' in the Enlightenment could be used in an imprecise way to denote the views of any debunking, rationalist critic of Christianity. To give it greater precision, one must proceed ostensively: it is the kind of religious outlook displayed by paradigmatic English thinkers regarded then and now as deists, thinkers such as Charles Blount and Matthew Tindal, among others. What is typical of these thinkers is the claim that natural religion – a simple religion based on reason alone – is sufficient for salvation and revealed religion therefore unnecessary. Kant's own philosophy of religion appears to be very close to this, so it is deeply unhelpful for him to declare that he is not a deist but a theist. The ground given for his declaration is that the deist believes in a lifeless, blind divine substance, whereas the theist believes in a living, providential God (see, for example, *Lectures Theology* 28:1001 and 1047). Kant, as noted in an earlier chapter, must have known of the philosophy of the English deists, if not through translations (Tindal's *Christianity as Old as the Creation* was translated into German in 1741), then through the work of his teacher Knutzen. Typical of deistic summaries of true religion is this seven-point statement of natural religion from Blount:

1. That there is an infinite, eternal God.
2. That he governs the world by providence.
3. That our duty is to worship and obey him.
4. Worship consists in prayer and praise to him.
5. Obedience to God consists in following the rules of reason and virtue.
6. The expectation of rewards and punishments after this life is grounded on God's providence.
7. If we err from these rules we can repent and expect mercy. (Blount 1695:197–8)

Note that Blount's God is providential and thus not the lifeless being of a merely transcendental theology. What is also notable about the above list is that it does not include much that is in the Apostles' creed and that, in both what it contains and does not contain, it comes close to the tenets of Kant's own Critical religion. The fundamental agreement is to be found in the underlying assumption that the truths of religion are truths of reason and that these truths in no way depend on revelation in history for their grounding. Both Blount and Kant agree that true religion is a rational, moral religion produced by reason. Tenet (7) does not exactly correspond to Kant's own account of what to expect when we realise that our performance always leaves us short of the moral perfection demanded by reason and the providential being controlling reality. He speaks of the need for divine grace at this point. The deists do not. We will return to this below.

It is arguable that typical deistic thinkers were committed to naturalism, as Kant defines it. Their fundamental claim that natural religion is sufficient for the guidance of life does not indeed formally rule out revelation. Some deistic thinkers, such as Toland in *Christianity not Mysterious*, leave open the possibility that Kant allows when he states that a religion may be subjectively revealed though objectively natural. Toland distinguishes the uses of revelation as a source of information and as a ground of assent. He states that we should not confound the way we have come to knowledge of a thing with the grounds we have to believe it. My source of information as to a fact may be someone's testimony or the record of it in a book. My proper ground of assent to it will be reason and the proofs it provides that the fact is genuine (see Toland 1696:38). This very point is the one that Kant relies on to draw his subjective v. objective revelation distinction. The sub-title of Tindal's *Christianity as Old as the Creation* proclaims that the Gospel is a republication of the religion of nature and the thought therein allows in principle that the Gospel might contain revelation. Tindal states that 'the business of the Christian dispensation was to ... restore ... the true, primitive, and natural religion' (1730:379). Tindal's tongue may have been firmly in his cheek when he wrote that. A common deistic assertion is that revelation is out: given that natural religion is sufficient, there is no need of revelation and the idea of revelation can only serve to cloak the introduction of superstition into the world. So argues Peter Annet in *The Resurrection of Jesus Considered* (1743:18).

A significant point of difference between Kant and the deists is that they are preoccupied with divine justice and the problem it poses for the idea of revelation. If God is just, he will not give some parts of the human race a knowledge of himself and his requirements on conduct through revelation while leaving other parts without such help. Granted that there are defects in natural religion, or in its reception by human beings, a just God will not seek revelation in history as the remedy for them. So to act raises the justice problem again: why are some parts of the world and epochs in history given this aid and others not? Thomas Chubb is one who makes this point: 'But seeing divine revelation has not been afforded to all, and therefore by it has not been a supply to the aforementioned general defect; from hence, I think, I justly infer ... that either reason is, or else that it ought to be, a sufficient guide in matters of religion' (1731:14). I can find no place in the Kantian corpus where he reflects on divine justice in this way, or argues for the sufficiency of natural, moral religion from premises about divine justice. It will readily be admitted that reflections on divine justice do provide a prima facie objection to admitting the need for what Kant describes as 'subjective revelation'.

The deists may or may not have been naturalists rather than Kantian pure rationalists – though we have seen that Kant himself casts doubt on the viability of pure rationalism. There is one obvious difference between deistic philosophical theology and Kantian: Kant makes explicit mention of need for divine grace, the deists do not. This is connected with another difference. Typical eighteenth-century deists reject the Christian picture of the fall of the human race, whereas Kant, we have seen, considers that the story of the Fall represents the important truth that human beings are mired in a radical evil. Deists cannot see beyond the historical and moral problems in the account of Adam and Eve and our inheritance of their guilt by the rest of the race (see Tindal 1730:389–91). They have no way of embracing Kant's symbolic reinterpretation of the Fall and are generally much more optimistic about human nature. They do confront the problem that arises when God makes his final reckoning and discovers that no one has an unblemished record. Blount is typical in the way he copes with this gap between law and performance: God will grant eternal bliss to those who show 'penitence and resolution of amendment' (1695: 199–200). God will thus take a good heart and sincere commitment to the moral law in lieu of perfect performance. This resolution of the problem of universal human failing fits in well with a widespread picture in deism of God as a wise distributor of happiness rather than a wrathful punisher of sin. A major contrast to Kant!

But wait: we noted in the Chapter 7 that for all Kant's toying with the possibility of transforming and justifying grace, the only form of divine grace he gives any substantive work to is what we styled 'distributive grace'. And this form of grace is remarkably like the benevolent justice the God of Blount and other English deists dispenses in the after-life. Like the deist God, Kant's God will take goodness of heart in lieu of perfect moral performance. Kant *appears* to have a different view of divine justice. Kant tells us in *Lectures Ethics* that the holy, just God will not, like a 'benevolent ruler', simply waive away our crimes, remit our punishments and thereby dole out a mere 'lenient justice' (27:331). 'Lenient justice' is just what the deist God is dispensing, for his chief property is his benevolence. Kant, instead, wants to speak of a mysterious 'supplement' God makes to human nature that enables God to bridge the moral gap while continuing to be a strict judge. But we have seen that nothing concrete comes from this thought. In both the second *Critique* and the first part of the *Religion* Kant's God appears to act just like the deist God and dole out lenient justice. (That Kant's rejection of lenient justice is weak is argued in detail in Frierson 2003:115ff.)

We can perhaps find a substantive difference between Kant and deism in this: the role of mystery in religion. The title of John Toland's most famous book *Christianity not Mysterious* of 1696 is indicative of the rational optimism that is absolutely central to deistic thought. There are no truths in religion, or morality, that are above, let alone contrary to, reason. God, the world, human nature and our duties are all capable of rational comprehension. This rational optimism provides a major plank in the deistic rejection of revelation. There is no need for it, given that all that we need to know is so easily discoverable. There is for the deists a detectable correspondence between God's nature and the structure of reality. There is a rational and providential order to reality that is the perfect conduit into the rational order in the mind of God. The Light of Nature in us makes the reason in God and the reason in nature plain to us (see, for example, Tindal 1730:67). This is just the epistemic optimism that the Critical Philosophy is bent on rebutting: belief in a pre-established harmony between human reason and reality. Deistic thought is a paradigm of that heteronomous view of reason that Kant's own autonomous conception seeks to overturn. As a consequence, Kant's philosophical theology has room for something utterly alien to deism: the thought that there are ideas in religion that we are in some manner committed to even though we cannot prove them or even fully comprehend them. Not least of these ideas is that of God. We know that for Kant even our awareness of morality is something tinged with mystery. Moral awareness and action is a reflection of our supersensible, intelligible, free natures that cannot be captured in a scientific, empirical investigation into human nature. This means, as shown in earlier chapters, that Kant can surround the moral with the aura of the holy, the sublime, the supernatural. This aura is famously present in the conclusion to the second *Critique* ('Two things fill the mind with ever new and increasing admiration and reverence ... ', 5:161). A consequence of this is that the commonplace thought – in reason and revelation discussions – that reason's hold upon morality and God is a form of general revelation has greater rhetorical force in Kant than in typical religious rationalists. This association, via morality, of religion with supersensible mysteries also makes the rhetoric of notions like grace and of the Holy Spirit available to Kant in a way that it could not be for any deist.

That there is a mysterious, 'mystical' streak in Kant's treatment of religion and morality cannot be denied when we bear in mind the way in which he connects both with the sublime. In a significant passage in *The Conflict of the Faculties* (7:58–9), Kant himself acknowledges that there is something supersensible in our moral nature that is readily taken as the sign of something supernatural at work in us. He introduces this thought by telling us that 'There is namely something in us, that we cannot cease to wonder at, when we have once had it before our eyes, and this is that which at the same time raises *humanity* in its idea to a dignity we should never have suspected in the human being as an object of experience'. It is not the mere fact that we are creatures of reason and thus subject to the moral law that is the source of this wonder. It is rather the supremacy of the supersensible over the sensible in us. The supremacy is shown in 'the ability that we have through morality to bring our sensuous nature to so great a sacrifice, that we *can* do what we *ought* to do, where we easily and clearly conceive it'. The supremacy of the supersensible over the sensible is shown in the way the latter is nothing when it comes into conflict with the former. Such is our degree of wonder at the moral disposition in us that 'we can excuse those, who, because the *supersensible* in us is inconceivable, while it is practical, are led to consider it *supernatural*, i.e. as something, which is not at all in our power and [not] belonging to us, but as much more the influence of another and higher spirit'. Kant goes on to say that we cannot literally take our power of acting on moral maxims against self-interest to be supernaturally based, since the resultant acts 'would not be our deed'. This is his standard problem with transforming grace. But, as noted in Chapter 6, at least the supersensible, mysterious character of moral action gives some links to the notions of grace and of 'the spirit of Christ' (7:59). A Tindal or a Blount could not conceivably have written any of this.

There is more to the rhetorical differences between Kant and the deists than the above. Deistic writing on religion – from Blount to Voltaire to Paine – is characterised by ridicule of Christianity, its institutions, its scripture. It is an essential deistic tactic to open up Christianity for questioning by showing one facet or another of it in a ridiculous light (for ample illustration of this in English authors see Herrick 1997). This spirit of ridicule directed at Christianity is absent from Kant's published works. This is surely not out of mere fear of the censor. We have seen above that Kant can speak like any good Enlightenment rationalist of superstition and enthusiasm in established religion, but the fact that his rationalism is different, less optimistic, less facile than that of the deists prevents the strategy of ridicule being employed by him as a major weapon in his critique of historical, ecclesiastical faiths. A further reason for this difference lies in the fact that he can sincerely admit a positive role for these faiths in the history of the human race.

The last point made above reveals a major difference between the philosophical and religious history of Kant and that provided by deism. Deism's account of human history is very simple. Once upon a time all human beings were free and rational. The growth of wealth and political power has produced subjection and superstition. The history of religion is the history of the loss by the race of an original, pure, rational religion through the evils of priestcraft. Along come the free-thinkers and deists to recover what is lost and cast out priestcraft and superstition. Toland got this view across in some particularly weak poetry in his *Letters to Serena*:

> Natural religion was easy first and plain,
> Tales made it mystery, offerings made it gain;
> Sacrifices and shows were at length prepared,
> The priests ate roast meat and the people starved. (Toland 1704:130)

We have seen in this chapter that Kant's developmental, progressive view of history sets the human race the task of creating a fully free, morally governed society as a task. Prior to the realisation of the end of history, ecclesiastical, historical faiths can serve as the vehicles for the moral, rational religion. They are not sad departures from an initial pure, perfect, universal natural religion. They are (or can be if moral religion is really implicit in them) stepping stones toward the full flowering of the ends of reason in history. They cater for the, apparently temporary, need for human beings to have something sensibly tenable in their grasp of moral religion and its goals. This stance clearly gives Kant another ground for a positive appreciation of the scriptures and symbols of Christianity at least. The stance provides a further reason for not pursuing the strategy of ridicule so typical of deism.

Conclusion

A review of Kant's relation to deism allows a final drawing together of the threads in Kant's philosophical theology. We have seen that his account of God depends for its form on the conception and descriptions of God standard in much rationalist philosophical theology. The picture of God that comes down from the Greek philosophical tradition through Scholasticism to his closer forebears, such as Locke and Leibniz, is present in Kant's Critical philosophy of religion. But it is united with the Critical conception of reason as autonomous. Thus, for example, the traditional philosophical proofs of God are rejected, even while the descriptions of God they prompt are taken over by Kant. The autonomous conception of reason underscores the rejection of these proofs and ties in with the notion that the concept of God is grounded in reason's need for orientation in thought. As an orienting notion, the concept of God is constructed by us, not read off from facts. As an orienting notion, the concept of God is subjective and heuristic in its fundamental character. Its subjective and heuristic character means that we cannot sensibly ask whether God is really like how we picture him in philosophical and in popular thought. All this marks Kant's philosophical theology as fundamentally different from that of traditional philosophical rationalism, even though, like that tradition, he is committed to regarding the world as a rational and teleological whole and to using the concept of God to articulate that commitment. The Critical philosophy of religion alters our whole perspective on the philosophical concept of God more than it challenges points of detail in it. This change of perspective is but another consequence of the wholesale change in philosophical outlook produced by Kant's Copernican revolution in philosophy.

Orientation, heuristic and subjective thinking, the change of perspective: all these, if fully acknowledged, should settle the question of whether Kant's philosophical theology is compatible with the literal truth of Christianity. His philosophical theology simply does not permit of the divine–human interchange in the history of the race and in the life of individual human beings that Christianity demands. But just as Kant can provide a rationale and use for the language of traditional philosophical theology, so he can for Christian symbolism. That use is connected with his ruminations on the mystery of radical evil and our response to it. In this he is like other German rationalists of the eighteenth century, such as Wolff, who wanted a harmony between a purified Christianity and reason, and who, unlike the deists, rejected the application of a hostile, debunking rhetoric toward Christian writings and symbols.

In reflecting on Kant's relation to deism and Christianity, we have returned to a theme aired at the start of this study: the tensive, ambiguous character of Kant's thought about religion. So much of what he wants to say about the nature of true religion is antithetical to Christianity. It is very similar to deism. On the other hand, much of his thinking stems from a desire to preserve what he sees as essential elements in the Christian world-view. It is designed to preserve important Christian concepts and elements of Christian discourse.

Bibliography

Kant sources

Kant's writings are published in German in *Gesammelte Schriften*; volumes 1–22 edited by the Preussischen Akademie der Wissenschaften, volume 23 by the Deutschen Akademie der Wissenschaften zu Berlin, volumes 24 onward by the Akademie der Wissenschaften zu Göttingen. The volumes are now published by Walter de Gruyter, Berlin. The first 23 volumes are available on line in an electronic addition courtesy of the University of Bonn at <http://www.ikp.uni-bonn.de/kant/>. The electronic edition includes all the major and minor works, the correspondence and the *Handschriftlicher Nachlass*. Volumes 24–8 of the Academy Edition are not included, and it is in those that notes of Kant's lectures by his colleagues and students are found.

Dates are given below for works published in Kant's lifetime.

Answer to the Question: What is Enlightenment? [*Beantwortung der Frage: Was ist Aufklärung?*, 1784, *G.S.* vol. 8].
Anthropology from a Pragmatic Point of View [*Anthropologie in pragmatischer Hinsicht*, 1798, *G.S.* vol. 20].
Conjectures on the Beginnings of Human History [*Muthmaßlicher Anfang der Menschengeschichte*, 1786, *G.S.* vol. 8].
Correspondence [*Briefwechsel*, *G.S.* vols 10–13].
Critique of Pure Reason [*Kritik der reinen Vernunft*, 1781/1787, *G.S.* vols 4/3].
Critique of Practical Reason [*Kritik der praktischen Vernunft*, 1788, *G.S.* vol. 5].
Critique of Judgement [*Kritik der Urtheilskraft*, 1790, *G.S.* vols 20 and 5].
The End of All Things [*Das Ende aller Dinge*, 1794, *G.S.* vol. 8].
Groundwork of the Metaphysics of Morals [*Grundlegung zur Metaphysik der Sitten*, 1785, *G.S.* vol. 4].
Idea for a Universal History with a Cosmopolitan Purpose [*Idee zu einer allgemeinen Geschichte in weltbürgerlicher Absicht*, 1784, *G.S.* vol. 8].
Immanuel Kant's Logic [*Immanuel Kant's Logik: Ein Handbuch zu Vorlesungen* (ed.: G.B. Jäsche) 1800, *G.S.* vol. 9].
Lectures on Ethics [*Vorlesungen über Moralphilosophie*, *G.S.* vol. 27].
Lectures on Logic [*Vorlesungen über Logik*, *G.S.* vol. 24].
Lectures on Metaphysics [*Vorlesungen über Metaphysik*, *G.S.* vols 28 and 29].
Lectures on Rational Theology [*Vorlesungen über Rationaltheologie*, *G.S.* vol. 28].
Metaphysical Foundations of Natural Science [*Metaphysische Anfangsgründe der Naturwissenschaft*, 1786, *G.S.* vol. 4].
Metaphysics of Morals [*Die Metaphysik der Sitten*, 1797, *G.S.* vol. 6].
Moral Mongrovius II [*G.S* vol. 29].

New Elucidation of the Metaphysical Principles of Cognition [*Principiorum Primorum Cognitionis Metaphysicae Nova Dilucideatio*, 1755, G.S. vol. 1].
On the Common Saying: That May Be Correct in Theory, But it Is of No Use in Practice [*Über den Gemeinspruch: Das mag in der Theorie richtig sein, taugt aber nichts für die Praxis*, 1793, G.S. vol. 8].
On the Miscarriage of all Philosophical Trials in Theodicy [*Über das Mißlingen aller philosophischen Versuche in der Theodicee*, 1791, G.S. vol. 8].
Opus Postumum [G.S. vols 21 and 22].
Proclamation of the Imminent Conclusion of a Treaty of Perpetual Peace in Philosophy [*Verkündung des nahen Abschlusses eines Tractats zum ewigen Frieden in der Philosophie*, 1796, G.S. vol. 8].
Prolegomena to Any Future Metaphysics That Will Be Able to Come Forward as a Science [*Prolegomena zu einer jeden künftigen Metaphysik, die als Wissenschaft wird auftreten können*, 1783, G.S. vol. 4].
Reflexionen [G.S. vols 17, 18, and 19].
Religion within the Boundaries of Bare Reason [*Die Religion innerhalb der Grenzen der bloßen Vernunft*, 1793/1794, G.S. vol. 6].
The Conflict of the Faculties [*Der Streit der Facultäten*, 1798, G.S. vol. 7].
The Only Possible Ground of a Demonstration of the Existence of God [*Der einzig mögliche Beweisgrund zu einer Demonstration des Daseins Gottes*, 1763, G.S. vol. 2].
Toward Perpetual Peace [*Zum ewigen Frieden*, 1795, G.S. vol. 8].
Über Wunder [G.S. vol. 18].
What Does it Mean: to Orient Oneself in Thinking? [*Was heißt: Sich im Denken Orientiren?*, 1786, G.S. vol. 8].
What Real Progress Has Metaphysics Made in Germany since the Time of Leibniz and Wolff? [*Welches sind die wirklichen Fortschritte, die die Metaphysik seit Leibnizens und Wolff's Zeiten in Deutschland gemacht hat?*,1804, G.S. vol. 20].

Non-Kant sources

Adams, R. M. (1999), *Leibniz: Determinist, Theist, Idealist*, New York, Oxford University Press.
Adams, R. M. (2000), 'God, possibility and Kant', *Faith and Philosophy*, vol. 17, 425–40.
Allison, H. E. (1983), *Kant's Transcendental Idealism*, New Haven, Yale University Press.
Allison, H. E. (1990), *Kant's Theory of Freedom*, Cambridge, Cambridge University Press.
Allison, H. E. (1996), *Idealism and Freedom*, Cambridge, Cambridge University Press.
Alston, W. P. (1991), *Perceiving God*, Ithaca, Cornell University Press.
Annet, P. (1743), *The Resurrection of Jesus Considered*, London.
Aquinas, St T. (1964), *Summa Theologiae*, vol. 3, tr. T. McDermott, London, Eyre and Spottiswood.

Aristotle (1941), *The Nicomachean Ethics*, in R. McKeon ed., *The Basic Works of Aristotle*, New York, Random House.

Audi, R. (1991), 'Faith, belief, and rationality', in J. E. Tomberlin ed., *Philosophical Perspectives 5: the Philosophy of Religion*, Atascedero, Ridgeview, 213–39.

Beck, L. W. (1969), *Early German Philosophy*, Cambridge, MA, Harvard University Press.

Bennett, J. (1974), *Kant's Dialectic*, Cambridge, Cambridge University Press.

Blount, C. (1695), *The Oracles of Reason*, in *Miscellaneous Works*, Part I, London.

Byrne, P. (1998), *The Moral Interpretation of Religion*, Edinburgh, Edinburgh University Press.

Chubb, T. (1731), *A Discourse concerning Reason with Regard to Divine Revelation*, London.

Descartes, R. (1970), *Meditations on First Philosophy*, in *Philosophical Writings*, tr. E. Anscombe and P. Geach, London, Thomas Nelson and Sons.

Denis, L. (2003), 'Kant's critique of atheism', *Kant-Studien*, vol. 94, 198–219.

Edgley, R. (1969), *Reason in Theory and Practice*, London, Hutchinson.

Everitt, N. (1995), 'Kant's discussion of the ontological argument', *Kant-Studien*, vol. 86, 385–405.

Ferreira, M. J. (1983), 'Kant's postulate: the possibility *or* the existence of God?', *Kant-Studien*, vol. 74, 75–80.

Forgie, J. W. (1994), 'Pike's *Mystic Union* and the possibility of theistic experience', *Religious Studies*, vol. 30, 231–42.

Frierson, P. (2003), *Freedom and Anthropology in Kant's Moral Philosophy*, Cambridge, Cambridge University Press.

Gale, R. (1994), 'Why Alston's mystical doxastic practice is subjective', *Philosophy and Phenomenological Research*, vol. 54, 869–83.

Green, R. M. (1978), *Religious Reason*, New York, Oxford University Press.

Grier, M. G. (2001), *Kant's Doctrine of Dialectical Illusion*, Cambridge, Cambridge University Press.

Guyer, P. (2000), *Kant on Freedom, Law and Happiness*, Cambridge, Cambridge University Press.

Hanna, R. (2004), 'Kant's Theory of Judgement', in E. N. Zalta ed., *The Stanford Encyclopaedia of Philosophy (Fall 2004 Edition)*, <http://plato.stanford.edu/archives/fall2004/entries/kant-judgment/>.

Hare, J. E. (1996), *The Moral Gap*, Clarendon Press, Oxford.

Hare, J. E. (2000a), 'Kant's divine command theory and its reception within analytic philosophy', in D. Z. Phillips and T. Tessin eds, *Kant and Kierkegaard on Religion*, Basingstoke and London, Macmillan, 236–77.

Hare, J. E. (2000b), 'Kant on recognising our duties as divine commands', *Faith and Philosophy*, vol. 17, 459–78.

Hare, J. (2001), *God's Call*, Grand Rapids, Eerdmans.

Heine, H. (1979), *Zur Geschichte der Religion und Philosophie in Deutschland*, *Werke*, vol 8, Hamburg, Hoffman and Campe Verlag.

Herrick, J. A. (1997), *The Radical Rhetoric of the English Deists : The Discourse of Scepticism 1680–1750*, Columbia, University of South Carolina Press.

Hume, D. (1976), *Dialogues concerning Natural Religion*, J. V. Price ed., Oxford, Clarendon Press.
Kain, P. (2004), 'Self-legislation in Kant's moral philosophy', *Archiv für Geschichte der Philosophie*, vol. 86, 257–306.
Kenny, A. (1992), *What is Faith?*, Oxford, Oxford University Press.
Kuehn, M. (2001), *Kant: a Biography*, Cambridge, Cambridge University Press.
Lawrence, J. P. (2001), 'Moral mysticism in Kant's religion of practical reason', in P. Cicovacki ed., *Kant's Legacy: Essays in Honour of Lewis White Beck*, Rochester, University of Rochester Press, 311–31.
Leibniz, G. (1956), *Philosophical Papers and Letters*, tr. L. E. Loemker, Chicago, University of Chicago Press.
Locke, J. (1975), *An Essay concerning Human Understanding*, P. Nidditch ed., Oxford, Clarendon Press.
Locke, J. (1999), *The Reasonableness of Christianity as Delivered in the Scriptures*, Oxford, Clarendon Press.
Maimonides (1963), *The Guide of the Perplexed*, tr. S. Pines, Chicago, Chicago University Press.
Mariña, J. (1997), 'Kant on grace: a reply to his critics', *Religious Studies*, vol. 33, 379–400.
Mariña, J. (2000), 'Making sense of Kant's highest good', *Kant-Studien*, vol. 91, 329–55.
Meynell, H. (1982), *The Intelligible Universe*, London, Macmillan.
Neiman, S. (1994), *The Unity of Reason*, New York, Oxford University Press.
O'Brien, K. S. (2000), 'Kant and Swinburne on special revelation', *Faith and Philosophy*, vol. 17, 535–57.
Oppy, G. (1995), *Ontological Arguments and Belief in God*, Cambridge, Cambridge University Press.
Palmquist, S. (1989), 'Immanuel Kant: a Christian philosopher', *Faith and Philosophy*, vol. 6, 65–75.
Palmquist, S. (1992), 'Does Kant reduce religion to morality?', *Kant-Studien*, vol. 83, 129–48.
Palmquist, S. (2000), *Kant's Critical Religion*, Aldershot, Ashgate.
Quinn, P. (1984), 'Original sin, radical evil, and moral identity', *Faith and Philosophy*, vol. 1, 188–202.
Quinn, P. (1986), 'Christian atonement and Kantian justification', *Faith and Philosophy*, vol. 3, 440–62.
Savage, D. (1991), 'Kant's rejection of divine revelation in his theory of radical evil', in P. J. Rossi and M. Wreen eds, *Kant's Philosophy of Religion Reconsidered*, Bloomington, Indiana University Press, 54–76.
Strawson, P. (1966), *The Bounds of Sense*, London, Methuen.
Stroble, P. E. (1993), 'Without running riot: Kant, analogical language and theological Discourse', *Sophia*, vol. 32, 56–72.
Sullivan, R. L. (1989), *Immanuel Kant's Moral Theory*, Cambridge, Cambridge University Press.
Swinburne, R. (1997), *Simplicity as Evidence for Truth*, Milwaukee, Marquette University Press.

Swinburne, R. (2001), *Epistemic Justification,* Oxford, Oxford University Press.
Swinburne, R. (2004), *The Existence of God*, 2nd edn, Oxford, Clarendon Press.
Tindal, M. (1730), *Christianity as Old as the Creation*, London.
Toland, J. (1696), *Christianity not Mysterious*, London.
Toland, J. (1704), *Letters to Serena*, London.
Vallicella, W. F. (2000), 'Does the cosmological argument depend on the ontological?', *Faith and Philosophy*, vol. 17, 441–58.
Vorländer, K. (1977), *Immanuel Kant: der Mann und das Werk*, Hamburg, Felix Meiner Verlag.
Walsh, W. H. (1975), *Kant's Criticism of Metaphysics*, Edinburgh, Edinburgh University Press.
Ward, K. (1972), *The Development of Kant's View of Ethics*, Oxford, Blackwell.
Wike, V. S. (1994), *Kant on Happiness in Ethics*, Albany, State University of New York Press, 1994.
Wood, A. W. (1970), *Kant's Moral Theology*, Ithaca, Cornell University Press.
Wood, A. W. (1978), *Kant's Rational Theology*, Ithaca, Cornell University Press.
Wood, A. W. (1991), 'Kant's deism', in P. J. Rossi and M. Wreen eds, *Kant's Philosophy of Religion Reconsidered*, Bloomington, Indiana University Press, 1–21.
Wood, A. W. (2001), 'Kant versus eudaimonism', in P. Cicovacki ed., *Kant's Legacy: Essays in Honour of Lewis White Beck*, Rochester, University of Rochester Press, 261–81.
Zagzebski, L. (1987), 'Does ethics need God?', *Faith and Philosophy*, vol. 4, 294–303.

Index

Adickes, E., 5
Allison, H., 17, 18, 133
analytic v. synthetic judgements, 26–7
Annet, P., 169
anti-realism, 5
appearances v. things in themselves, 13–14
    see also transcendental idealism
Aquinas, St Thomas, 31, 34, 70–1, 72
arguments from probability (to God), 44–51
arguments to and from design, 37
Aristotle, 97
asymptotic goals, 95
atheism, 91–3, 95, 96, 97
    dogmatic, 91–3
    sceptical, 91–2
autonomy v. heteronomy of the will, 83

Bayes's theorem, 48
Beck, L. W., 7
belief, *see* faith
Bennett, J., 33, 61, 80
Berkeley, G., 15
blessedness, 109–10
Blount, C., 168, 169
Buddhism, 93

categories, 58–60
    schematised v. unschematised, 58
causality, 58
change of heart, the, 114, 115, 145–47
Christianity, 6, 7, 10, 153, 157–58, 160, 171–72, 173
Christian philosophy, 2
Chubb, T., 169
cognition, 58–61, 74, 75
concept empiricism, 32, 61, 66
    see also principle of significance
Copernican Revolution in philosophy, the, 12
cosmological argument, 31–6

deism, 6, 10, 73, 153, 167–73

Descartes, R., 11, 23
Dialogues concerning Natural Religion, 9, 26, 46
dogmatism, 4

ecclesiastical faith, 162, 167, 172
Enlightenment, the, 8
Epicureanism, 81, 84
ethical commonwealth,
    see moral community, the

faith, 46, 52, 89, 90
Ferreira, M. J., 90, 91

God, and analogy, 65, 68, 69–72
    and anthropomorphism, 39, 44, 46, 51, 63, 64, 65, 67, 68, 70, 71
    and conscience, 131
    and probability, 44–51
    and simplicity, 48–51
    and the moral community, 137–39, 142–47
    as highest original good, 85–6
    as holy lawgiver, 125, 128, 131–37
    as just judge, 125
    as moral governor, 125
    as necessary being, 29–30
    as a regulative principle, 79–82
    concept of, 8–9
    in *Opus Postumum*, 125–26
grace, 112, 139–51, 169–71
Guyer, P., 5, 126

happiness, 83–6, 101–10
    see also, highest good
Hare, J. E., 2, 12–27, 138–39
Heine, H., 2–3
highest good, 84, 85, 95–9, 101–10, 117–20
    see also happiness, virtue
holiness, 110–17, 119
    see also virtue
humanity as highest end, 83, 85–6

Hume, D., 9–10, 11, 12, 26
hylozoism, 81

immortality, postulate of, 112–13, 115–17

Jacobi, F. H., 77–8
Jesus Christ, 113, 140, 150, 158–59, 160, 165, 167
Judaism, 160, 161
judgement
    determinative, 79, 81
    reflective, 79, 81

Kalam argument, 22
Kant's *Weltanschauung*, 7–8
kingdom of ends, 137
knowledge, 52
Knutzen, M., 10, 168
Kuehn, M., 7, 9

Lavater, C. J., 6
Leibniz, G. W., 11, 30–1
Lessing, G. E., 77
Locke, J., 42, 53, 159, 160, 164, 165

Maimonides, M., 71
Mariña, J., 124
materialism, 4
Mendelssohn, M., 5, 77–8
metaphysics
    general and special, 11–12, 14, 15
Meynell, H., 80
miracles, 160–67
Mongrovius, C. C., 5
moral community, the, 106–7, 118, 137–39
    and Kingdom of God, 118–19
moral proof, 83–99, 120–21
    in *Critique of Practical Reason*, 84–99
    in *Critique of Pure Reason*, 97–8
moral religion, *see* natural religion
moral religion v. religions of rogation, 148
mystery, 170–71
mysticism, 55

natural ends, 80–82
Neiman, S., 47

ontological argument, 20–31
opinion, 52

orientation in thinking, 77–79

Palmquist, S., 2
pantheism, 93
philosophy of history, 161, 172
physico-theological proof, 37–40, 48
Pörschke, K. L., 7
principle of non-contradiction, 20, 21
principle of significance, 57, 61
    see also concept empiricism
principle of sufficient reason, 31, 34, 35, 36
problem of evil, 122–23
proof from possibility, 40–4
purposiveness, 80–2

Quinn, P., 145–46

radical evil, 98, 142–47
real possibility, 43, 60, 73–4, 92
reason, defined, 8
    autonomy of, 36, 39, 47
    heteronomy of, 36, 39, 170
Reimarus, H. S., 10
religion, 122
    and history, 156–57
    as the recognition of all duties as divine commands, 125, 127, 128–31
    natural, 10, 153–59, 161, 163, 165, 167, 168, 169
    revealed, 153–55
    true religion, *see* religion, natural
religion of reason, *see* religion, natural
religious experience, 52–5
religious scepticism, 2–3
religious language, 1, 61–72
    in *Critique of Judgement*, 64–71
    in *Critique of Practical Reason*, 67, 74
    in *Critique of Pure Reason*, 61–4
    in *Prolegomena to Any Future Metaphysics that May Present Itself as a Science*, 70
    in *Religion within the Boundaries of Bare Reason*, 68
    see also God
revelation, 155–56, 160–69
    and naturalism, 154, 163–67
    and pure rationalism, 154, 159–67
    and supernaturalism, 154, 155–56

Scheffner, J. G., 7
Spinoza, B., 96
Spinozism, 77, 81
Swinburne, R. G., 39, 45, 46, 48, 49
St Anselm, 23
Stoicism, 84, 93
St Paul, 159
Strawson, P. F., 57, 80
sublime, the, 54–5, 170–71
superstition, 53, 54
synthetic a priori, the, 12

teleology,
    moral, 83–4, 85
    natural, 77–82
theism, 73
theodicy, 122–23
theological morality, 98, 125, 127–28
theology
    cosmo-, 44, 46
    moral, 44, 98, 125, 127
    natural, 44
    onto-, 44, 46
    transcendental
thinking, 58–61
Tindal, M., 10, 168, 168
Toland, J., 10, 168–69
transcendental idealism, 15–18
transparency of belief, 88–9

verification principle, 61
virtue, 83–8, 110–17, 123–24
    see also highest good
    see also holiness

Ward, K., 1
Wizenmann, T., 88, 121
Wolff, C., 1
Wolffianism, 9
Wood, A. W., 4–5, 80, 108